Smuggled Chinese

Clandestine Immigration to the United States

D1021468

In the series

ASIAN AMERICAN HISTORY AND CULTURE

edited by Sucheng Chan, David Palumbo-Liu, and Michael Omi

Smuggled Chinese

Clandestine Immigration to the United States

KO-LIN CHIN

Foreword by

DOUGLAS S. MASSEY

TEMPLE UNIVERSITY PRESS

Philadelphia

Temple University Press, Philadelphia 19122
Copyright © 1999 by Temple University
All rights reserved
Published 1999
Printed in the United States of America

⊗ The paper used in this publication meets the requirements of the American
National Standard for Information Sciences—Permanence of Paper for Printed
Library Materials, ANSI Z39.48-1984

Library of Congress Cataloging-in-Publication Data

Chin, Ko-lin.
    Smuggled Chinese: clandestine immigration to the United States /
Ko-lin Chin; with a foreword by Douglas S. Massey.
        p.   cm. — (Asian American history and culture)
    Includes bibliographical references and index.
    ISBN 1-56639-732-4 (alk. paper). — ISBN 1-56639-733-2 (pbk.: alk. paper)
        1. Chinese—United States—Social conditions.   2. Illegal aliens—United
States—Social conditions.   3. Immigrants—United States—Social conditions.
4. Smuggling—United States.   5. United States—Emigration and immigration.   6. China—Emigration and immigration.   I. Title.   II. Series.
E184.060474   1999
304.873061–dc21
                                                            99-36088
                                                            CIP

For my father-in-law,
  Wen-ching Lin,

  and

In memory of my mother-in-law,
  Ai-mei Chow

Contents

Foreword ix
DOUGLAS S. MASSEY

Preface xv

Acknowledgments xix

I. LEAVING FOR THE BEAUTIFUL COUNTRY

1 In Search of the American Dream 3

2 In Search of the Beautiful Country 9

3 The Social Organization of Human Smuggling 28

II. FOLLOWING THE SNAKEHEADS

4 The Air Route 49

5 The Sea Route 62

6 The Land Route 79

III. CLIMBING THE MOUNTAIN OF GOLD

7 Safe Houses 97

8 Life in the Mountain of Gold 111

9 Stemming the Tide 132

Glossary   167

Appendix A: Research Methods   171

Appendix B: Tables   175

Notes   187

References   199

Index   217

DOUGLAS S. MASSEY

Foreword

THE CURRENT ERA of mass migration constitutes a sharp break with the past. No longer dominated by outflows from Europe to a handful of former colonies, immigration is now truly a global phenomenon. Since 1950 the number and variety of sending countries has increased and the global supply of immigrants has shifted from Europe to developing nations in Africa, Asia, and Latin America. The variety of destination countries has also grown. In addition to traditional immigrant-receiving societies such as the United States and Canada, countries throughout Western Europe began to attract significant numbers of immigrants during the 1960s; and by the 1970s even the countries of Southern Europe had switched from the exportation to the importation of labor. After the rapid escalation of oil prices in 1973, capital-rich nations in the Persian Gulf region likewise began to sponsor massive labor migration; and by the mid-1980s labor importation had spread into Asia, not just to Japan but to newly industrialized "tigers" such as South Korea, Taiwan, Hong Kong, Malaysia, and Singapore.

Although *all* countries in the world now participate in international migration to a measurable extent, the number of countries for which transitional movements are significant is still rather small. There are only five well-established international migration systems operating in the world today, each consisting of a stable set of sending nations that contribute steady streams of immigrants to one of five core receiving areas: North America, Western Europe, the Persian Gulf, Asia and the Pacific, and the Southern Cone of South America. To this list, we might also add an emerging regional system in Africa composed of flows from Sub-Saharan and Asian nations into post-apartheid South Africa. To the immigrants participating in these well-structured systems, we must add some 13 million refugees and displaced persons, three quarters of whom are in poor nations of Africa and Asia. As of 1990, the stock of immigrants around the globe stood at some 120 million persons, 45 percent of whom were in developed countries and 55 percent of whom were in developing nations.

As volumes have risen and origins and destinations have diversified, international migration has become a topic of consuming interest to citizens and policy makers throughout the world. In response, social scientists have intensified their efforts to comprehend the phenomenon and have made considerable progress in developing a sound theoretical basis for understanding the forces behind the resurgence of international migration at century's end. Contemporary international migration originates in the social, economic, political, and cultural transformations that accompany the penetration of markets into non-market or pre-market societies. In the context of a globalizing economy, the entry of markets into peripheral regions disrupts existing social and economic arrangements and brings about the displacement of people from customary livelihoods, creating mobile populations of workers who actively search for new ways of earning income, managing risk, and acquiring capital. International migration does not stem from a *lack* of economic development, but from development itself.

One means by which people displaced from traditional livelihoods seek to assure their well-being is by selling their labor in emerging markets. Because wages are generally higher in urban than in rural areas, much of this process of labor commodification is expressed in the form of rural-urban migration. But wages are even higher in developed countries overseas, and the larger size of these wage differentials inevitably prompts some adventurous people to sell their labor in international markets by moving abroad and looking for work.

International wage differentials are not the only factor motivating people to migrate, however. Evidence also suggests that people displaced in the course of economic growth move not simply to reap higher lifetime earnings by relocating permanently to a foreign setting. Rather, households struggling to cope with the jarring transformations of early economic development use international migration as a way of managing risk and overcoming barriers to capital and credit. In developing countries especially, markets or government programs for insurance, futures, capital, credit, and retirement are poorly developed, and households turn to international migration in order to compensate for these widespread market failures. By sending members abroad to work, households diversify their labor portfolios to control risks stemming from unemployment, crop failures, or price fluctuations.Foreign labor also permits households to accumulate cash for large consumer purchases or productive investments, or to build up savings for retirement.

While the early phases of economic development in poor nations promote emigration, post-industrial transformations in wealthy nations yield a bifurcation of labor markets. Jobs in the primary labor market provide steady work and high pay for native workers, but those in the secondary labor market offer low pay, little stability, and few opportunities, thus repelling natives and generating a structural demand for immigrant. This process of labor market bifurcation is most acute in global cities such as Los Angeles and New York, where a concentration of managerial, administrative, and technical expertise leads to a concentration of wealth and a strong ancillary demand for low-wage services. Unable to attract native workers, employers turn to immigrants and at times initiate immigrant flows directly through formal recruitment.

Although instrumental in initiating immigration, recruitment becomes less important over time because the same processes of economic globalization that create mobile populations in developing regions and generate a demand for their services in global cities also create links of transportation, communication, politics, and culture to make the international movement of people cheap and easy. Immigration is also promoted by foreign policies and military actions taken by core nations to maintain international security, protect foreign investments, and guarantee access to raw materials, entanglements that create links and obligations that generate ancillary flows of refugees, asylees, and military dependents.

However an immigration stream begins, it displays a strong tendency to continue because of the growth and elaboration of migrant networks. The concentration of immigrants in certain destination areas creates a "family and friends" effect that channels later cohorts of immigrants to the same places and facilitates their arrival and incorporation. If enough migrants arrive under the right conditions, an enclave economy may form, which further augments the specialized demand for immigrant workers.

The spread of migratory behavior within sending communities sets off ancillary structural changes, shifting distributions of income and land and modifying local cultures in ways that promote additional outmigration. Over time, the process of network expansion tends to become self-perpetuating because each act of migration causes social and economic changes that promote additional international movement. Moreover, as receiving countries implement restrictive policies to counter rising tides of immigrants, they simply create a lucrative niche into which enterprising agents, contractors, and other middlemen move to create migrant-supporting institutions, providing migrants with yet another infrastructure capable of supporting and sustaining international movement.

Current knowledge about the forces behind international migration thus suggests that movement to the United States and other core immigrant-receiving nations will grow, not decline, in the next century. None of the conditions known to play a role in initiating migratory flows— wage differentials, market failures, segmentation of labor markets, the globalization of the economy—is likely to moderate anytime soon; and once begun, the forces that perpetuate international movement—social network formation, the emergence of global transportation and communication infrastructures, and other processes of cumulative causation—ensure that it will continue into the foreseeable future.

The key player likely to intervene in these flows is the state, and social scientists have recently sought to understand theoretically and substantively the origins and determinants of immigration policy. In general, this work predicts a growing move toward restriction among developed nations. The globalization of markets and technological change have not only accelerated immigration, they have also combined to raise income inequality and/or unemployment throughout the developed world, a mix of conditions that pushes governments toward the implementation of restrictive measures. The shift to such an immigration policy regime has been aided by the end of the Cold War, which removed a major ideological prop for expansive immigration policies.

The likely result will thus be a growing move toward restrictive policies throughout the developed world, with core receiving nations employing increasingly repressive measures to hinder the entry of immigrants, discourage their long-term settlement, and promote their return. The ability of states to deter immigrants and, hence, control the volume and composition of international migration is nonetheless constrained by a variety of important influences. Globalization itself limits the power and influence of nation states to control transnational movements of labor as well as of capital, goods, and information. Likewise the emergence of an international human rights regime constrains the ability of political leaders to respond to the racial and ethnic concerns of voters, or to impose harshly restrictive measures on immigrants and their dependents. These constraints are particularly salient in nations with well-established constitutional protections for individual rights and strong, independent judiciaries.

Little systematic research exists to measure exactly how successful governments can expect to be in limiting and controlling immigration over the next century. To date, virtually all research has focused on Latin American immigration to the United States, with disproportionate attention paid to the very special case of Mexico-U.S. migration. For this reason Ko-lin Chin's study of Chinese emigration to the United States assumes great theoretical and substantive importance. Using a combination of quantitative surveys and detailed ethnographic fieldwork conducted at places of both origin and destination, he is the first to document, analyze, and theoretically understand the growing flow of international migrants from China. His data not only bear upon salient theoretical debates concerning the causes and consequences of immigration, but they address for the first time the issue of enforcement and its consequences.

Although migratory flows to the United States are now largest for countries in Latin America, the latent potential for immigration is greatest in Asia, where the forces that initiate and sustain international migration have only begun to operate. The potential for Chinese immigration alone is enormous. Even a small rate of emigration, when applied to a population of more than a billion people, can be expected to produce a flow of immigrants dwarfing that now observed from Mexico. If international migrants are indeed created by economic development and market penetration, then China's rapid growth and headlong movement into the global market contain the seeds of an enormous future migration. Social networks linking China and developed nations overseas are now being formed and in the future will serve as the basis for an even larger movement of population. Immigration from China and other populous, rapidly developing nations in Asia have an unrecognized latent potential to transform world migration flows and to shape the racial and ethnic composition of developed nations in the next century. No topic could be more important as we move into the new millennium.

Preface

MOST AMERICANS became keen observers of the plight of illegal Chinese immigrants in June 1993 when the *Golden Venture*, a human cargo ship with more than 260 passengers aboard, ran aground in shallow waters off a New York City beach (Gladwell and Stassen-Berger 1993a). Eager to complete their dream journey to the United States, ten Chinese citizens drowned while attempting to swim ashore (Fritsch 1993). The stories of desperation filled the evening news and left the American public hungry for answers as to why so many would risk their lives for a chance to come to America.

Perhaps some answers lay in the headlines of four years earlier, when the Chinese government cracked down on a pro-democracy movement in June 1989. The world watched as Chinese soldiers fired on students and other protestors in Tiananmen Square (Kristof and WuDunn 1994). Were the *Golden Venture* passengers disenchanted supporters of democracy or were they, like their predecessors 150 years ago, immigrants who were trying to improve their economic lives? Or perhaps the Tiananmen Square uprising and the surge in illegal immigration were both symptoms of China's underlying political, economic, and social problems.

The *Golden Venture* tragedy made news, but what of the many other clandestine arrivals and deaths that occur as the result of such smuggling operations? In an attempt to understand the desperation that fuels the lucrative and dangerous trafficking in Chinese immigrants, or "human snakes," this book examines the motivations for and methods of covert immigration, the social organization of human smuggling, the experiences of smuggled immigrants after their arrival in the United States, and the issues of controlling clandestine immigration. (Although Chinese who enter the United States legally but stay illegally after their visas have expired are described as illegal or undocumented immigrants by immigration authorities and scholars, their experience is quite different and will not be addressed here.)

RESEARCH METHODS AND PLAN OF THE BOOK

Although many studies on international migration have been conducted, most focus on Mexican immigrants or the impact of undocumented workers on the American economy (Weintraub 1984; Cornelius 1989; Bean et al. 1990; Delgado 1992). Willard Myers (1992, 1994, 1996, 1997), the director of the Center for the Studies of Asian Organized Crime in Philadelphia, has written extensively about the problem of Chinese human smuggling, but his work is based on his clients' immigration files and interviews with U.S. authorities. Based on informal interviews with a small number of illegal immigrants in New York and a trip to China, Peter Kwong (1997), a professor in Asian Studies, wrote a book on the labor aspect of illegal immigration, arguing that the rise of Chinese illegal immigration is mainly due to unfair American labor practices. Even though a number of academics (Bolz 1995; Zhang and Gaylord 1996; Wang et al. 1997) have also written on Chinese human smuggling, no researcher has yet examined the causes and processes of this smuggling using extensive quantitative and qualitative data.

This study employs multiple research strategies, including a survey of three hundred smuggled Chinese in New York City, interviews with key informants who are familiar with the lifestyle and social problems of illegal Chinese immigrants, a field study in the Chinese immigrant community of New York City, two research trips to sending communities in China, and a systematic collection and analysis of media reports. Readers interested in the details of how I conducted my research will find them in Appendix A.

In Chapter 1, I present the problems associated with illegal Chinese immigration and explain why U.S. authorities are concerned with this issue. Chapter 2 begins with a description of Chinese enthusiasm for emigration to the United States—whether legal or illegal—and looks at the sending communities and at various other factors associated with immigration. The major reasons for clandestine immigration are then examined in the context of existing theories about international migration.

In Chapter 3, I focus on the individual and group characteristics of the smugglers themselves—their modes of operation and the extent of their affiliation with Chinese organized crime and street gangs. I also examine the relationship between smuggling networks and the authorities in both China and the transit countries. This chapter challenges the popular belief that traditional Chinese gangs and organized crime groups are heavily involved in human smuggling.

Chapters 4, 5, and 6 examine the three routes of entering the United States, by air, sea, and land. Chapter 4 describes how Chinese immigrants leave China by air, which transit countries they are likely to pass through and what happens to them there, and how and where they enter the United States.

The social context and organization of sea smuggling is the subject of Chapter 5. How are the passengers recruited and transported? What happens as the ships cross the Pacific or Atlantic oceans to arrive in America? How are the passengers ferried to American shores? And how do illegal immigrants cope with violence, rape, hunger, and natural disasters on their travels across the ocean?

In Chapter 6, I explain how smugglers transport Chinese to either Mexico or Canada and thence to the United States over land. The chapter concludes with a comparison of the three main smuggling routes. When the illegal immigrants arrive in the United States, most of them are confined in so-called safe houses by the smugglers until their smuggling fees have been paid (U.S. Senate 1992). In chapter 7, I discuss the likelihood that a Chinese immigrant will be confined in a safe house, the factors associated with the probability of detention, and the length of confinement. I also discuss the tactics that human smugglers employ to force their captives to pay their passage fees.

Chapter 8 looks at the experiences of Chinese immigrants after they leave the safe houses and begin to settle in New York City. Their experiences include finding work, adjusting to new lifestyles, involvement in illegal activities, and further vulnerability to victimization. The common psychological conditions of new immigrants and their future plans are also described.

In Chapter 9, I examine the countermeasures adopted by government officials and law enforcement authorities in the sending, transit, and receiving countries. This chapter concludes with a discussion of the problems immigration authorities face in trying to control clandestine immigration and suggests policies that might ameliorate the smuggling of Chinese.

Acknowledgments

I AM GRATEFUL to the individuals who have contributed to this study. First of all, I would like to thank my mother-in-law, Ai-mei Chow, for teaching me whatever I know about the culture of the Fujianese and helping me to appreciate it. I also thank my father-in-law, Wen-ching Lin, for accompanying me on my research trips to China. Because he was born and raised in Fujian, his presence not only helped me to establish rapport with my research subjects but also enabled me to set up a network through his friends and relatives. This book is dedicated to Ai-Mei and Wen-ching.

Special thanks go to Professor Robert Kelly of Brooklyn College and the Graduate Center of the City University of New York, the co-Principal Investigator of this research project and a long-time mentor and friend. Bob and I have worked together in other projects and, as always, he provided me with all the guidance I needed to complete this study.

I am also very grateful to those who conducted the interviews for me in New York: Mei-qing Ren, Yu Lin, Hui-qin Zou, Jhou-long Luo, Chen-tao Huang, Yin-chi Zheng, and Shu-zhen Wang. Without their ability to communicate with the subjects in the dialect of Fuzhou and their intimate knowledge of the process and plight of illegal immigration among the Chinese, I would never have been able to collect the data I needed. I am especially thankful to Mei-qing Ren for arranging and conducting some of the interviews in China. I also would like to express my gratitude to my research subjects in New York City and China.

Ronald Clarke, Dean of the School of Criminal Justice at Rutgers while I was working on this project, has always been very supportive of my research. To him, I express my sincere gratitude. I also am thankful to my colleagues at the School of Criminal Justice, especially James Finckenauer, Jeffrey Fagan, Freda Adler, and Gerhard Mueller, for their encouragement and support.

Thanks to Cynthia Nahabedian, Jennifer Scott, and Justin Ready, three doctoral students at the School of Criminal Justice who helped me with data management. I also want to thank Caroline Herrick and Suzanne Wolk for editing the manuscript. My appreciation is also extended to Tamryn Etten-Bohm, who read the draft of this book and gave me many invaluable suggestions for improvement.

My sincere gratitude to Janet Francendese, Editor-in-Chief of Temple University Press, and Janet Greenwood, Editorial Director of Berliner, Inc., for helping me to get this book published. I am also extremely grateful to Michael Omi of the University of California, Berkeley, and to Michael Welch of Rutgers University for their suggestions in improving this book.

Last but not least, I am indebted to my wife Catherine for her support. It was she who suggested that I study the issue of illegal immigration among the Chinese, provided me with many research questions (and sometimes answers), and made sure her relatives in China would help me with my research.

Support for this research was provided by Grant SBR 93-11114 from the National Science Foundation. The opinions are those of the author and do not necessarily reflect the policies or views of the National Science Foundation.

Smuggled Chinese

Clandestine Immigration to the United States

I. LEAVING FOR THE BEAUTIFUL COUNTRY

1   In Search of the American Dream

A YEAR AFTER the United States established diplomatic relations with the People's Republic, China liberalized its immigration regulations in order to qualify for most-favored-nation status with the United States (Dowty 1987).[1] Since 1979, tens of thousands of Chinese have legally immigrated to the United States and other countries (Seagrave 1995). U.S. immigration quotas allow only a limited number of Chinese whose family members are U.S. citizens or who are highly educated to immigrate to or visit America (Zhou 1992). Beginning in the late 1980s, some of those who did not have legitimate channels to immigrate began turning to human smugglers for help (U.S. Senate 1992).

After the Chinese government's crackdown on the pro-democracy movement in June 1989, many students and intellectuals fled China to avoid persecution (Kristof and WuDunn 1994). That exodus, the resurrection of left-wing political leaders after the incident, and rampant corruption among government officials left many ordinary Chinese disillusioned with government promises for economic and political reform (Wen 1992). In the aftermath of the crackdown, the number of Chinese who left their country illegally reportedly surged (Arpin 1990; Chan et al. 1990; Kamen 1991a; Mydans 1992). According to U.S. immigration authorities, the number of illegal Chinese immigrants arrested jumped from 288 in 1988 to 1,353 in 1990 (Lorch 1991). Immigration officials in Taiwan, Hong Kong, Macau, Japan, Australia, Hungary, Romania, Italy, Spain, the Netherlands, and Canada were also alarmed by the dramatic increase in the number of undocumented Chinese arriving in their countries (Boyd and Barnes 1992; Dubro 1992; Eager 1992; Lee 1992; Tam 1992; Stalk 1993; Vagg 1993; Dobson and Daswani 1994; Chang 1995; Craig 1995; International Organization for Migration 1995; Smith 1997; Yates 1997).

The United States ranks high among the settlement choices of smuggled Chinese (Kristof 1993).[2] In New York City's Chinatown, the destination for almost all smuggled Chinese in the United States, the arrival of large numbers of undocumented Chinese has resulted in the expansion into what is known as Little Italy and into the eastern part of the lower east side of Manhattan, an area once populated by Jewish immigrants (City of New York Department of City Planning 1992; Bernstein 1993). Smuggled Chinese choose New York City because most of them have friends and relatives living there and most smuggling networks in the United States are also there (Burdman 1993a).

Smuggled Chinese arrive in the United States by land, sea, or air routes (Smith 1997). Some travel to Mexico or Canada and then cross U.S. borders illegally (Glaberson 1989). Others fly into major American cities via any number of transit points and make their way to their final destination (Lorch 1992; Charasdamrong and Kheunkaew 1992; U.S. Senate 1992). Entering the United States by sea was an especially popular method between August 1991 and July 1993 (Zhang and Gaylord 1996). During that time, thirty-two ships carrying as many as 5,300 Chinese were found in waters near Japan, Taiwan, Indonesia, Australia, Singapore, Haiti, Guatemala, El Salvador, Honduras, and the United States (Kamen 1991b; Schemo 1993; U.S. Immigration and Naturalization Service 1993), though in the aftermath of the *Golden Venture* incident, the use of the sea route diminished significantly (Dunn 1994).

U.S. immigration officials estimated that at any given time in the early 1990s, as many as 4,000 Chinese were waiting in Bolivia to be shuttled to the United States by smugglers (Kinkead 1992); several thousand more were believed to be waiting in Peru and Panama. American officials maintained that Chinese smuggling rings have connections in fifty-one countries that were either part of the transportation web or were involved in the manufacturing of fraudulent travel documents (Freedman 1991; Kamen 1991a; Mydans 1992).[3] According to a senior immigration official interviewed in the early 1990s, "at any given time, thirty thousand Chinese are stashed away in safe houses around the world, waiting for entry" (Kinkead 1992: 160).

Unlike Mexican illegal immigrants who enter the United States at relatively little financial cost (Cornelius 1989), illegal Chinese immigrants reportedly must pay smugglers about $30,000 for their services (U.S. Senate 1992). The thousands of Chinese smuggled out of their country each year make human trafficking a very lucrative business (Mooney and Zyla 1993; Smith 1997). One case illustrates the point: A forty-one-year-old Chinese woman convicted for human smuggling was alleged to have earned approximately $30 million during the several years of her smuggling career (Chan and Dao 1990d). In 1992, a senior immigration official estimated that Chinese organized crime groups were making more than $1 billion a year from human smuggling operations (U.S. Senate 1992). Others suggest that Chinese smugglers earn more—about $3.2 billion annually—from the human trade (Myers 1994).

Because few Chinese can afford the high cost of illegal immigration (Li 1997), those who want to come to the United States must seek help from friends and relatives in China to raise the money for a down payment, which is reported to be 10 to 20 percent of the entire fee. When that is not enough, as it usually is not, they seek financial commitments from friends, relatives, or other "guarantors," often business owners in the United States, to pay the balance upon their arrival. Once here, they repay their guarantors by working in places such as restaurants or garment factories.

Although most illegal immigrants work hard to repay their debts, some have disputes with their "snakeheads," the term commonly used for human smugglers (Kifner 1991), perhaps about a delay in the smuggling process, a dispute over the amount they owe, or difficulty paying the balance.[4] Those unable to pay may be kidnapped and tortured by Chinese gang members hired by smugglers to collect the smuggling fee (Lorch 1991); their relatives and friends who guaranteed their payment may also be at risk for this treatment (Strom 1991). Their illegal status and high debt render them vulnerable in other ways. Chinese gangs and criminal groups may recruit them as drug couriers (Chan and Dao 1990a), enforcers in illicit businesses (Kifner 1991), or prostitutes to ensure payment of their debts (Y. Chan 1993b). Smuggled Chinese experience great difficulty in adapting to their new social setting because of cultural differences, language barriers, and unfamiliar work environments (Burdman 1993d). Largely limited to employment in restaurants and garment factories owned by Chinese businessmen, illegal immigrants generally work long hours for unlawfully low wages and without health insurance and other benefits (Kwong 1997). Most find themselves living in crowded and dilapidated apartments in conditions that recall the notorious tenements of the nineteenth century (Rimer 1992).

When illegal Chinese immigrants are victimized by criminals or exploited by employers, they are understandably reluctant to seek help from law enforcement and government agencies (Kinkead 1992).

Because most of them have left their families behind in China, they have little emotional support in times of need (Myers 1997). According to social workers, many Chinese illegals, frustrated and depressed about their predicament, indulge in heavy gambling or drinking (Hatfield 1989). Illegals also have limited access to legitimate recreational activities, a lack that has led to the proliferation of brothels and gambling dens in New York City's Chinatown (Chin 1996). The increased demand for illegal services has in turn enabled the Chinese underworld to expand its criminal operations (Lay 1993). As I will show in later chapters, these illegal immigrants envisioned a very different life for themselves when they left their homes. It is no wonder, then, that they experience enormous stress in the settlement process (Kinkead 1992).

CONCERN OVER ILLEGAL CHINESE IMMIGRATION

According to official U.S. estimates, approximately half a million Chinese were residing in the United States illegally in 1991 (English 1991). This number includes smuggled Chinese not only from China but also from Taiwan, Hong Kong, and other countries. It also includes not only those transported by human traffickers but also those who entered the country with valid non-immigration visas and then remained illegally after their visas expired.

Estimates of the annual number of smuggled Chinese immigrants vary from ten thousand to one hundred thousand (Smith 1997). The latest estimate, made by the Interagency Working Group (1995) that was established by the White House to monitor the Chinese human trade, suggests that smugglers bring in up to fifty thousand Chinese per year.

It is fair to say no one really knows for sure how many Chinese have been smuggled into the United States over the past decade (Smith 1997), but according to official statistics, the number of illegal immigrants from China in the United States is relatively low compared to the number of illegal immigrants from other countries. INS data show that in terms of the number of illegal immigrants in the United States, China ranks twenty-first among countries of origin (City of New York Department of City Planning 1993).

If the number of undocumented Chinese in the United States is relatively low compared to other ethnic groups, why has the arrival of illegal Chinese become a major concern for U.S. law enforcement and immigration authorities? For one thing, the illegal passage of Chinese immigrants appears to be relatively more risky than that of other immigrant groups. Many smuggled Chinese have reportedly lost their lives in accidents in transit countries or on U.S. borders (Smith 1997). Those who do make it to the United States safely may be subject to kidnapping and torture at the hands of debt-collectors and other criminals who prey upon them. Smuggling-related violence among the Chinese has captured the attention of authorities because these incidents are widely reported in the media (Kifner 1991; Strom 1991; Rabinovitz 1992; Fiason 1993c; Dunn 1995).

In addition, the ways Chinese enter the United States are unlike those of other immigrant groups. Even though a substantial number of Italians and Poles live illegally in New York City, they tend to enter the United States legally, or at least quietly (City of New York Department of City Planning 1993). The arrival of illegal Chinese immigrants, by contrast, often draws attention, especially arrival by boat. Between January 1992 and July 1995, for example, thirty-six ships crowded with Chinese passengers were detected near U.S. waters. Other, undetected ships sailed right through San Francisco Bay and unloaded hundreds of Chinese on the city's dock (Brazil et al. 1993). From the U.S. Coast Guard's perspective, United States national security is seriously threatened by the armada of human smuggling ships (U.S. Coast Guard 1996). In the aftermath of the *Golden Venture* incident, President Clinton characterized Chinese human smuggling as a threat to national security and authorized the National Security Council to direct the U.S. response (Freedberg 1993).

There is also the matter of Chinese organized crime, which has grown in tandem with illegal Chinese immigration, much to the concern of U.S. authorities (Booth 1991; Lavigne 1991; Dubro 1992; Chin 1990, 1996; Kleinnecht 1996). Many in the law enforcement community are convinced that members of Chinese organized crime groups are actively involved in human trafficking (U.S. Senate 1992; Burdman 1993b; Boltz 1995). The United Nations, for example, has estimated that as many as fifty Hong Kong-based triad groups or criminal organizations are responsible for trafficking as many as one hundred thousand illegals per year to the United States, raking in billions of dollars for their services (Schmid 1996). As one anonymous law enforcement official quoted in the *San Francisco Chronicle* put it, human smuggling empowers the Chinese underworld:

"If they said, 'We'll smuggle anybody to the United States for free,' I wouldn't be concerned for a minute. [But] this is a huge revenue source, a portion of which is flowing directly into these criminal organizations and strengthening their power to expand, power to corrupt, power to bribe" (Burdman 1993b: A1). Not only do these criminal groups reap financial gains, they also gain potential recruits through the arrival of a large number of young, aggressive males. In addition, U.S. authorities are concerned that smuggled Chinese are being used by smugglers to carry heroin and other drugs into the United States in exchange for a discount in their smuggling fees (Wren 1996; Smith 1997). Thus, unlike illegal immigration among other nationalities, unlawful immigration by Chinese is considered by U.S. law enforcement authorities to be a factor in the growth of Chinese organized crime worldwide (Smith 1997).

Currently, for reasons discussed in the next chapter, most Chinese who are smuggled into the United States come mainly from the Fuzhou area, located on the northeast coast of Fujian Province. U.S. authorities fear that arrival of a large number of Chinese from Fujian Province may trigger an outflow of Chinese from other provinces such as Zhejiang (Kwong 1997).[5] The U.S. policy is basically to stop the influx of illegal Chinese immigration before it gets out of control.

Finally, U.S. authorities are unhappy with the abuse of the U.S. political asylum program by smuggled Chinese who apply for political asylum once they arrive in the United States (Weiner 1993; Greenhouse 1994). The Refugee Act of 1980 makes a person eligible for asylum if he or she has suffered past persecution or has a well-founded fear of persecution on account of race, religion, nationality, membership in a particular social group, or political opinion (Ignatius 1993). The number of Chinese applications not only clogs the already overwhelmed asylum program but also undermines the system's ability to determine the authenticity of applicants' claims (Conover 1993).[6]

There are many theories on the causes of international migration (Massey et al. 1993). Researchers are concerned with the push and pull of both legal and illegal immigration because they want to know what motivates people to leave their homes for foreign lands (Todaro 1976; Piore 1979; Todaro and Maruszko 1987; Morawska 1990; Stark 1991; Gurak and Caces 1992; Taylor 1992). In the next chapter, I examine the circumstances and forces that lead many Chinese to leave their families and risk their lives for the elusive promise of a better life in America.

2   In Search of the Beautiful Country

According to various sources, people in the Fuzho area of China in the early 1990s were simply engulfed with desire to emigrate (Kamen 1991a; Kinkead 1992; Myers 1992; Burdman 1993a; Hood 1997). In the words of a Chinese journalist who visited Fuzhou, "Everybody went crazy. The area was in a frenzy. Farmers put down their tools, students discarded their books, workers quit their jobs, and everybody was talking about nothing but going to America. . . . If people found out someone had just successfully arrived in the United States, his or her home will be crowded with people, both acquaintances and strangers, to come to collect information about going to America" (*Sing Tao Daily*, December 2, 1996: 26).[1]

To understand why this type of frenzy for immigration to the United States developed in the Fuzhou area, it is necessary to examine what it means to be a *meiguoke* or Guest from the Beautiful Country, especially in the eyes of the immigrants' families and friends. The United States is called *Meiguo* in Mandarin, meaning "Beautiful Country." *Ke* means "guest," underscoring the status accorded to Chinese *from* the United States who are *in* China. Even though immigrants are considered by members of the host country to be living at the margin of society, immigrants tend to see themselves differently (Mahler 1995). In fact, the perceptions of the host society are largely irrelevant to immigrants. They typically follow the views of their countrymen in China in explaining their new life in America to themselves (Chen 1993).

Most of my respondents stressed that their arrival in the United States had a significant impact on their families in China. A twenty-four-year-old male explained why it is so important to have a family member living in the United States: "[Since I left China], my family has changed for the better. My younger brother opened a store and my brother-in-law started a business because they were able to borrow money. They did so simply because I am here. No doubt my family's social status has improved, and people now respect us." According to another respondent, the desire to be a spouse of a *meiguoke* had blinded many females in the Fuzhou area to the risks of illegal immigration:

> For us, coming to America means generating honor for our families in China. You know what? When a woman's husband is in America, people around her respect her, are willing to lend her money, and do favors for her. Many women may have cried in public after they heard that a neighbor's husband was killed when the *Golden Venture* was stranded, but shortly after that, they dried their tears and talked about how wonderful America is. Many women [in the Fuzhou area] are poorly educated. I think that's why they cannot understand how difficult it is for their husbands to survive in America. You tell them the hardships illegal immigrants have to face in the United States, and it will go in one ear and out from the other.

Having a family member in the United States not only confers status and respect, it also brings material changes to the family. A forty-three-year-old male painted a rosy picture of a family with a member in the United States: "After I left China, the living standards of my family improved dramatically. My family bought a new house for 100,000 yuan [or *renminbi*, equivalent to approximately $12,000]. Members of my family are happy every day. That's what we call 'A slave turn around completely and become a master.'"

Although it is extremely cumbersome and costly to be smuggled from China to the United States, many young Chinese from the Fuzhou area are eager to take a chance because they are convinced that this is the only way that they and their families can dramatically change their economic and social status within China. For many people in the sending communities, a family has "hope" only if it can produce a *meigouke*. Those who do not see it this way may also end up going to the United States illegally simply because their families and relatives pressure them to do so.

Why don't Chinese who are eager to come to the United States immigrate legally? The reason is simple—most of them are not eligible. They can come legally only if immediate family members who are U.S. citizens or permanent residents sponsor them. Even then there are many restrictions and requirements (age and income, for example) that they or their family members in the United States may not meet. The waiting period, moreover, especially for those sponsored by siblings, can be as long as two or three decades.

THE FUZHOU AREA

According to U.S. authorities, most undocumented Chinese in the United States come from the Fuzhou area of Fujian Province (U.S. Senate 1992; Interagency Working Group, 1995).[2] According to the 1990 Chinese census, the population of Fujian was approximately 30 million. The population per square mile in the province was 248, more than twice the national average of 118 (Chao and Chan 1993). When the late Chinese leader Deng Xiaoping adopted the "open-door policy" in the late 1970s, Fujian Province, along with neighboring Guangdong Province, was selected to experiment with a market-oriented economy (United Daily's Mainland China News Center 1993). Although Fujian is considered to have lagged behind Guangdong in economic reform, the province is, in many respects, more developed than the rest of China (Duffy 1993; Lyons 1994).

The two seaports and urban centers of Fujian Province are Xiamen and Fuzhou, and the province has long been characterized as the home of outward-looking people who are active in sea trade and smuggling (Sun 1992; Seagrave 1995). Xiamen has been strategically developed by the Chinese authorities to attract Taiwanese investors because Xiamenese speak *minanhua* (the dialect of southern Fujian), the same dialect spoken by people living in Taiwan. The Fuzhou area, encompassing three cities and six counties, is situated in the northeastern part of Fujian Province. According to Myers (1992) and Burdman (1993a), most undocumented Chinese in the United States come from Changle City, Tingjiang Township, Mawei District, Fuzhou City, and Lianjiang County, all which are in the region of Fuzhou.

Changle City

Almost half of my three hundred respondents came from Changle City (see Appendix B, Table 1). Peter Woolrich (1993), a journalist who traveled to Changle, observed that young people there were bored and frustrated because they were getting nowhere even after China's economic reforms. Because of Changle's proximity to Hong Kong, young Changlenese were aware that a better world existed, and they were determined to go to America to fulfill their dreams.

One of the well-known sending communities in Changle City is Houyu Township. According to Pamela Burdman (1993g), a *San*

Francisco Chronicle reporter who visited Houyu, there were very few men left in the township because they had all gone to America. In Houyu, Burdman observed, pretty young wives, their children, and elderly villagers lived in new, spacious houses built with wealth from overseas.

Changle residents are considered by northern Chinese to be aggressive, hard-working, outward-looking people who are determined to find fortune far from their homeland. Men are taught at a very young age to be aggressive in earning money, and once they became independent, they go where the money is. Getting a good education has never been an important goal for young Changle males (L. Chan 1994).

In the early 1990s, smuggling of goods and people became one of Changle's major economic activities, and many young and middle-aged males left Changle for the United States. Those who remained behind were viewed by their friends and neighbors as lazy and stupid (Chen 1993). According to a longtime Chinese government employee:

> Right after China adopted the "open policy," many Changle residents began to become involved in smuggling goods from Hong Kong and Taiwan into China. People from all over China, including government officials, traveled to Changle to buy relatively cheap imported goods. As a result, the people from Changle earned plenty of money from the smuggling business. However, shortly after the emergence of the smuggling industry, authorities in Beijing decided to crack down on smuggling activity in Changle. Consequently, the smuggling business was transplanted to Chingjiang, Sishi [both in Fujian Province], and Wenzhou [in Zhejiang Province].
>
> The rich residents of Changle invested the money they earned from smuggling into *xiangzhen chiyeh* [village and township enterprises]. However, due to heavy taxes, most of these businesses lost money and were forced to shut down. At that time, those people who had overseas connections began to immigrate to the United States, with the help of smugglers. Once a small number of people began to leave illegally, the word soon spread out, and this created a major social force. That force became the catalyst of mass illegal immigration by people from Changle.
>
> The alien smuggling industry emerged and was perpetuated in Changle mainly because the well-to-do residents of Changle could afford the price. Look at where I am from [Minghou]. People in Minghou are relatively poor; they simply cannot afford to pay the $30,000 smuggling fee. What about the well-to-do people from Chingjiang, Sishi, and Wenzhou? Well, the first two groups have no American connections because most of their relatives live in Southeast Asia. Besides, local and overseas Chinese from Chingjiang and Sishi have made a concerted effort to invest their money

in the economic development of their villages instead of establishing an alien smuggling industry. That's why Jingjiang and Shihsi are better developed than Changle. The people of Wengzhou have followed the path of the people of Changle. That's why there are also many illegal immigrants from Wenzhou in the United States and some European countries.

Other respondents in my sample came from Tingjiang, Mawei, Fuzhou City, and Lianjiang County. Tingjiang is a town located between Mawei District and Lianjiang County with a population of 36,647. It is estimated that approximately 1.6 million Chinese in Hong Kong, Macau, and Taiwan have roots in Tingjiang (L. Chan 1994). Mawei, a district of Fuzhou City, is separated from Changle by the Mingjiang River. The population of the district was 44,000 in the early 1990s. In 1985, authorities in Beijing ordered the establishment of a special economic zone in Mawei. The area is a major commercial seaport known for its shipbuilding industry and its navy base (L. Chan 1994). Fuzhou City is a slightly special case in that although some residents have emigrated abroad, many are unwilling to leave clandestinely, mainly because they are generally better educated and have better jobs than people from Changle City and Tingjiang Township. Lianjiang County, which consists of nineteen towns, is located to the north of Fuzhou City. Most illegal immigrants from the county are from Guantou Township, which is adjacent to Tingjiang Township.

There are two other major sending communities in the Fuzhou area. The first is Fuqin City, which is made up of twenty-one towns. There is a large number of overseas Chinese-owned factories in the area; as a result, entry-level job opportunities are abundant (L. Chan 1994). Although some Fuqin City residents have managed to go to the United States illegally, most have chosen to go to Japan, also illegally (Gu 1993). The other sending community is Pingtan County, located east of Fuqin City. Many of its residents have illegally immigrated to Taiwan, which is only about seventy sea miles away (Chang 1995). Table 2 (in Appendix B) illustrates the connections between sending communities in China and the main receiving communities in Asia and the West.

PUSH FACTORS

Given that unlawful immigration to the United States is both costly and risky for Chinese, why are so many of them eager to immigrate?

Poor Economic Conditions in China

According to neoclassical economic theory, people emigrate because they are earning very little in their home countries (Harris and Todaro 1970). Many immigration researchers have also concluded that the opportunity to earn vastly better wages is the biggest incentive for immigrants (Mahler 1995). For most of the Chinese in my sample, the United States is an ideal place to make money because U.S. dollars are *haoyong* (good to use or worthy). Even when the amount of money they earn in the United States may not allow them to live comfortably in America, their wages have enormous buying power in China. Besides, if they remain in China, they are unlikely to earn the amount of money they can make in the United States, wages in China being relatively low (Kristof and WuDunn 1994).

About 61 percent of my respondents said they came to the United States for only one reason—to make money (see Appendix B, Table 3). Another 25 percent stated that their primary motive was to make money but also mentioned one or more non-monetary reasons for coming. Most respondents were impressed with the amount of money they could make in America. According to a part-time elementary school teacher who made about $12 a month in China, "I can make a lot of money in America. A day's wages in the United States could be equivalent to half a year's salary in China."[3] My respondents made an average of about $100 a month in China, but in the United States they earned an average of $1,359 a month—more than their annual income in China.

Some respondents were simply obsessed with possessing U.S. money and living in the affluent American society. In the words of a thirty-seven-year-old male from Fuzhou City, "When I was in China, I thought U.S. dollars were the best thing on earth. I often dreamed about having plenty of U.S. money. I heard that everything was so nice in America, you can even find gold in the streets." Others I interviewed came to the United States mainly because they were barely surviving in China, even though their neighbors might have prospered after China began improving its economy in the late 1970s. A forty-three-year-old Changle male explained, "I was a farmer in China. My family barely had enough food to eat. Every year, we reaped about eleven to twelve *tang*s [bundles] of rice, but about 10 *tang*s were taken away by the government. That left us with only a couple of *tang*s. My annual income was not even close to 200 yuan [approximately $28]."

Some of my respondents came to America not because they were poor but because they needed to find a quick way to solve their financial problems. According to a twenty-nine-year-old male from Changle, "I came to America because I owed a lot of money after I was deported to China from Japan for illegal immigration. It cost me about $5,000 to be smuggled to Japan. I was also fined almost $2,000 by the Chinese government upon my return. To repay the debts, I sold the car I relied on to make a living as a deliveryman, but it was not enough. I had no choice. I had to take another chance [in coming to America] to solve my financial problem."

For most of my respondents, America symbolized the "Mountain of Gold" where their chances of improving their standard of living would significantly increase.

Maximizing Household Income and Minimizing Risk

My data support the new economic theory of migration, which holds that families or households, not individual actors, make migration decisions in order to maximize expected income, minimize risks, and loosen constraints associated with a variety of market failures (Stark and Bloom 1985). Both my quantitative and qualitative data suggest that members of a subject's immediate and extended family played a crucial role in the subject's decision to leave China, because he or she depended on them for financial support to finance the illegal passage. Without that support, few respondents could come up with the $30,000 smuggling fee.

Another reason for immigrating to the United States was the desire to minimize the risk associated with Chinese economic policy. Although their living standards had improved after China adopted the open-door policy in the late 1970s, some of my respondents were unsure how long the reform policy might last. The lessons on the Cultural Revolution had not been lost on these people.[4] If China decided at some point to close its doors and return to a policy of economic collectivization, they could lose their possessions and be subjected to persecution because of their wealth. Having a family member established abroad, they believed, was the best way to protect themselves and their wealth.

Some respondents who considered themselves affluent viewed the acquisition of a foreign passport as the best protection from the Chinese government. A foreign passport would give them "overseas Chinese" status even if they lived in China, and this, they believed, would protect their wealth from arbitrary confiscation by the Chinese government. A foreign passport would also confer the economic privileges accorded to overseas Chinese by the Chinese government.[5]

Finally, some of my well-to-do respondents came to the United States because their status here could be used to protect and justify their families' wealth in China. Their families were making a substantial amount of money in China, but their income-generating activities might not be considered totally legitimate under Chinese law. In the event of an investigation by Chinese authorities, wealth could be explained by cash gifts from a family member abroad.

According to Massey et al. (1993), the new economic theorists suggest that families send workers overseas not only to increase income in absolute terms but also to improve income relative to other households, an argument supported by my data. Some of my respondents came to America because so many people from their area had immigrated to the United States that they felt they had no choice but to follow if they did not want to fall behind their neighbors in relative economic terms.

The Dislocation of Labor

World systems theory suggests that transnational migration is a result of the expansion of capitalism from its core in Western Europe, North America, Oceania, and Japan to other peripheral countries. The incorporation of these peripheral regions into the world market economy causes internal disruptions and dislocations that in turn generate immigration (Morawska 1990). According to Ong et al. (1994), Asian immigration to the United States should be understood in the context of developing global capitalism. Because of the economic crisis in the American capitalist economy in the 1960s, the Pacific Rim economy has been "restructured" by American industrialists to take advantage of the cheap labor available in Asian countries. As some of these countries industrialize, professionals and unskilled workers move from Asia to the United States, mainly to fill the demand for a semi-coerced labor force in a changing U.S. capitalist economy.

The displacement in Fuzhou, for example, is rooted in distant and recent history. For many centuries, economic development in Fujian Province in general and the Fuzhou area in particular has been hampered by the shortage of arable land (Chao and Chan 1993). As a result of China's open-door policy and restructuring into a market-oriented economy in the late 1970s, a large amount of farmland in the Fuzhou area has been converted into industrial areas or special economic zones, displacing farmers from their land (Zhang and Gaylord 1996). Poorly educated farmers cannot compete with young, better-educated females for factory jobs in the rapidly expanding manufacturing industries (WuDunn 1992).

As the Fuzhou area, like the Guangdong Province, became the destination for millions of young, desperate workers from inland areas such as Sichuan and Hunan Provinces (Li 1997), displaced farmers and local workers faced additional competitive pressures and looked eagerly for a way out (Burdman 1993i; Han 1993).

Fishermen, too, felt trapped in a dying occupation. According to a journalist who visited Guantou, "residents say fishing, Guantou's traditional industry, is no longer profitable because fish stocks have been depleted. Many fishermen now subsist on farming, shopkeeping, construction and odd-jobbing" (Leicester 1993: 11). Moreover, as China confronted the painful task of closing inefficient state enterprises, the urban unemployment rate increased (Kristof and WuDunn 1994), forcing many people in the Fuzhou area to leave China and seek jobs elsewhere.

PULL FACTORS

The dual market theory of international migration suggests that pull factors in the receiving countries, especially the chronic need for foreign workers, are more important than push factors in the sending communities (Piore 1979).

Job Opportunity and Higher Wages

The prevalence of working people in my sample (about 89 percent of my respondents) supports the common belief among the Fujianese that a person willing to work should have little trouble finding a job in the United States. Would-be Chinese immigrants are supported by households willing to put up $30,000, relatives and friends willing to borrow money, and loan-shark networks eager to finance clandestine trips, mainly because all of them are confident that a Chinese immigrant in the United States, will soon begin to earn money and repay the debt.

Although most will make less than an average U.S. wage earner does, undocumented Chinese still believe that coming to the United States is worthwhile. According to dual market theorists:

> The disjunction in living standards between developed and developing societies means that even low wages abroad appear to be generous by the standards of the home community; and even though an immigrant may realize that a foreign job is of low status abroad, he does not view himself as being a part of the receiving society. Rather, he sees himself as a member of his home community, within which foreign labor and hard currency remittances carry considerable honor and prestige. (Massey et al. 1993: 442)

Most illegal Chinese immigrants are more concerned with their families' well-being than with their own, a tendency somewhat at odds with American individualism. As a thirty-five-year-old Changle male said, "I am sacrificing myself to bring happiness to my family."

Other respondents in my sample said that a person living in the United States signifies hope for his or her immediate and extended family. A thirty-one-year-old Changle male explained, "When my family learned that I was leaving for the United States, they were excited. Why? Because I was going to earn U.S. dollars. Besides, my family members could come to join me later. Even though this might be a long-term plan, at the very least the economic status of my family would improve instantly. Since I left, everybody in my family has been full of hope for the future."

Political Asylum

Many immigration experts suggest that the U.S. political asylum program is a major pull factor for illegal immigration. After the Chinese government crackdown on student protests in June 1989, President George Bush issued an executive order allowing all Chinese students studying in the United States to become permanent residents. Later, many non-student Chinese living in the United States also were welcomed to stay permanently. According to Jack Shaw, the associate commissioner of the Immigration and Naturalization Service, "The executive order is a major impediment [to stemming illegal immigration]. It creates the appearance of a magnet" (Hood 1993c: 2). Bush's Executive Order of 1989, coupled with the Immigration Reform and Control Act (IRCA) of 1986, which allowed illegal immigrants who entered the United

States before 1982 to become permanent residents, created an impression among people in the Fuzhou area that the United States passes amnesty laws for illegal immigrants every time a new president is elected.

There is evidence that many from the Fuzhou area choose to come to the United States instead of to other countries because they know they have a chance to apply for political asylum after they arrive here.[6] If they chose to immigrate illegally to Japan or Taiwan, they would pay a lot less to smugglers and have a significantly less traumatic passage, but most prospective immigrants still prefer the United States because they are unlikely to be arrested and deported (Hong and Vandenburgh 1995).[7]

In America, immigrants who apply for political asylum are protected from detention and deportation until their applications are reviewed. About 84 percent of my respondents, regardless of whether or not they had been persecuted by the Chinese government, applied for political asylum.[8] While their asylum cases were pending, illegals were issued a C-8 immigration card that allowed them to remain in the United States and be legally employed (Ignatius 1993). If their petitions for asylum are rejected months or even years later, illegal immigrants still have the option of residing illegally in the United States, confident that immigration authorities are unlikely to make a concerted effort to find them. There is a saying among residents of the Fuzhou region: "Once you enter America, you have succeeded."[9]

PERPETUATION OF CLANDESTINE IMMIGRATION

Even after the causes of massive transnational migration subside, other factors may emerge to sustain the movement of people. Many scholars of international migration have suggested that the spread of migrant networks and the development of institutions supporting transnational movement make additional movement more likely, a process known as cumulative causation.

The Spread of Migrant Networks

According to network theory, migration increases when people believe they are going to a place where they will find friends, relatives, and a community of shared origins—in short, as taking less personal risk

(see Massey et al. 1993). The arrival in New York City of tens of thousands of Fujianese resulted in the development of a well-established
Fujianese community in New York (Kinkead 1992). On the lower east
side of Manhattan, buildings once occupied by Cantonese, Italian, and
Jewish residents have become the homes of newcomers from the Fuzhou
region (Kwong 1997). Likewise, many stores in Chinatown are owned
by business people from the Fuzhou area. Two streets in Chinatown—
East Broadway and Eldridge—have become so dominated by people
from Fuzhou that they are called "Fuzhou No. 1 Street" and "Fuzhou
No. 2 Street." As the population of people from the Fuzho area continues to grow in New York City, hundreds of restaurants, immigration
consultant offices, clinics, accounting firms, and driving schools have
been established in Manhattan's Chinatown to cater to their needs
(Kwong 1997).

Through networking, Fujianese come to learn about the outside
world. They become discontented with the living standards they
accepted in China and realize that they can do better in their adopted
homeland. A history teacher in Fujian told an American journalist why
the Fujianese are eager to go abroad: "We're on the coast. So while we're
better off, we also know more than people in other parts of China what
we're missing" (Kristof 1993: A1).

Reunification with loved ones is another sustaining factor for immigration. After the first wave of illegal Chinese immigrants settled in
America, their children followed in their parents' footsteps (Myers
1997) and wives, after being separated from their husbands for several
years, went to the United States illegally to reunite with their husbands
(Hood 1993b). A twenty-four-year-old female subject from Fuzhou City
said:

> I left China mainly for nonfinancial reasons. When I was in China, I met
> an overseas man in a barbershop where I was working, and we developed
> a very close relationship.[10] Later, he went back to America. When he was
> about to leave, he promised he would return in a year to marry me and
> bring me to America. However, I did not hear from him thereafter. I
> believed he looked down on me. Later, through a customer, I found a
> snakehead from Tingjiang. After I made a $1,000 down payment, the
> snakehead helped me go to Hong Kong as a tourist [and later to Amer-
> ica].

Smuggling Networks

The development of smuggling networks is another sustaining factor in illegal immigration. According to Massey et al., the strong demand for international migration creates "a lucrative economic niche for entrepreneurs and institutions dedicated to promoting international movement for profit, yielding a black market in immigration" (1993: 450). The clandestine immigration of Fujianese is supported by a number of organizations, ranging from smuggling networks and labor export companies in China to travel agencies and hotels in transit countries to arrangers (or snakeheads) and debt collectors in the United States (Kwong 1997). Without the support of these organizations and networks, the movement of tens of thousands of Chinese peasants and laborers to the United States would not be possible.

The Cumulative Effect

According to the theory of cumulative causation, once some families in a certain area begin to emigrate and improve their income, other families will feel relatively deprived and thus feel spurred to emigrate themselves (Taylor 1992). Feelings of deprivation are exacerbated when overseas Chinese visit China. When folks at home meet their friends and relatives from abroad, they are often stunned by their visitors' wealth. A thirty-year-old male from Tingjiang said, "In China, I lived in a so-called overseas village, where many families have overseas connections. When overseas Chinese came back, they spent money like water, and looked really *san chi* [arrogant]. That's why I envied the American lifestyle before I came here."

In the Fuzhou area, there is an insurmountable economic gap between households with one or more family member overseas and those without a family member abroad. Many families with relatives abroad dwell in new houses full of expensive furniture and home appliances, while others live in huts with little furniture and few modern amenities (Woolrich 1993b). For the relatively deprived, the only way to *fanshen* (restore one's social status) is for a family member to go abroad and send home foreign currency. Otherwise they will be viewed by neighbors, friends, and even relatives as foolish, lazy, or incompetent (Kwong 1997).

Although most of my respondents said they came to America to make money, they also acknowledged that they were under enormous pressure to immigrate. Most poorly educated people from rural areas were conditioned by Chinese authorities to act in concert with state-sponsored social movements and to follow the lead of others for fear of being left out. Being left out could mean individual as well as family disgrace. A thirty-eight-year-old woman with very little education explained:

> Before I came here, I imagined that America would be a wonderful place to live. I thought that if I ever had the opportunity to come to the United States, my life would not be wasted. Because so many people from my area have come to America, if I didn't, I would have been looked down on by others. My neighbors would have thought that everyone in my family was useless. When my friends and relatives in America learned that I was planning to join them, they said, "Come! The United States is better than China."

A thirty-five-year-old man from Changle noted the great increase in immigration from his area: "It's like if a family does not have a member here, it's a disgrace."

OTHER FACTORS RELATED TO CHINESE IMMIGRATION

My respondents offered a variety of more individual reasons for immigrating; although their personal circumstances varied, they referred to broad categories of mostly non-economic factors that are rarely discussed in the literature on the causes of international migration.

Personal Problems

Examining immigration from a psychoanalytic perspective, Grinberg and Grinberg (1989) suggest that people leave home not only because of social forces but also because of individual traumas and the belief that a change in living environment will alleviate the pain associated with their country of origin. Some of the immigrants in my sample left China because they were experiencing personal problems too awful to cope with. Some, for example, did not get along with their spouses but did not want to get a divorce.[11] Others said they left China because of trouble with the law. In the words of a thirty-eight-year-old male from Changle, "I was involved in a fight, and I knew I would be in trouble [arrested] sooner or later. So I decided to come to America. Before I left China, I hid in a place far away from home. I was making about $250 a month as a water and electric technician, and you can say I was living a very comfortable life. However, to avoid trouble, I had to leave China." Another subject, a thirty-five-year-old male, left out of fear of government reprisals. "I owned a massage parlor in China. Even though I made about $2,000 a month, I did not like the business because I knew I couldn't be in it for long. There was no stability in this kind of business. I was once imprisoned for fifteen years. I was wary that China might change her liberal policy, and that I might be jailed again [for my sex business]."

Official Extortion and Corruption

Some of my respondents who were *getihus* (private entrepreneurs) in China said they immigrated because they were upset by official exploitation. A twenty-nine-year-old store owner from Fuzhou City said, "Before I came to America, my idea of America was a free country where a person can earn a lot of money by working hard. In China, if you make money, you end up being extorted by police and tax collectors." Another subject, a thirty-five-year-old factory owner from Fuzhou City, explained why he came to America: "I was the owner of a machine factory. I earned about $6,000 a year. Naturally, I lived a comfortable life in China. I owned a car and a motorcycle. You can say I came here for political freedom. In my hometown, my income made a lot of people *yanhong* [eyes turned red with envy]. Many government employees came to 'extract oil' [ask for money] from me. I refused some of them. In retaliation, they charged me with a crime I did not commit. That's why I left in a hurry. I made up my mind in a few days."

Dissatisfaction with the Chinese government is largely a result of official corruption and a sense of powerlessness among ordinary Chinese who lack *guanxi* (connections) (Bian and Logan 1996). Because most so-called good jobs in China are in the public sector, most Chinese believe that without connections it is impossible to find a good job, no matter how qualified the applicant.[12] In the words of one illegal Chinese immigrant, "In China, if you do not have someone rich or powerful to rely on, you have no chance whatsoever to become successful. Here in the United States, as long as you are willing to work hard, you have a chance to make it" (*World Journal,* May 31, 1993: A3).

Guanxi not only helps people get government jobs, it also enables them to get by with their everyday activities. Most activities must approved by Chinese authorities, but people with *guanxi* can use the "back door" to get what they want. The majority, by contrast, have to endure all of the frustrations caused by inept and corrupt government employees. The only way out of this stressful situation for them is emigration abroad. They believe that when they return as overseas Chinese, government officials will treat them with more decency and respect.

Political Persecution

Some of my respondents said they left China for political reasons. A forty-year-old male from Fuzhou City expressed his dismay over China's recent political history:

> When I was in China, I considered going to America as going to heaven. Think about it. I suffered a lot during the Cultural Revolution, and before that, I survived the Big Famine.[13] That's why I was always looking for an opportunity to come to the United States. I have no feelings for China anymore. During the Cultural Revolution, I was wrongfully labelled as a "counterrevolutionary"[14] and tortured. I was *douzheng* [struggled against][15] for twenty days. Only after they couldn't find anything against me, did they send me home. Since then, whenever I think of the communists' tactics, it scares me. That's why I have longed for an opportunity to come to this free country.

Some respondents left China because they were persecuted under China's one-child policy.[16] A forty-three-year-old farmer from Tingjiang explained, "I came because I have four children. The Chinese government forced me to be sterilized and wanted to fine me. My life in China was miserable. I needed to get away. That's why I decided to come to the United States." Another subject, a twenty-seven-year-old male from Changle, left China because, as he put it, "I was victimized under the one-child policy, and I am disgusted with the communist regime. When my wife was pregnant with our second child, she was forced to have an abortion five days before she was about to give birth."

There is no doubt that people are distraught about the denial of human rights in China. Even though most of my respondents did not elaborate on this issue, I presume that government oppression may be an underlying cause of the massive legal and illegal immigration of Chinese.[17]

Circumstantial Factors and Childhood Expectations

The desire to immigrate can be either spontaneous or long-standing (Grinberg and Grinberg 1989). Some of my respondents came to the United States almost by chance. A thirty-one-year-old woman from Changle gave this almost unbelievable account of how she came to the United States virtually on the spur of the moment:

> Come to think of it, I was quite *hutu* (silly). One day, two friends came to say farewell because they were about to leave for the United States. They told me it cost very little to initiate a trip to the United States. They said I only need to pay a little snakehead about $60 and he would allow me to board the ship. The $60 would cover the bus fare from Fuzhou to Guangzhou. No need to provide anything else. My friends also said I would need to pay a big snakehead $30,500 when I reach the United States. So I left with them, without notifying my family. After I arrived in Guangzhou, I called home and told my family I was leaving. They cried and asked me not to go, but it was too late.

Most of my subjects, however, had thought of the United States since their early childhood. As one said, "Before I came here, I was crazy about the United States. For me, coming to the United States is the most important goal of my life." A fourteen-year-old girl from Changle described her lifelong desire to emigrate to America:

> My parents were in the meat business, and they were very rich. My schoolmates were always talking about going to the United States. Some of them have migrated to the United States legally, and one of them used illegal methods. When I told my parents I wanted to go to America, they were against it because I was so young. Then I started creating problems at home, like frequently arguing with my parents. Soon they were convinced that they had no choice but to let me go.

The desire to come to the United States is so strong among some Chinese that they have wildly inflated expectations of the place. A twenty-four-year-old male from Changle said, "Before I came, I thought America was a very prosperous country, that it was a heaven filled with gold. In America, you could gain weight by just drinking water." Some young subjects were so determined to come to the United States they did not even bother seek employment after graduating from high school. These youths from affluent families were confident that once they found the opportunity to leave, their families would provide them with the money to go.

Tricked by Snakeheads

A small number of Chinese immigrants embark on a clandestine trip to the United States because they are tricked by smugglers, especially by little snakeheads (recruiters) whose only motive is to collect fees from big snakeheads. Some of my respondents were told by their little snakeheads that they would become legal residents if they reached the United States before July 1, 1993, or that illegal immigrants are granted amnesty every four years, with the election of a new president. According to Chinese authorities, illegal immigration by Chinese would not have become a major problem if such greedy snakeheads did not exist.

In sum, it appears that personal factors (specific motives and family pressures) and structural factors (socioeconomic and political conditions as well as opportunities abroad) combine to motivate Chinese to make the illegal passage to the United States. Whereas structural factors might explain the prevalence of illegal immigration, personal factors seem to play a key role in determining who will actually immigrate.

The causes of illegal immigration among the Chinese raise additional questions. First, why are people from the Fuzhou area the primary illegal immigrants to the United States? My study suggests several reasons. For one thing, there are many first- and second-generation Fujianese and Cantonese in almost every corner of the world, and once China adopted its open-door policy, people from these two groups became more likely to immigrate than did people from other Chinese groups who had no overseas connections. The development of a human smuggling industry in the Fuzhou area facilitated the illegal movement of the local population, whereas people from Beijing and Shanghai, who also immigrate in large numbers, have access to legitimate channels.

Second, will people from other parts of China also initiate a covert international movement? U.S. and European officials concerned about this likelihood want to identify the factors that may trigger it. It is important to point out that although most undocumented Chinese living in the United States, Japan, and Taiwan are from the Fuzhou region, many undocumented Chinese from other areas live throughout the world. For example, many illegal Chinese in Hong Kong are from Guangdong Province (Vagg 1993), and most undocumented Chinese in Italy are from Zhejiang Province (W. Chan 1993; Y. Chu 1996). As only part of the massive immigration of Chinese (Smith 1997), the causes and impact of illegal Chinese migration to the United States must be examined in relation to legal Chinese immigration, as well as both legal and illegal immigration of Chinese to Hong Kong, Japan, Taiwan, and Western Europe.

Finally, are illegal Chinese immigrants in the United States really economic or political refugees? Even though my subjects did not elaborate very much on the political aspects of their decision, it seems clear that lacking the right to vote, being deprived of freedom of speech and opportunity, being subject to exploitation by government officials, and the dismal prospects for those without *guanxi* all are significant forces in the decision to migrate.

3 The Social Organization of Human Smuggling

UNLAWFUL ENTRY of Chinese nationals into the United States is not a recent phenomenon. After the Chinese Exclusion Act (1882), a result of widespread racism against the Chinese, barred Chinese from entering the United States (Saxton 1971; Salyer 1995), illegal smuggling brought some twenty thousand Chinese into the country annually in the last years of the nineteenth century (Tsai 1986; Storti 1991). In one method, Chinese immigrants fraudulently claimed that they were children of naturalized Chinese (Sung 1967).[1] Some Chinese women were also brought into the United States to work in the brothels of San Francisco's Chinatown (Martin 1977).

In more recent years, family members living in the United States have helped illegal immigrants. After the United States established formal relations with China in 1979, many overseas Chinese began to visit their families and relatives in China and were shocked by the level of poverty there. Out of sympathy or guilt, or simply to impress their long separated families and friends, the overseas Chinese gave money or expensive gifts to their relatives (Kwong 1997), no doubt leaving a lasting impression on the local Chinese that all overseas Chinese were well-to-do. This perception inspired other Chinese to start going abroad in the early 1980s. At the beginning, most Chinese were brought into the United States across the Canadian or Mexican borders (Myers 1996).

As already mentioned, in the wake of the 1989 Tiananmen Square violence, political asylum was extended to Chinese students in the United States. Later, as U.S. government officials became concerned about human rights conditions in China, they also granted political asylum to most Chinese who could demonstrate that they were persecuted under China's one-child policy (*Sing Tao Daily*, September 2, 1992). The U.S. government's lenient immigration policy, coupled with the indifferent attitude of local Chinese authorities toward illegal immigration, resulted in an influx of illegal Chinese immigrants in the early 1990s.

As illegal Chinese immigration to the United States exploded in the early 1990s, Chinese smugglers reacted by developing more daring methods. Instead of transporting a relatively small number of immigrants via air, they discovered a way to move hundreds of illegal immigrants by ship across the Pacific Ocean. Sea smuggling was developed in 1989, and it expanded rapidly over the next three years before subsiding in the aftermath of the *Golden Venture* incident.

THE SMUGGLERS

Little is known about the people and organizations involved in smuggling Chinese to the United States. Law enforcement authorities know little about human smugglers' individual characteristics, such as their country of origin, immigration status (if they are in the United States), or occupation. They are also uncertain whether smugglers are members of Chinese triads, tongs, or street gangs.[2] Nor is there much data on the structure of people-trafficking organizations. How, for example, are trafficking rings organized? How are smugglers linked to Chinese government officials? How do they develop smuggling routes? Moreover, there is no credible information on the connection, if any, between human smuggling and heroin trafficking, although American authorities assume that some Chinese crime groups are involved in both (U.S. Senate 1992; Myers 1994).

My subjects often distinguished between big snakeheads and little snakeheads. Big snakeheads (or arrangers/investors), often Chinese living outside China, generally invest money in a smuggling operation and oversee the entire operation but usually are not known by those being smuggled. Little snakeheads, or recruiters, usually live in China and work as middlemen between big snakeheads and customers; they are mainly responsible for finding and screening customers and collecting down payments.

Big Snakeheads

According to a Chinese police officer I interviewed, there is no "typical" big snakehead:

> Big snakeheads can be categorized according to their education level, citizenship, and closeness to Chinese government officials. There are well-educated and poorly educated big snakeheads, foreign-based and

China-based big snakeheads, and "good" and "bad" big snakeheads. In general, big snakeheads who help people to *sidu* [to leave China legally and enter another country illegally] are closely associated with Chinese authorities because they need to obtain passports and other travel documents [e.g., exit permits] from government units. Big snakeheads who help people to *toudu* [to leave China and enter another country both illegally] are unlikely to be affiliated with authorities because they do not need to acquire travel documents for their clients. Some "big snakeheads" are basically con men whose main purpose is to cheat customers out of their down payments. Finally, there are snakeheads who know they are unable to smuggle people to the United States, yet they guarantee their customers safe arrival in the United States. These snakeheads smuggle people out of China by any means and then sell them to snakeheads in transit points for the final leg to America.

Some of my respondents said that all contacts were made through little snakeheads and that they never met their big snakeheads. A female big snakehead explained why big snakeheads generally do not deal directly with their clients:

> At the very beginning, I was involved in smuggling people from Fuzhou to Hong Kong. During that time, I always talked to my clients face to face. Once, I brought a small group of people to Shenzhen and was about to help them enter Hong Kong. All of a sudden, my clients' guarantors and relatives in Hong Kong changed their minds and said they were not going to pay the smuggling fees on my clients' behalf.[3] I had no choice but to bring those would-be immigrants who were already in Shenzhen back to their villages in Tingjiang. Since I had to spend money transporting them from Tingjiang to Shenzhen, I was supposed to keep the down payment, which was about $2,500 per person. Yet I returned to everybody half of their down payments. Nevertheless, my clients were not happy; they wanted the entire down payment back. Therefore, there was a major disagreement among us. My clients called and threatened me. Later, when I visited Tingjiang, a group of people stopped me and forced me to return their money. Since that incident, I made up my mind that I would not interact directly with my clients anymore. I asked an assistant to deal with my clients, and I remained behind the scenes.

Some of my subjects did not even know who their big snakeheads were. Subjects who did meet, or who knew, their snakeheads had mixed impressions. Most tended to see them as respected business people rather than as criminals. According to a twenty-five-year-old male from Changle: "Big snakeheads are mainly wealthy business owners. That's why people trust them. They are not criminals. Big snakeheads have got to have a good reputation."

Snakeheads were often Chinese Americans closely connected to authorities in the Fuzhou area.[4] Originally from the area, these snakeheads played an active role in contributing money to their hometowns, according to many of my respondents. A twenty-five-year-old male construction worker from Fuzhou City considered his snakehead a small capitalist who had returned to China and made generous donations to improving the local infrastructure.

Many respondents thought of snakeheads as philanthropists and appreciated their services. The $30,000 fare to America was worth it, in their opinion. In the words of a forty-three-year-old male from Tingjiang, "I look at human smuggling as benevolent work because a snakehead can help people out of their predicament." A nineteen-year-old woman from Changle described snakeheads as "good people because, in a way, they help China solve her overpopulation problem."

Respondents who encountered no hardships on their voyage normally had only good things to say about their snakeheads, especially if they were well-treated once they reached New York. A forty-four-year-old male from Tingjiang described his experience:

> [One of] my snakeheads was a classmate of mine who was living in Hong Kong. He obtained a Chinese passport for me and helped me to get to the first transit point. After I arrived in New York City, another person and I were kept in [another] snakehead's house where the two of us shared a bedroom. The meals were good, and we were allowed to watch TV and talked to each other. The [New York] snakehead treated us very well; he prepared meals for us every day. He even said: "If you are short of a couple of thousand dollars don't worry. Pay me later when you have the money." Besides, everything went very smoothly on the way to America. We lived and ate well throughout the trip. We were also able to enjoy ourselves. For instance, in Bolivia, we visited quite a few tourist attractions. Before we left Bolivia, the snakehead there even threw us a farewell party. Everybody in the group considered this to be a nice trip.

Other respondents, however, saw their snakeheads as "ordinary people" out to make money. A few regarded big snakeheads as selfish, untrustworthy people who cared nothing for the needs and feelings of their customers. Respondents who were unhappy with their snakeheads felt they had been misled or lied to. Some were told that they would fly to the United States but were later coerced into taking the sea route or crossing the rugged China-Myanmar border. Some who were smuggled by sea had been told that they would be transported on luxurious ocean liners. One snakehead promised that the ship would be "furnished with a theater, a free bar, and a swimming pool."

After arriving in New York City, some subjects were forced to pay more than the price set in China and overcharged for phone calls to China. Some snakeheads "sold" their clients to other snakeheads at various transit points when they were unable to obtain fraudulent travel documents for them.

Most of my respondents, however, viewed big snakeheads as smart and capable business people with power, wealth, good reputations, and connections. They were described as people who were *paitou* (had an aura of wealth), *lihai* (shrewd), *youbanfa* (highly capable), *kekao* (reliable). Most big snakeheads were Fuzhou-born overseas Chinese living in the United States, Hong Kong, or Thailand, though Taiwanese in Taiwan, Brazil, Panama, and Bolivia were also said to be active in human smuggling. My respondents also said that a small number of high-ranking or retired Chinese officials were involved in smuggling.

Little Snakeheads

Little snakeheads, also called *lakejia* (recruiters), are often local Chinese rather than overseas Chinese. All kinds of people seemingly can become little snakeheads, including low-level government employees, close friends or relatives of big snakeheads,the unemployed, and even housewives. Most of my respondents saw them as opportunists primarily interested in encouraging people to immigrate while downplaying the hardships and associated dangers.

Quite a few of my respondents expressed outrage when asked about their little snakeheads, feeling they had been fooled. Because little snakeheads are paid a fee for each passenger they recruit, they often mislead their potential "clients" by guaranteeing a safe and comfortable passage to America. Most people in the Fuzhou area have never been even to Beijing or Shanghai, let alone abroad, and are gullible. A twenty-four-year-old female teacher who had an arduous boat trip and border crossing from Mexico said, "The little snakehead told me that it was going to be a safe trip. You can say he glamorized everything about the trip. He sounded *tian hua luan duo* [flowers dropping from the sky, all very rosy] when he tried to persuade me to leave China."

Although several respondents thought their little snakeheads had kept their promises, most were much more positive toward the big snakeheads who were relatively inaccessible to them than toward the little snakeheads with whom they had to deal directly. Their greatest displeasure, however, was reserved for crew members and enforcers on smuggling ships and debt collectors in New York City.

GROUP CHARACTERISTICS

A smuggler I interviewed in 1994 insisted that nobody really knows how many Chinese smuggling groups exist worldwide, but she guessed approximately fifty. Other estimates vary widely, from only seven or eight (*Sing Tao Daily*, July 14, 1990) to as many as twenty or twenty-five (Chan et al. 1990; Burdman 1993b). According to some observers, Chinese people-trafficking groups are well organized, transnational criminal enterprises that are active in China, Hong Kong, Taiwan, Thailand, and the United States (Myers 1992; U.S. Senate 1992; Burdman 1993b), but there are little empirical data to support this observation.

A smuggler I once asked to characterize a Chinese smuggling network said, "It's like a dragon. Although it's a lengthy creature, various organic parts are tightly linked." According to my subjects, in addition to big and little snakeheads, a smuggling organization includes many roles:

1. Transporters. Transporters in China help immigrants traveling by land or sea make their way to the border or smuggling ship. Transporters based in the United States are responsible for taking smuggled immigrants from airports or seaports to safe houses.
2. Corrupt public officials. Chinese government officials accept bribes in return for Chinese passports. Law enforcement authorities in many transit countries are also paid to aid the illegal Chinese immigrants entering and exiting their countries.
3. Guides and crew members. Guides move illegal immigrants from one transit point to another and aid immigrants entering the United States by land or air. Crew members are employed by snakeheads to charter or work on smuggling ships.
4. Enforcers. The enforcers, themselves mostly illegal immigrants, are hired by big snakeheads to work on the smuggling ships. They are responsible for maintaining order and for distributing food and drinking water.

5. Support personnel. These are local people at the transit points who provide food and lodging to illegal immigrants.
6. Debt collectors. A U.S.-based debt collector is responsible for locking up illegal immigrants in safe houses until their debt is paid and for collecting smuggling fees. There are also China-based debt collectors.

According to data collected in New York City and the Fuzhou area, a close working relationship links the leaders and others in the smuggling network, especially the snakeheads in the United States and China. More often than not, all those in the smuggling ring belong to a family or extended family or are good friends. If a smuggling group is involved in air smuggling, the group may also need someone to work as a snakehead in such transit points as Hong Kong or Thailand.

When I visited Fuzhou, I interviewed a number of people who belonged to a ring that smuggled Chinese by air. A woman in charge of a government trade unit in Fuzhou City recruited customers and procured travel documents. She interacted only with government officials who helped her obtain travel documents; her assistant dealt with customers directly, recruiting, collecting down payments, signing contracts, and so forth. She recruited a partner, a childhood friend and member of the Public Security Bureau, who was responsible for securing travel documents for the smuggling ring's clients. A female relative in Singapore acted as a transit point snakehead. She traveled to countries such as Thailand, Indonesia, and Malaysia to set up transit points in those countries.

The primary leader and investor in the ring, based in New York, was responsible for subcontracting with members of a Queens-based gang to keep immigrants in safe houses and collect their fees after arrival in the United States. If the fee was to be paid in China, the female snakehead's assistant in China would collect it. It was unclear to me how profits were distributed among members of the smuggling ring or how money was actually transferred from one place to another.

Most smuggling groups reportedly specialize in either air or sea smuggling. According to Zhang and Gaylord (1996), only groups with ties to organized crime groups in Asia engage in the complicated, large-scale operations of sea smuggling, but snakeheads involved in air smuggling may venture into sea smuggling. A thirty-two-year-old housewife from Fuzhou City who left China by boat alleged that her snakehead was involved in both.

Not all sea smugglers are affiliated with criminal groups, Zhang and Gaylord notwithstanding. A forty-year-old male store owner from Changle described his female snakehead, who specialized in sea smuggling, as "a Taiwanese with a good reputation who came to China to be a snakehead. She was involved in sea smuggling for the first time when I was recruited by her. After that, she transported several boatloads of people to the United States. . . . She visited Fuzhou often. After our ship arrived in Los Angeles, [her] husband and a group of people picked us up."

Some U.S. authorities are convinced that Chinese smugglers of immigrants also bring heroin from southeast Asia into the United States (U.S. Senate 1992). Senator William Roth, Jr., the Delaware Republican who directed a Senate investigation of Asian organized crime, claimed that some human smugglers are former drug dealers (Burdman 1993b), and there is some evidence to support this view. One of the first groups of Chinese to be charged with human smuggling had previously been indicted for heroin trafficking (*Centre Daily News,* May 9, 1985), and a Chinese American who owned a garment factory in New York City's Chinatown was charged with both heroin and human trafficking (*Sing Tao Daily,* October 10, 1992). Moreover, during an undercover operation, Chinese smugglers offered heroin to federal agents posing as corrupt immigration officers in exchange for travel documents (DeStefano 1994). U.S. officials also claim that smuggled Chinese are asked by snakeheads to carry heroin into the United States, presumably to finance their illegal passage (Chan and Dao 1990d). Mark Riordan, INS assistant officer for Hong Kong, suggested that "smugglers make even more when illegals who can't raise the fee carry heroin in exchange for their trip" (Chan and Dao 1990b: 14).

I asked my respondents whether their snakeheads asked them to carry drugs or to commit crimes to subsidize their illegal passage. Of the three hundred respondents, only one admitted that he was asked by his snakehead to transport two bags of opium from the Golden Triangle to Bangkok, Thailand. None of those who left China by sea saw any illicit drugs aboard the sea vessels. It is not clear whether human smugglers are typically involved in heroin trafficking. Based on my interviews, I conclude that only a small number are.

OPERATIONAL FEATURES

To fully understand how a human smuggling group functions, one would want detailed information about their several operations. How do smugglers in China find and screen their clients? How do they obtain passports and visas for their clients? How do they arrange sea vessels to transport their clients to the United States or to a transit point? How do smugglers in China coordinate with smugglers at transit points along the way? How do smugglers at final transit points coordinate with traffickers in ports of entry? Do smuggling rings occasionally work together or do they work independently? I was unable to obtain such specific data in the course of my research and can only describe in general how the process worked for my subjects.

Contacting and Screening Clients

Of the three hundred respondents, only eleven said they were initially approached by little snakeheads. The majority (74 percent) initiated contact with their little snakeheads through friends or relatives in China (see Appendix B, Table 4). Some subjects (12 percent) found their snakeheads through relatives and friends living abroad. About 30 percent of those who reached the United States in 1988 and before found their foreign-based snakeheads through friends and relatives who were living abroad. My data suggest that smugglers began moving their recruiting activities from abroad to China in the early 1990s, primarily by hiring friends and relatives in China to recruit customers. By various accounts, big snakeheads normally pay recruiters or little snakeheads somewhere between $500 and $1,000 per recruit (Burdman 1993a).

As we have seen, little snakeheads were usually family members, relatives, or good friends of big snakeheads. When little snakeheads had trouble recruiting customers themselves—often the case with sea smuggling, when hundreds of customers must be recruited within a short period—they turned to family members and friends to act as a second tier of little snakeheads. Occasionally, my subjects said, snakeheads asked former clients now in the United States to recruit friends and relatives in China.

Preparing for the Journey

The U.S. media have reported that since 1989, when modern smuggling by sea began, smugglers have allowed many of their customers, without the need of a guarantor or a down payment, to board smuggling ships (Lawrence 1993; Y. Chan 1993b), but only twenty-eight (9 percent) of my subjects were allowed to leave China without a guarantor or a down payment, and some had to have both. It appears, however, that from 1989 to 1993 these requirements were not strictly enforced, and by 1993 the need for a guarantor was not as critical as it had been before 1989. Especially for those smuggled by ship, a down payment was usually sufficient.

The average down payment of my respondents was $3,069, but the mode was $1,000. According to a subject who left China by ship, the down payment was made this way: "Once I got on the ship, I turned over my identification card to the little snakeheads and they went to my home, collected the $1,000, and returned my identification card to my family."[5]

After the down payment is made and/or the name and address of a guarantor is provided, the smuggler and customer may sign a contract.[6] Many rules are stipulated in these contracts, but it is not clear how closely the signing parties follow them. One chilling aspect of these contracts is the understanding by both parties that the smugglers can hold their clients hostage if the clients, upon arrival in America, do not come up with the smuggling fee.

After a contract is signed, there is a waiting period before departure. About 20 percent of my subjects waited a week or less, and more than half waited less than a month. Only about 15 percent had to wait for more than three months. The average waiting period remained at about two months between 1988 and 1993, but waiting times differed significantly with smuggling method. The average waiting period was twenty-nine days for subjects who left China by ship, forty-six days for those entered the United States by land, and seventy-three days for those who left by air.

Smuggling Fees

My respondents paid an average of $27,745 for their illegal passage, ranging from a minimum of $9,000 to a maximum of $35,000. The average smuggling fee in 1988 was $22,956 and increased about $2,000 each year after that, with the exception of 1992 and 1993. By 1993, the average smuggling fee was $29,688 (see Appendix B, Table 5).[7] Of the three routes, air travel was the most expensive ($29,070), followed by the sea route ($27,560). The least expensive was the land route ($26,276). Between 1988 and 1993, the smuggling charge for the air route increased the most (from $23,500 in 1988 and earlier to $31,230 in 1993).

ORGANIZED CRIME, GANGS, AND THE HUMAN TRADE

Law enforcement and immigration officials in the United States have asserted that Chinese triads, tongs, and street gangs are involved in human smuggling (U.S. Senate 1992) and claim that Hong Kong-based triads are responsible for the massive movement of undocumented Chinese to the United States via Hong Kong (Torode 1993a). As Bolz (1995: 148) put it, "Triads have taken over the smuggling of illegal immigrants from smaller 'mom and pop' organizations as an increasingly attractive alternative to drug trafficking because it promises multibillion dollar profits without the same severe penalties if caught."

There is indeed evidence that certain triad members are involved in the human trade. One human smuggler has testified in court that a triad member in Hong Kong was involved in human smuggling (Torode 1993c), and authorities in California are convinced that the California-based Wo Hop To triad was responsible for the arrival of eighty-five undocumented Chinese on a smuggling boat discovered near Long Beach, California, in 1992 (*Sing Tao Daily*, March, 6, 1992). However, no triad member or organization, either in Hong Kong or the United States, has ever been indicted for human smuggling.

U.S. authorities have also claimed that the U.S.-based tongs or community associations, especially the Fukien American Association, are active in the human trade, citing the testimony of New York City police at the 1992 U.S. Senate hearings on Asian organized crime (U.S. Senate,1992). Leaders of the Fukien American Association, however, have denied that their organization has ever been involved in the illegal alien trade. The president of the association in 1992, labelled by journalists the "Commander-in-Chief of Illegal Smuggling," announced at a press conference that his organization "does not have control over certain individual members and therefore can not be held responsible for their illegal activities. It is unfair to blacken the name of the Fukien

American Association as a whole based on the behavior of some non-member bad elements which are not under the control of the Association" (Lau 1993: 5).

Since 1991 U.S. authorities have also asserted that Chinese and Vietnamese street gangs are involved in smuggling. After a 1991 article in the *San Francisco Examiner* linked Asian gangs and human trafficking (Freedman, 1991), numerous media accounts depicted Chinese gangs in New York City as collectors of smuggling payments. Gang members allegedly picked up illegal immigrants at airports or docks, kept them in safe houses, and forced them to call their relatives to make payments. For their services, gangs reportedly were paid between $1,500 to $2,000 per smuggled immigrant. None of these news articles implied that gangs were involved in transporting immigrants from China to America (Strom 1991).

After the *Golden Venture* incident, U.S. immigration officials and law enforcement authorities began to view Chinese gang members not as "service providers" to smugglers but as smugglers themselves who were capable of transporting hundreds of illegal immigrants across the Pacific Ocean (Lay 1993; Wang 1996) and charged that the Fuk Ching gang was responsible for the *Golden Venture* tragedy itself (Burdman 1993b; Faison 1993a; Gladwell and Stassen-Berger 1993b; Treaster 1993). According to the authorities, the gang not only invested money in the purchase of the *Golden Venture,* but also was directly involved in recruiting prospective immigrants in China.

In a crack-down on Chinese gangs, members of the White Tigers, the Green Dragons, and the Fuk Ching were indicted for transporting people from borders and coastal areas to New York City and collecting debts for human smugglers. According to court materials in a murder case involving the Fuk Ching gang, Ah Chu, a snakehead, paid a member of the Fuk Ching $500 a head to pick up five illegal immigrants near the Mexican border. Ah Chu also gave this gang member $150,000 to go to California, where he paid a group of Mexicans $500 for each illegal alien they brought in. According to the gang member, Ah Chu was not member of the Fuk Ching but a partner or friend of the big boss, Ah Kay. The gang member also made two trips to Boston to pick up illegal aliens, transporting seven people by van from Boston to New York on each trip. For this and for serving time in another case, Ah Kay allegedly paid him $10,000 (Superior Court of New Jersey 1995).

At the trial, a street-level leader of the Fuk Ching acknowledged that his gang boss paid him $3,000 for transporting 130 illegal immigrants from Boston to New York in a Ryder truck, adding that his gang had smuggled three hundred immigrants from China to the United States. Another Fuk Ching defendant testified that he received $200 to $300 a week for watching the "customers." No Chinese gang members, however, not even members of the Fuk Ching gang—who were widely believed to be the most active in human trafficking—were charged with transporting illegals from China to the United States. Nevertheless, U.S. authorities completed an undercover operation called "Operation Sea Dragon" and concluded that "a highly sophisticated, compartmentalized network of Asian gangs in different parts of the United States" was deeply involved in human smuggling (Branigin 1996: A12).

When asked what role Chinese gangs play in the human trade, a Chinese American immigration officer told me that in the past, Chinese gangs had only collected fees for smugglers but that more recently they have been getting into the smuggling business themselves. They now "plan the trips, invest the needed capital, and collect the debt in America."

Although tongs and gangs allegedly are involved in the human trade, little is known about the nature and extent of their involvement, other than what is suggested by these anecdotal accounts. Nor is it clear whether smuggling operations are sponsored by tongs and gangs jointly or carried out by individual members on an ad hoc basis. Some observers, including some law enforcement authorities, disagree that smuggling organizations are closely linked with gangs or tongs and regard the connection as, at best, haphazard. One Hong Kong police officer claimed that "Some of these people are in triads, but it isn't so organized. It's just a question of a couple of people with the wherewithal to put together a criminal scheme to smuggle illegal immigrants" (DeStefano et al. 1991: 8). Another observer concluded that "Contrary to popular belief, people who deal in this business are normally shop or business owners, not gang or 'Mafia' members" (*The Nation*, November 9, 1994: A2).

Asked by a reporter how he was related to members of organized crime, a New-York based smuggler denied any connection between snakeheads and gang members:

> What do you mean by "members of organized crime groups"? These people [debt-collectors] are nothing more than a bunch of hooligans who like

to bully people in Chinatown. These guys are getting out of control; they are willing to kill people for money. Yet, people like us who are in this business could not conduct our business without them. Most illegal immigrants are decent people; however, there are also some criminals. If I don't hire thugs to collect money, I may not get paid. . . . When the immigrants I smuggle arrive here, my debt collectors will go to the airport to pick them up and lock them up somewhere. They collect the smuggling fees, and I pay them $2,000 per immigrant (Nyo 1993: S4).

Willard Myers has also concluded that traditional organized crime groups such as the triads, tongs, and gangs do not dominate the human trade. In criticizing U.S. law enforcement strategies against the trade in Chinese human smuggling, Myers (1994: 4) has suggested that "Chinese transnational criminal activity is carried out as a form of entrepreneurial activity by and among persons who are linked by language (dialect group) and lineage (ancestral birth place), who may or may not be a member or affiliate of an organization recognized by law enforcement."

The testimony of my respondents, while a limited sample, tends to support the conclusion that human smuggling is not closely associated with organized crime, as has commonly been alleged in criminological literature (Maltz 1994). No doubt members of triads, tongs, and gangs are, to a certain extent, involved in trafficking Chinese, but I believe that their participation is neither sanctioned by nor even known to their respective organizations. Triads, tongs, and gangs are frightening terms that are often used to generate panic and can result in discrimination against ethnic and racial minorities. The "organized crime and gang" problem is perpetuated by the law enforcement community to justify greater investment in the traditional criminal justice apparatus. The media contribute to this view because organized crime and gang problems are easily sensationalized for public consumption. My data, however, suggest that the Chinese trade in human smuggling is not a form of organized crime but rather a "business" controlled by many otherwise legitimate groups, both small and large, working independently, each with its own organization, connections, methods, and routes. A smuggler once told me, "It's like a Chinese story about eight angels crossing a sea: every angel is extremely capable of achieving the goal due to her heavenly qualities." No one of these groups, however, dominates or monopolizes the lucrative trade. When U.S. authorities in New York indicted eighteen Chinese for human trafficking, they found that these people belonged to five smuggling groups, with several defendants belonging to more than one group (DeStefano 1994).

I also found, contrary to the assertions of Myers (1994), Hood (1993c, 1997), and Zhang and Gaylord (1996), that immigrant smuggling is not necessarily dominated by ethnic Chinese from Taiwan but is a global business initiated by Chinese Americans of Fuzhou extraction and supported not only by Taiwanese but also by Chinese and non-Chinese in numerous transit countries. In short, the human trade is in many ways like any other legitimate international trade, except that it is illegal. Like any trade, it needs organization and planning, but it does not appear to be linked with traditional "organized crime" groups.

GOVERNMENT CORRUPTION AND HUMAN TRAFFICKING

Reasoning that China is a tightly controlled society, U.S. authorities have suspected Chinese law enforcement authorities, as well, of involvement in the smuggling of immigrants to the United States (U.S. Senate 1992; Burdman 1993c; Engelberg 1994). In such a well-policed state, how could smugglers covertly transport tens of thousands of people and escape the notice of Chinese authorities? They must either be accepting bribes or be actively involved themselves in transporting people out of China.

An officer of the INS enforcement division told me that "People in the Fujian Public Security Bureau have to be involved in alien smuggling. They take bribes from smugglers and either turn a blind eye on illegal immigration or provide logistical support. The INS has evidence to show that Chinese law enforcement authorities are behind alien smuggling." Some of my subjects made the same point. A female immigrant who was deported back to China by Mexican authorities told me that a group of smugglers transported her and hundreds of others from Fuzhou City to a seaport on Chinese military trucks. She believed that the military trucks were used by the snakeheads to avoid inspection by local authorities.

There are many legitimate channels available to Chinese citizens who wish to travel abroad—for instance, advanced study, leaving China as exported laborers, participating in an official or business delegation, visiting relatives abroad, or joining a Hong Kong or Macau tour. It is reported that Chinese government officials and government-owned travel agencies are actively facilitating the departure of a large number of Chinese immigrants through such means (Burdman 1993c). To understand how allegedly corrupt officials might be involved in the human trade, one needs to examine the nature and operation of some of the government-sponsored labor and economic affairs organizations in the Fuzhou area.

In China, there is a fine line between illegal immigration and legally exported labor (*United Daily News,* May 12, 1989). In the coastal areas, there are numerous government-sponsored labor-export companies that work closely with foreign-based labor-import companies to move tens of thousands of Chinese workers overseas, mainly to Southeast Asian countries where there is a labor shortage (Kwong 1997). It is not always clear, however, which components of their operations are legal and which are illegal, nor is it always clear whether these companies are involved in the human trade on an organizational level or whether individual employees are involved unbeknownst to their employers.

Whatever the case, those of my subjects who left China with the aid of a labor-export company professed satisfaction with the company's services. A thirty-five-year-old computer clerk from Fuzhou City told this story:

> I sought help from a company, a government agency specializing in exporting labor, to leave China. The company worked along with a company in Singapore to help people leave China as laborers. When I got in touch with the company, it was agreed that I should pay the company $2,000 for a passport and an application fee. After I reached the United States, I would pay an additional $26,000. They told me it would take about seven days to get to the United States and it would be safe. After the meeting with the company, I left China within twenty-four days. I flew to Singapore from Fuzhou, with a Chinese passport and a Singapore visa. They were all genuine documents. After staying in Singapore for two weeks, the Singapore company provided three of us with photo-sub Singapore passports [passports on which the original holder's picture is replaced with the respondent's picture] to fly to Los Angeles via Germany.

It is possible that employees of these state-run labor-export companies are bribed by snakeheads behind the backs of company officials. A government employee from Fuzhou City said:

> In China, I worked for a government agency [a labor-export company]. The main purpose of the agency was to make money by means of assisting

people to go abroad as export labor. I used my position in the company to help a friend obtain tourist passports. My friend told me he was only helping his friends and relatives to immigrate. I wasn't quite sure what was he doing exactly. Later, I learned that those who left China with the passports I provided to him had attempted to go to the United States illegally via a third country. How did that happen? Well, while they were attempting to board a plane in Indonesia with fake travel documents, they were arrested and deported back to China. The Public Security Bureau investigated the case and discovered that I was the one who supplied them with the Chinese passports. They accused me of being a snakehead. My boss ordered me to quit while the investigation was going on. I had nowhere to appeal. In China, the punishment for being a snakehead is severe—equal to the punishment for murderers and drug traffickers. After evaluating all my options, I decided to flee China.

Government employees may play another role in facilitating the illegal movement of Chinese. Since China adopted the open-door policy and implemented economic reforms in the late 1970s, the government has sent many official delegations abroad to strengthen international ties. Human smugglers seized the opportunity to bribe the people who decide the makeup of these official delegations. A forty-four-year-old male from Changle explained how his big snakehead got him and others included in a business delegation to the United States by writing to officials at the local governmental department in charge of the visit.

Reports of government employees' involvement in smuggling have also appeared in the Chinese media, as when a newspaper reported that four high-ranking Xian City officials had been convicted of trafficking in people. According to the report, the officials knowingly allowed twenty-three people from Fuzhou to leave China with official passports as members of a business delegation. The report revealed that smugglers paid the chairpersons of the city's Economic Affairs Committee and Foreign Affairs Committee about $90,000 for making the arrangement (*Wen Wei Pao*, November 6, 1993). Another Chinese media account revealed that the director of the Public Security Bureau angrily denounced "some labor export companies for helping Chinese to go abroad illegally, [who] were in reality 'slave traders' who were only interested in collecting a certain amount of money from the immigrants and allowed the people they helped export to run wild in the world community" (Zi 1993: S5). In a 1997 media account, 150 officers and soldiers of the Shenzhen's Border Patrol Army who were bribed by human smugglers were arrested for allowing more than 8,000 Chinese citizens to leave China illegally (*World Journal*, October 17, 1997).

According to a number of my respondents, their snakeheads were either former or current Chinese government employees. One described his snakehead as "a government employee working as a middleman for a big snakehead who was his relative." The snakehead of another respondent was "a government official responsible for recruiting customers locally [who] referred them to his younger brother who lived abroad."

Government officials in transit countries are allegedly bribed by human smugglers as well, either to look the other way or to provide help to immigrants (DeStefano 1997). When asked whether smugglers make kickbacks to immigration police in Thailand, one smuggler replied, "That's the essential part of the business" (*The Nation*, November 9, 1994: A2). One of my respondents said that public officials assisted him in Thailand. "Because we had no documents, we were arrested by the Thai police and detained for seven days. Later, our snakehead bribed the Thai officers to release us." Another respondent recalled how he passed through Thailand: "I got past Thai immigration by means of *maiguan* (buying checkpoint). That is, my snakehead slipped a $100 bill in my passport. A Thai immigration officer took the money, stamped my passport, and I went through."

Immigration officers in other countries were also reported to have accepted bribes from smugglers. In 1993, immigration officers in Hong Kong were involved in a bribery case involving people trafficking (Gomez and Gilbert 1993) and in 1995 an immigration officer stationed at the Buenos Aires airport was arrested for aiding Chinese smugglers (*World Journal*, October 14a, 1995).

Some of my respondents reported that Mexican authorities played an important role in facilitating the movement of Chinese to the United States via Mexico. A corroborating newspaper account reported an incident in which Mexican authorities, presumably after being bribed, allowed Chinese immigrants in their custody to "escape." "There were about 300 Chinese confined in a detention center in Mexicali. They were not worried at all because they had been told by their snakeheads that their Mexican guards would all 'fall asleep,' after which they would be transported to the airport for deportation. One night, as predicted by the snakehead, all the guards suddenly 'disappeared,' and the Chinese escaped. They all eventually crossed the border and entered the United States" (*World Journal*, August 25, 1993:A1). The Washington, D.C.-based American Interagency Working Group (1995) has also concluded that the trade in illegal immigrants is supported by rampant corruption among officials in various transit countries such as Belize, Panama, Guatemala, and the Dominican Republic.

There is no shortage of evidence that government officials, both within China and at various transit points, help to facilitate the clandestine movement of people abroad. Let us now look more closely at the specific means by which illegal immigrants make their way from China to "the promised land" of America.

II.   FOLLOWING THE SNAKEHEADS

4   The Air Route

THE ILLEGAL MOVEMENT of tens of thousands of Chinese immigrants halfway around the globe is inevitably a chaotic and perilous affair. Whether made by air, sea, land, or—as is almost always the case—by some combination of the three, the voyage from China to the United States is invariably fraught with difficulty and hardship for illegal Chinese immigrants. From the initial down payment and procurement of travel documents to long stays in transit countries to the final arrival in America and confinement in safe houses, the journey is arduous, risky, and stressful, and it is often plagued by unforeseen logistical difficulties.

For obvious reasons, most of my respondents preferred to travel by air, but since passports and visas for air travel are difficult to come by, the first leg of their trip out of China was often made by sea or overland.[1] Many of them traveled overland to Hong Kong or Myanmar, flew from there to Mexico or Canada, and crossed the U.S. border by land. Others made the journey primarily by sea, boarding smuggling ships off the coast of China and sailing directly across the Pacific Ocean to California, where they boarded a plane to New York.[2] Forty-eight percent of my respondents flew into the United States. Another 40 percent entered the United States by crossing the U.S.-Mexican or U.S.-Canadian border overland. Only 12 percent arrived in the United States by boat, although, because of the publicity given to ships crowded with Chinese immigrants, this method of travel has most greatly alarmed U.S. authorities.

Although the next three chapters are organized by the type of travel used, few immigrants were transported by one means only; almost all used some combination of methods to reach their destination, and there will necessarily be some overlap in the discussion of the various routes. When I speak of respondents who used the air route, I am talking about those people who traveled primarily, though not exclusively, by air.

PATTERNS OF AIR SMUGGLING

Of the 143 respondents in my survey who flew to the United States, 138 (96 percent) either flew out of China or left by land through Hong Kong or Myanmar. Only seven who left China by air flew directly to the United States. Most of those who went through Hong Kong and all who went through Myanmar subsequently went to Bangkok, where local snakeheads gave them travel documents to continue on to the United States or another transit point. Many Western reporters confirm that Bangkok is the hub for illegal passage to America (Dao and Chan 1990; Boyd and Barnes 1992; Chan 1993).

Respondents who did not go through Bangkok were most likely to pass through another Asian city from which they then flew to the United States. Although few traveled through as many as nine transit points, most went through at least two or three, mostly in Asia. Of the seven most common transit points, five are in Asia; but undocumented Chinese also pass through countries in Europe, Africa, Central America and the Caribbean, or Australia on their way to the United States.

Even for those who made the fewest stops along the way, the trip was not quick or easy. Most spent about a week in their first transit point and about a month in the second; some, however, languished in the second for several months to a year, perhaps because of difficulties in obtaining travel documents or because they had been "sold" to snakeheads in the second transit point. Once they obtained travel documents, most respondents spent only a few days in any additional transit points. On average, respondents arrived in the United States 106 days after leaving China. Ten respondents waited a year or more in various transit points before they landed in the United States.

Of the 143 respondents who flew to the United States, only one said he came alone. Most traveled in small groups of three to four immigrants, unaccompanied by a guide or snakehead. If a group was guided, the guide was mostly likely to be a Chinese who spoke English and either Mandarin or the Fuzhou dialect.

These 143 air travelers made their way into the United States from forty-four final transit points, the most common being Bangkok (twenty), Tokyo (eleven), and Germany (ten, city unknown). Ninety-five of them, or 66 percent, flew into Kennedy airport in New York,[3] and another thirty-six (25 percent) flew into Los Angeles. Other arrival cities included Miami (five), Honolulu (four), San Francisco (two), and Chicago (one). Fifty-eight percent arrived with genuine or forged travel documents. Among the eighty-three who arrived with passports from fifteen countries, passports issued by Taiwan (twenty-four), Singapore (fifteen), and the People's Republic of China (fourteen) predominated. Most of those who had passports also had tourist visas, usually counterfeit. Those with genuine Chinese passports often possessed bona fide business visas issued by U.S. consulates in China. Two respondents said they entered the United States with contrived green cards or advanced parole certificates.[4]

A substantial number of my respondents presented no travel documents at all to U.S. immigration officers. In the pre-*Golden Venture* era, for reasons that will be discussed in Chapter 9, these people were usually detained for a few hours or a few days and released.[5] As instructed by their snakeheads, most had destroyed their fake travel documents before their planes landed in the United States and told airport officials that they had no passport or visa.[6] In some instances, snakeheads acting as guides confiscated fake travel documents after immigrants boarded the last plane, presumably for use in future smuggling operations (J. Chu 1994).

LEAVING CHINA

Overland

The majority of my respondents, whose first destination was Hong Kong, usually traveled from Fuzhou City to Shenzhen by bus and entered Hong Kong through the border checkpoint called the Lauhu Bridge Station.[7] For a thirty-one-year-old male from Changle, the trip was relatively uncomplicated.

> There were altogether ten of us. From Fuzhou, we took a bus to Shenzhen to enter Hong Kong. After spending two days in Hong Kong, we flew to Singapore and stayed there for seven days. We then flew to Thailand, and remained there for twenty days. From Thailand, we flew to New York. We all carried photo-sub Chinese passports [passports that have been altered by photo substitution] and tourist visas. We passed through the JFK airport immigration counter undetected.

A forty-three-year-old farmer was not as fortunate and spent almost a year in Thailand in hiding and under guard.

> I gave the snakehead a $1,000 down payment and my Chinese passport. With my passport, the snakehead obtained a Thai visa for me. I took a bus to Shenzhen and entered Hong Kong. After staying in Hong Kong for seven days, I flew to Thailand with a visa issued by the Thai consulate in China. While I was in Hong Kong, I stayed at a friend's house. In Thailand, I was initially put up in a cheap hotel called the XXX Hotel. Two immigrants had to share a bed. I stayed there for two months, and my snakehead gave me 100 *baht* [approximately $4] a day for meals. After two months, the snakehead moved us out of Bangkok because our visas had expired. We were asked by the snakehead to stay inside a pigpen in a rural area. The snakehead also sent some enforcers to guard us and would not allow us to go outside. After spending ten months in Thailand, I left with a Singapore passport. I boarded a flight to Miami via Frankfurt. A little snakehead [a Singaporean] guided me and twelve other illegal Chinese immigrants throughout the trip.

Some immigrants in my sample left China with fake foreign passports and some, as I mentioned, traveled through several transit points. In stark contrast to the farmer who had to hide in a pigsty, a twenty-two-year-old single female from Changle did not find her complex journey at all unpleasant.

> My snakehead, a well-known overseas Chinese originally from my village, provided a male Chinese and I with passports to go to Hong Kong via Shenzhen. In Hong Kong, the snakehead checked us into an expensive hotel. The living accommodations were good, and we were allowed to leave the hotel. Later, the snakehead gave us Hong Kong passports to go to Thailand. He also gave me an address in Thailand. When we arrived in Bangkok, someone from Fuzhou met us at the airport and took us to a Chinese hotel. There, too, we were allowed to tour the city. The next day, the snakehead arrived. Later, we used the same Hong Kong passports to fly to Paris. In Paris, the snakehead bought us new clothes. He asked me to mix my personal belongings with those of the male to create the impression that the two of us were on a honeymoon. In Paris, we also stayed in a luxurious hotel. Two days later, we flew to New York. We did not encounter any problem at the airport. The snakehead also flew along with us. I think it was a nice trip. The snakehead disguised us like we were a wealthy couple. Before we boarded the plane in Paris, he even arranged for the two of us to visit a nice hair salon to make sure we looked good.

Myanmar (formerly Burma), a country neighboring China, seems to have been selected as a transit country to reach the major staging ground of Bangkok for two reasons (see Figure 1 for a map of East Asia). First, the rapidly developing trade along the China-Myanmar border since the late 1980s has resulted in a tremendous amount of border-crossing between Myanmar's Shan State and China's Yunnan Province (Porter 1992). Second, the route is the best alternative for immigrants whose snakeheads could not provide them with Chinese passports to travel to Hong Kong, but it is by no means an easy one.

Typically, immigrants travel by bus to the city of Kunming, the capital of Yunnan Province, and then are transported to Bangkok. In danger of being arrested and returned to China, they risk their lives on the rugged terrain. A twenty-five-year-old male respondent from Fuzhou City explained how he came to the United States via Myanmar:

My snakehead asked me to pay him about $1,000 before my departure. I also had to deposit another $1,000 into my bank account so that when I arrived in Thailand, my bankbook would be turned over to my snakehead and he would then retrieve the money from my bank. The original plan was this: my snakehead in China would transport me from China to Thailand and help me get in touch with another snakehead in Thailand who would transport me to America for an additional $24,000. Six other immigrants and I took the train from Fuzhou to Kunming. On the way from Kunming to Shi Ta, we were hidden in a truck to get past the checkpoints to Jin Yun. However, at the Mun Hai checkpoint, Chinese border patrol guards arrested us. After being detained for a week, we were released when our families wired us about $110 each to pay the fines. Then we went back to Jin Yun and got in touch with the original snakehead. This time, we also hid in a truck and we successfully got past the Mun Hai checkpoint. Later, a Burmese guide—an army lieutenant—helped us cross the mountains and enter Burma. It took four days and three nights to cross the border. From Burma to Thailand, we disguised ourselves as Burmese soldiers. We wore army uniforms and rode on military motorcycles. We flew from Thailand to the United States, using fake Taiwan passports and genuine tourist visas. A Singaporean and an Indonesian, both of whom spoke Mandarin, accompanied us to America.

Most of my respondents who journeyed through Myanmar had nightmarish stories to tell. A thirty-five-year-old factory owner from Fuzhou City recalled:

From Kunming, we climbed mountains and crossed rivers for a week to get to the Burmese border. While we were crossing the border, we were chased by Chinese border patrol officers. In the process, our guide fled and abandoned us. We were not familiar with the area at all. So we decided that each of us should chip in $100 to hire local Burmese to escort us to Thailand. We eventually found a group of Burmese who were

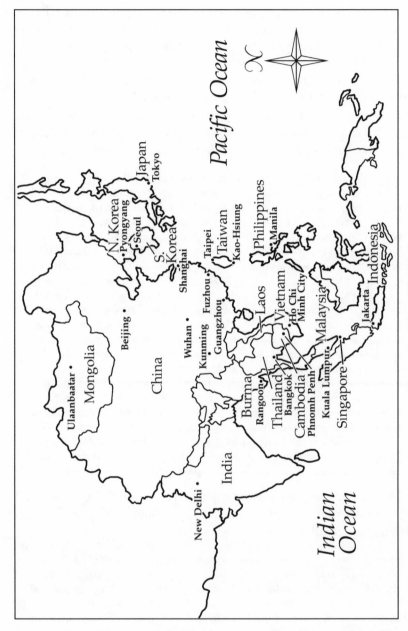

FIGURE 1. Map of East Asia

willing to help us, but they took away all our money and personal belong-
ings. They said it would be troublesome to carry all our stuff to Thailand.
In return, they provided us with Burmese clothes. After dressing like
Burmese, we took off.

To avoid the Burmese authorities, the local guides brought us to Thailand through the jungle. For twelve days, we ate and slept in the jungle.
Sometimes we had to climb more than twenty hills a day. We traveled at
night and slept during the day. We might have lost our direction in the
jungle, because the trip, which should have taken only seven days, actually took sixteen days. Since we had limited dried food, we had to eat
roots, wild fruits, or cow waste for about ten days. We also drank the
murky water along the roadside. We went through like that for ten days
and every one of us looked like a savage. We all had long hair and dirty
faces. Our clothes were filthy.

While climbing the hills, we often fell down. Burmese who thought we
were aborigines also often chased us. Once, we all ran when we were
chased by the Burmese. Unfortunately, a seventeen-year-old boy fled the
wrong way and was captured. He was beaten severely by the local people, probably because they thought he was a jungle person. Not long after
we made it to Thailand, that boy also arrived; he had wounds all over his
body. When we saw the poor boy, our eyes were filled with tears. We
stayed in Thailand for seven days, and we flew to New York with Taiwan
passports.

It is not clear how many Chinese immigrants have died while
attempting to get to Bangkok via Myanmar. According to a media
account, seven Chinese immigrants lost their lives in the Burmese jungle on their way to Thailand (*World Journal*, February 21, 1992: 3). Several of my respondents told harrowing stories of sickness and near star-
vation in the jungle and mountains. Others suffered at the hands of
authorities. Almost all suffered some form of hardship or deprivation,
and some underwent a seemingly unending series of trials. One twenty-
nine-year-old construction worker from Tingjiang watched his compatriots beaten by the Chinese border patrol near the Burmese border.
During the year it took him to make his way from China to the United
States, he was arrested three times, sent back to China once, cheated out
of $2,000, and traveled by horseback, in the back of trucks, and on foot
before finally arriving in Hawaii by plane via the Philippines.

Incredibly, a small number of my respondents left China on their
own and then looked for snakeheads at transit points en route. A forty-
five-year-old man from Changle left home in December 1990 and traveled from Fuzhou to Guangdong and from there to Kunming, Nang

Chang, and finally Mu Lien. He managed to pass through three Chinese checkpoints by pretending to be mute but was finally arrested at Ray Mao. He escaped, leaving his identification card behind, and crossed the border into Burma thirteen months after his original departure. With the help of local Burmese and through his own ingenuity, he eventually made it to Thailand with $2 in his pocket. He stayed in Thailand for three months before seeing an ad in a Chinese newspaper offering help in obtaining travel visas. Since he had no guarantor in America, he had to agree to pay $30,500. He stayed for a time in Singapore and Malaysia and finally flew to Los Angeles with a group of illegal Chinese posing as Taiwanese tourists. They were detained in Los Angeles for a few days and then released.

Because China and Myanmar are eager to promote border trade (Chapman et al. 1992), both governments are probably unlikely to restrict the movement of citizens across the border. Consequently, it is likely that snakeheads who are unable to obtain Chinese passports for their clients will have to rely increasingly on the route via Myanmar.

By Air

Of the 143 respondents who arrived in the United States by air, most left China via the land route, but a substantial number flew out. Compared with those who traveled overland, especially through Myanmar, those who flew enjoyed their trip. Xiamen, Shanghai, and Beijing were key departure points for exit by air, especially for those with official Chinese passports, which, predictably, deflect suspicion.[8] A forty-four-year-old college-educated male from Fuzhou City left China through Beijing: "I flew to Beijing from Fuzhou and then to Los Angeles via Tokyo. I left with a Chinese official passport. There were four of us, two would-be illegal immigrants and two Chinese government officials. The people who invited us to America met us at the airport. I don't think the hosts had a clue that two members of the delegation were smuggled illegal immigrants."

Most of my subjects who flew out of the Xiamen airport left China with Chinese passports and labor export visas. A male from Changle described his trip:

> After we boarded an airplane in Xiamen and flew to Hong Kong, the accompanying snakehead removed the Liberia labor export visa from the Chinese passport and inserted an Ecuador tourist visa. After we arrived

in Hong Kong, we did not go through customs and immigration and waited eight hours until we got on a flight to Ecuador. The snakehead did not come along. However, when we arrived in Ecuador, a Cantonese-speaking male came to pick us up. He checked us into a hotel, provided two meals a day, and did not allow us to go out. After seven days, the same person brought us to a bus station, and we took a bus ride to Colombia that lasted thirty-six hours. There, the guide put us in a rented house. The living arrangement was very good, but we had only two meals a day. The first two months, we were not allowed to go out. After four and a half months, the guide provided us photo-sub Taiwan passports and we flew to New York.

Respondents who left China from the Fuzhou airport were most likely to go to Singapore first. A twenty-eight-year-old Changle female related that she went first to Singapore using a Chinese passport and a Singapore visa. From there she and seven other immigrants flew to Los Angeles with photo-sub passports. They mixed in with a group of tourists from Singapore and passed through the INS without trouble.

According to my survey data, only one respondent who left China by sea entered the United States by air; the rest arrived in the vessels they boarded in China or entered by crossing the U.S.-Mexican border. The data showing that respondents who flew to the United States used many routes and passed through many transit points suggest that flexibility and contingency planning are indispensable in human trafficking.

VERSATILITY OF AIR SMUGGLING

Although smugglers did seem to have prearranged air routes for their customers, plans often went awry. Because they got paid only after their customers had reached the United States, however, they were determined to find transport in spite of whatever problems might arise. My respondents confirmed that their snakeheads could come up with new air routes in the event that original plans failed. Rerouting often meant even riskier travel and even longer delays, however. For example, a thirty-six-year-old government employee from Changle described his circuitous journey:

We took a bus to Shenzhen and were greeted by a little snakehead. From Shenzhen, we went to Hong Kong using Chinese passports and Singapore visas. A snakehead in Hong Kong applied for visas for us to go to

Thailand. After we stayed in Thailand for three months, the snakehead in Bangkok provided us with photo-sub Chinese passports and visas to go to Morocco. After a month in Morocco, we tried to get on a plane bound for the United States using Chinese passports and fake U.S. visas. However, authorities in Morocco discovered that we were using fake documents and would not allow us to board the plane. Later, our snakehead gave us visas to go Algeria. We stayed in Algeria for three months, not knowing what to do next. At that juncture, our snakehead found out that there was a way for us to go to the United States, but it required us to go to Spain first. So we climbed a few mountains to get back to Morocco from Algeria and stayed there for one month before the snakehead supplied us with Singapore passports with U.S. visas. We then went to the Spanish capital by bus and by boat. After staying there for about fifteen days, we flew to New York.

A forty-year-old man from Fuzhou City encountered hardship on three continents before finally arriving in the United States.

Through a business acquaintance, I met a Fujianese snakehead who was living in Panama. After he agreed to smuggle me to the United States, he asked me to pay him a $2,000 down payment. Once the payment was made, he got me a Chinese passport and a visa. After three months, I, along with two other immigrants, took a bus from Fuzhou to Shenzhen under the guidance of our snakehead. From Shenzhen, we went to Hong Kong. In Hong Kong, we ate and lived well. Four days later, we flew to Panama. After we arrived in Panama, our relatives in China paid our snakehead another $6,000 as stipulated by the agreement between the snakehead and us.

According to the original plan, we would remain in Panama for ten days, and the snakehead would prepare travel documents for us to fly to New York City. However, upon our arrival in Panama, we found that Panamanian immigration officers were very strict. Besides, our snakehead wasn't sure he could bribe the immigration officers there. So we were afraid to use fraudulent documents in Panama. As a result, our snakehead sold the three of us to another snakehead in Panama. For this reason, we ended up staying in Panama for more than three months. During that period, we lived in a cow barn. We ate things that looked like garbage. Later, the new snakehead obtained an Austrian tourist visa for me. He said it cost him $800 to get the visa because he bribed an Austrian embassy official in Panama. I left Panama alone for Austria. . . .

After remaining in Austria for seven months, I got in touch with the Panamanian snakehead again. He was not capable of getting travel documents that could enable me to fly directly to the United States from Austria. But he said he could help me fly to New York City from Panama. As a result, I flew back to Panama from Austria using the fake documents he provided. However, once in Panama, I had to wait another four months.

Again, I was forced to live a kind of life that is worse than being a cow or a horse, just like before. The snakehead was responsible for the eating and living accommodations, but what kind of living was that? I did not eat well or live well. Every day, the snakehead visited the prostitute houses or gambling places. He did not care whether his clients were alive or dead. Whenever I had something to say, he just yelled at me.

In that hell on earth, I suffered for another four months. Because the snakehead was not sure that he could arrange for a direct flight to New York City, he eventually arranged for us to first enter Colombia by sea, by means of a small boat. That small boat was like a leaf in the ocean, threatening to overturn at any time. As we crossed the sea, there was a big shark just about five meters from the boat. It was bigger than our boat. The shark was alongside us, and we were so scared we just closed our eyes and prayed. After five hours, we finally reached Colombia.

In Colombia, the snakehead arranged for a local person to guide us. We walked for about three hours, and then we got on a small plane that carried only seven passengers including the pilot. The small plane flew for about one and a half hours and landed in an unknown Colombian city. The guide took us to take the train there, and then to a bus, and then we walked. Two days later, we arrived in Bogota. This trip was considered short, but it was like we all died once. It was really an extremely dangerous trip. Now, whenever I recall what happened on the trip, I cry and cry. At that time, my family thought that I must have died on the road to the United States.

After staying in Bogota for a month (the food and living arrangements were awful), the snakehead finally got the travel documents ready. I left Bogota alone using a photo-sub Singapore passport and a ticket to Toronto. While I was passing through the JFK immigration counter on the way to Toronto, the INS officer asked me how come I had not filled out an entry form. I said I did not know how to. Eventually, I had nowhere to hide and got arrested.

Another respondent, a twenty-two-year-old unemployed male from Changle, also had to overcome many obstacles to arrive in the United States.

From Changle we took a bus to Fuzhou, accompanied by a local snakehead. His responsibility was to send us to Thailand, and another snakehead in Bangkok would help us to go to America. From Fuzhou, we went to Xiamen by bus and from there flew to Kunming. After staying in Kunming for about twenty days, the local snakehead found two Kunming residents to escort us to Burma. At the beginning of the trip, we climbed mountains. It was a trip filled with hardships and dangers. We climbed from late in the evenings till morning. The nights were long. There were poisonous mosquitoes and bugs everywhere. We also needed to cross a river that had strong currents, and when we crossed, there were blood-sucking bugs all over our bodies. It was really frightening.

We stayed in a cottage in Burma for twenty days, and we ate bad food. We almost died. Later, we climbed mountains to get to the Mekong River. From there, we boarded a small boat and sailed to another cottage and stayed overnight. The next day, a group of Thai people came and transported us into Thailand on a large boat. After we entered Thailand, they brought us to Bangkok on a bus. After staying in Thailand for forty days, we tried to enter Yugoslavia using fake Chinese passports and fake visas but were stopped at a Yugoslavian airport and deported back to Bangkok. The next time, we used photo-sub Malaysian passports and flew to Czechoslovakia via Yugoslavia. From Czechoslovakia, we took a train to Germany. From Germany, we flew to New York using fake Japanese passports.

These testimonies speak to the determination of the immigrants as well as that of the smugglers. Confronted with such tenacity, law enforcement officials in transit and receiving communities are ill-equipped to stop illegal Chinese from reaching their final destination.

THE UNITED STATES AS AN OPEN GATE

Each year, about 50 million passengers enter the United States through airports (U.S. Commission on Immigration Reform 1994: x), and most undocumented Chinese in my sample encountered few obstacles entering the United States this way. Because the INS had limited detention space prior to the *Golden Venture* incident in 1993, most of my respondents who entered U.S. airports without proper documents were released rather than detained. Even detention has little deterrent effect. Most of my respondents saw it as a minor hurdle they needed to go through to achieve their goal of coming to America. A forty-four-year-old Tingjiang male explained:

While we were confined at a detention center, we ate and lived well. We were provided with fresh milk, vegetables, and fruits. We had separate beds, and the rooms had wall-to-wall carpeting. They treated us well. They were not discriminative. You can say the detention center was like a hotel. Before we left Bolivia for the United States, our snakehead told us to call a lawyer if we were arrested in Los Angeles. The snakehead said the lawyer had an office near the detention center and specialized in representing illegal aliens. After the INS detained us, that lawyer bailed us out. It cost us $1,500 per person. My snakehead and I split the legal expenses.[9]

Another respondent, a thirty-three-year-old Changle male, explained how he was able to bypass immigration officers at JFK: "I arrived at JFK airport with a phony Taiwan passport and a tourist visa. When it was my turn to be inspected, I slipped through while the inspector was talking to other people. When I was about to exit the gate, I heard someone ask me to stop. I was so frightened, I started to run. I jumped into a taxi, and it took off."

Another subject, a twenty-nine-year-old government employee from Tingjiang, reported that he and his traveling companions were also able to enter the United States without having their travel documents inspected. "Six other illegal immigrants and me flew from Hong Kong to Los Angeles via Taiwan and Korea. We had Chinese passports and Dominican Republic visas. When we transferred planes in Los Angeles, we walked out of the airport without presenting any documents. I don't know how that could happen—all other passengers had to present travel documents."

If airport authorities discover illegal immigrants, it is the airline's responsibility to detain them in nearby hotels (Kamen 1992a). A twenty-nine-year-old factory worker from Mawei revealed how he and his companions were able to escape from the hotel where they were being detained: "When we arrived in New York and got arrested, we had to turn in our travel documents to immigration authorities, and then arrangements were made for us to stay in an airport hotel. We asked the guard to go out and buy something for us. Once he left, we sneaked out of the hotel and called a taxi to take us to Chinatown."

Although these accounts seem implausible, my data strongly suggest that once these immigrants were on a plane bound for the United States, they could count on staying in the country. Many of them who had been coached by their snakeheads managed to exploit lax U.S. travel regulations and sought political asylum fraudulently. The ease of international travel, coupled with the snakeheads' ability to bribe airport and immigration officials in almost all of the transit countries, enabled these Chinese illegals to travel relatively freely. It was fairly easy for them to board commercial airlines, for example. This is an issue that cannot be easily resolved. Even though the U.S. government has dispatched immigration officers to several international airports to work with airline employees to prevent passengers without proper travel documents from boarding U.S.-bound flights, it is not possible for U.S. authorities to be stationed at all international airports with direct flights to the United States. Most respondents who arrived in the United States without proper travel documents were well aware that if they were arrested and detained, they would eventually be released.[10]

5 The Sea Route

WHEN THE *Golden Venture* struck a sandbar near New York City in June 1993, hundreds of smuggled Chinese jumped into the frigid waters of the Atlantic Ocean. Ten passengers were drowned and many more injured. The arrival of illegal immigrants then became an issue not only for the United States but for the world community as well (Gladwell and Stassen-Berger 1993a).

Although the *Golden Venture* incident raised public interest and concern among U.S. authorities (Faison 1993a; Sontag 1993a; Weiner 1993; Hevesi 1994), reliable information about the illegal immigration of Chinese by sea is scarce. Law enforcement authorities cannot say how, for example, smugglers move large numbers of passengers from villages to staging seaports in China to mother ships in international waters, or how smugglers transport passengers by ship to the U.S. seashore and then to a final destination. Nor is there much information about how traffickers buy or rent ships or obtain food, water, and other supplies in seaports. They can only speculate about why traffickers turn to sea smuggling.

As we saw in Chapter 4, most of my respondents who left China by sea were first taken to a country in Central America and were subsequently smuggled into the United States overland. In this chapter, I will discuss the sea experiences of the few who left China and entered the United States by sea ($N = 35$) and those who left China by sea but entered the United States by land ($N = 122$), focusing on their sea voyages to South or Central America.

THE DEVELOPMENT OF SEA SMUGGLING

It is not clear when or why smugglers decided to transport Chinese immigrants to the United States by ship. When the Chinese human trade began to develop in the late 1980s, most Chinese either flew to the United States from a transit point or entered overland (U.S. Senate 1992). However, in the early 1990s news accounts reported that U.S. authorities were intercepting Chinese smuggling ships. In August 1991, the U.S. Coast Guard seized the *I-Mao*, a Taiwanese cargo ship carrying 131 passengers, near Long Beach, California (Kamen 1991b), and four months later another Taiwanese ship, the *Lo Sing*, was discovered near Guatemala with 216 passengers aboard. In the next eleven months, authorities detected sixteen ships carrying thousands of illegal Chinese immigrants in waters off the United States and neighboring countries such as Mexico and Guatemala. By 1998, forty-one ships carrying more than 6,300 passengers were intercepted.

Some were identified as smuggling ships long before arriving on U.S. shores, and their unimpeded journey to the East Coast of the United States in 1992 convinced American officials that the problem was a serious one, even if it took publicity surrounding the *Golden Venture* tragedy to bring the problem to public attention. In September 1992 a Taiwanese ship, the *Chin Wing*, reached Morehead City, North Carolina, packed with 151 passengers. First discovered in Mauritius, an island in the Indian Ocean, the *Chin Wing* eluded authorities there. It reached Port-au-Prince, Haiti, on August 15 and arrived at North Carolina on September 8, when the passengers were arrested by U.S. authorities as they were brought to shore. But it is not clear how a smuggling ship spotted so early and so far away from the United States could continue its voyage and reach its final destination.[1] The same month, another fishing boat unloaded two hundred Chinese passengers in New Bedford, Massachusetts, and U.S. authorities decided to take action against this rapidly developing problem. In February 1993, when the *East Wood* was discovered near the Marshall Islands, part of the U.S. Trust Territory of the Pacific Islands, the U.S. government sent all 528 Chinese aboard back to China (Woolrich 1993a). This unprecedented incident showed that U.S. authorities were determined to stop the influx of Chinese illegals by sea and set a precedent for dealing with similar incidents. By intercepting such ships before they reached U.S. waters and sending those aboard home from a third country, the United States prevented illegal immigrants from applying for political asylum, since only foreigners who actually enter the United States can apply.

Viewed as a major accomplishment for U.S. authorities, the *East Wood* incident nevertheless failed to deter Chinese from coming to the United States by sea. More fishing vessels were discovered carrying scores of passengers near Baja California (Mexico), San Diego, and San Francisco

(Asimov and Burdman 1993). Only three months after the *East Wood* incident, U.S. authorities were shocked to discover that Chinese smuggling operations were becoming more reckless. Instead of ferrying passengers from a mother ship to the U.S. shore on small boats, smugglers began to sail the mother ships right into U.S. seaports and unload hundreds of passengers on the docks. In May 1993, for example, a smuggling ship dropped 250 smuggled Chinese at a San Francisco Bay pier in the middle of the night and fled (Brazil et al. 1993: A1).

A month after the *Golden Venture* incident, three ships carrying more than six hundred passengers were discovered by the U.S. Coast Guard near Baja California (Devroy 1993) and towed to the Mexican shore; the passengers were immediately deported to China. Although Mexican officials were reluctant to let U.S. authorities use Mexico as a staging ground for deporting smuggled Chinese, they eventually complied under pressure from Washington. Likewise, after the *Jin Yinn* was found near San Diego, the ship and its 113 passengers were hauled to Guatemala for deportation (*World Journal*, May 7, 1994).

After the *Golden Venture* incident, U.S. resolve to stop the influx of illegal Chinese immigrants was strengthened. By that time, according to a senior U.S. government official, there was "almost an armada coming over here" (Rotella 1993: 1). The arrival of such a large number of ships led Jim Hayes, assistant district director for investigations at Los Angeles's immigration office, to conclude: "The way these boats have been coming in, I wouldn't be surprised if I saw one land in Topeka, Kansas. They seem to have the ability to show up anywhere" (Burdman 1993a: A1). Under pressure from the White House, the INS and other federal agencies established an interagency task force to deal with Chinese sea smuggling and the official U.S. position on illegal Chinese immigrants has changed dramatically since then. For the first time, for example, the passengers on the *Golden Venture* were detained for a protracted period of time while their petitions for political asylum were pending.

It is not known, however, how many ships have transported illegal Chinese immigrants to the United States and other transit points undetected. According to my survey of three hundred illegal Chinese immigrants, between October 1987 and September 1993 at least eighty-nine ships and some 16,000 passengers were involved in smuggling activity without being apprehended.[2] Of these, twenty-five ships reached the United States, fifty-two arrived in Mexico, and ten landed in Guatemala.

Chinese passengers dropped off in Mexico and Guatemala were later brought to the United States overland by smugglers.

Before U.S. authorities intercepted the *I-Mao* in August 1991, at least thirteen smuggling ships had entered the United States undetected. According to a forty-one-year-old female who arrived in San Francisco in 1987:

> I entered Hong Kong via Shenzhen with a Chinese passport and a Thai visa. Later, I flew to Thailand from Hong Kong. A Fujianese male met us [six men and two women] at the airport and checked us into a hotel. After staying in the hotel for thirty-four days, the snakehead told us that we would have to change plans. He said we would have to take a boat instead of flying to America. We were concerned for our safety on board a ship, but he said it was a cargo ship and there wouldn't be many passengers. Besides, he said the ship was well equipped. So we boarded a small boat, and it sailed for four hours to rendezvous with an Australian cargo ship in high seas. There were forty-eight illegal Chinese, including eight females. When the ship arrived near U.S. waters, we were worried that it might miss the small boat because the cargo ship was not supposed to be at that seaport, which was San Francisco. Two days later, the captain of the ship got in touch with our snakehead, and we were all excited. Later, a group of Americans and Mandarin-speaking Vietnamese transferred all forty-eight passengers to a small boat. When we got ashore, there were two buses waiting for us.

There are many factors thought to be associated with the development of smuggling Chinese by ship. For one thing, there is a long history of transporting Chinese workers to various countries by sea (Pan 1990). During the late nineteenth century, many young men from Xiamen were exported to Cuba to work. The abolition of the slave trade and the strong demand for cheap labor in Cuba led to the aggressive recruitment of cheap labor from China. Many so-called *ju jia,* or "piglets," lost their lives before they reached Cuba. Later, as the human trade became a lucrative business, merchants began to kidnap people in Xiamen and transport them to Cuba. According to Cheng-hsiung Wu (1988), an expert on overseas Chinese, the Fujianese were abused on the boats and in Cuba and were treated worse than were the black slaves they replaced.

More recently, the strong demand for illegal passage to the United States led smugglers from the Fuzhou area to devise a method that would transport large numbers of people at a huge profit (International

Organization of Migration 1996; Zhang and Gaylord 1996). The logical answer was large seagoing vessels, and unused fishing ships fit the bill nicely. Boyd and Barnes (1992: 6) have suggested that "Taiwan has emerged recently as a key route, largely because of the downturn in its fishing industry, which has left a surplus of boats. Vessels are on hire for about HK$40,000 [about $5,300] to smugglers."

TAIWANESE SHIPS

According to media accounts, law enforcement reports, and data collected for this study, most smuggling ships are Taiwanese sea vessels, though it is not clear what role Taiwanese ship owners play in the human trade. Some observers believe that they are actively involved; Myers (1994: 5) concluded, "In my five years of intensive study of the smuggling of Chinese aliens into the United States, I have found that Taiwanese are in total control of the global transportation networks whether by air or sea." Others disagree. A Taiwanese gang member who said he was "doing small business" in Fuzhou disputed Myers's assertion of "total control," though his own testimony suggests a high level of Taiwanese involvement:

> What do you mean we [Taiwanese] are the big snakeheads? Frankly, we are not qualified to be big snakeheads. How much connection do we have here in Fuzhou to run this kind of business? In the human trade, Taiwanese primarily play the role of *tongzi* [literally: bucket, or ship). They are suppliers of ships to big snakeheads. A ship costs between $200,000 to $300,000. The Taiwanese always make money playing this role, regardless of whether the operation is a success or a failure. The way it works is this: after a big snakehead has recruited enough passengers, he contacts a Taiwanese *tongzi* who is doing business in the Fuzhou area to find a ship. Once the two parties reach an agreement, the *tongzi* will go back to Taiwan, buy a ship, remold the ship into a smuggling ship, sail the ship to Hong Kong, register the ship, store the ship with food and water, and bring the ship off the coast of China. (Chen 1993: 7)[3]

Not all smuggling ships, however, are owned by Taiwanese or registered in Taiwan. The *Golden Venture* allegedly was bought by a snakehead in Singapore for $125,000. Undoubtedly Taiwanese play an active role in the trade, but they are clearly not the only ones.

SOCIAL PROCESSES OF SEA SMUGGLING

The clandestine transnational movement of hundreds of Chinese by ship appears to be a much more complicated operation than smuggling a few people at a time by air, and various phases of the operation need to be carried out in a significantly different way.

Recruiting Passengers

Sea smugglers, who are under pressure to enlist a large number of clients in a short period of time, must be much more aggressive than air smugglers in their recruiting practices. Once a ship has been arranged and a departure time set, little snakeheads must work quickly to locate and recruit customers. They cannot afford to transport half-full ships, so they often downplay the likely hardships of sea travel and exaggerate the positive benefits. Some of my respondents who came by sea felt cheated by their little snakeheads. A thirty-two-year-old male said:

> A little snakehead told me that I would be going to America on a huge ship and that it would take only about two weeks to get there. Moreover, he said I didn't have to make a down payment. So I boarded the mother ship. My family was very happy for me because the little snakehead said I would be traveling on a luxurious ship outfitted with a movie theater, a nightclub, and a swimming pool. Once I boarded the ship, I was scared. First of all, there was no theater or nightclub on the ship. Secondly, the ocean seemed endless.

Because little snakeheads were eager to find customers under almost any circumstances, there was often little time for preparation before departure. Some of my respondents left China in a haphazard way, as little as one day after meeting their little snakeheads, and were unable to prepare their families for the news. Some had to leave even without informing their families, which also caused them trouble in raising their passage fees upon arrival in the United States. According to my survey data, those who left China by sea were confined by U.S.-based debt collectors for an average of fourteen days, compared to eleven for those who left China by land and six for those who flew out. Length of confinement in the United States is a good indication of how well- or ill-prepared immigrants were to fulfil their financial obligations to their snakeheads.

Departing China

After customers have been recruited, they must be assembled and hidden before being taken to the mother ship. Normally, a few days before departure, big snakeheads inform little snakeheads that the ship is ready and little snakeheads instruct their clients to be prepared to leave. Most would-be immigrants keep their plans secret from neighbors to avoid the possibility of detection by local authorities. On the day of the departure (or the day before), little snakeheads inform their clients, usually by phone, that the ship will soon depart and direct them to a specified place, normally a hotel in Fuzhou City. Each little snakehead may handle a group of ten to twenty passengers. Later in the evening, little snakeheads transport their clients to a final staging ground near the shore; once there, their movements are restricted until they pay their smuggling fees.

A thirty-nine-year-old male construction worker recalled boarding a smuggling ship near Putian, a seaport south of Fuzhou City:

> I talked to a little snakehead and paid him a $1,000 down payment. The following day, I left home at 4:00 P.M. At about 5:00 P.M., I arrived in Fuzhou City. I waited there for two days, and several people joined me. We took an overnight bus to Putian. Gradually, other would-be immigrants joined us, and the number of people increased to thirteen. The following day, our snakeheads transported us to a boat by truck. On the boat, there were 245 people like me who were planning to leave China.

The clandestine transportation of hundreds of people from numerous villages, many in the Fuzhou area, to a staging point is a major challenge for smugglers. Many observers of Chinese human smuggling operations wonder how it is possible for snakeheads to notify, assemble, and transport such large numbers of people without being noticed by Chinese law enforcement authorities (Myers 1992, 1994). They conclude that Chinese officials must deliberately overlook the illegal exodus of Chinese emigrants. A female deportee explained to me in Fuzhou how she and her companions were transported to the seashore on military trucks. Even so, there was no guarantee that everything would go according to plan.

> I left in mid-May. I was told by my little snakehead at 1:00 A.M. to go to a bus stop. Those who lived far away from Fuzhou City had already been summoned to a hotel in Fuzhou City by the snakehead a day earlier. We were then transported to the seaside by huge military trucks. The

snakeheads rented the trucks because military trucks are not subject to inspection. That ship was supposed to transport more than three hundred passengers to America, but more than one hundred people were arrested while they were waiting for the military trucks to pick them up. In fact, once I heard that another group of people had been arrested, I wanted to give up and go home. But the military truck was quite tall. Once I got on, there was no way for me to get off. I had no choice but to move along.

The rental of military trucks to snakeheads suggests that some Chinese authorities do indeed look the other way, to say the least, when it comes to the illegal emigration of thousands of Chinese, for reasons that will be discussed later.

Boarding the Mother Ships

Prospective immigrants are ferried from the shore to the mother ship by small boats. The smuggling ships lie offshore in international waters, presumably to evade Chinese authorities, so it normally takes several hours for the small boats to reach them. Sometimes the rendezvous goes awry for reasons of bad weather or crossed signals and it takes several attempts before the passengers board successfully.

If the small boats can't find the mother ship in bad weather, they risk discovery by Chinese patrol guards. One of my respondents recalled:

We took a bus from Changle to Mawei. A number of small boats carried us to the mother ship. However, in the bay, the small boats circled around for more than five hours because they could not find the mother ship. On our return, we were caught by border patrol officers, and we were locked up. Later, our little snakeheads bribed the officials and more than one hundred of us were released. Three days later, the snakehead informed us that we were leaving again. This time, we took the bus to Fuqing Wankou County. A small boat sailed for about seven hours to transport us to the mother ship.

Traveling on a small, crowded boat for many hours in the dark, often seasick, unable to stretch or move around, was unpleasant, to say the least. One respondent recalled that his little boat traveled for two hours before reaching the mother ship. "Because most of us were seasick, the snakeheads were almost throwing us onto the mother ship. There were 203 passengers, including twenty-three women." Boarding in bad weather was a risky process; people already stiff from long confinement on the small boats could slip or fall and be swept into the sea. A thirty-six-year-old male from Fuzhou City recalled, "When we were transferred from the small boats onto the mother ship, a passenger was hit in the head by a heavy object. He died on the spot."

Another respondent, the twenty-two-year-old owner of a small grocery store, described trying to board a ship in a rainstorm. "It was quite dangerous boarding the mother ship from the small boat. A Tingjiang youth, a twenty-three-year-old male with dark skin, dropped into the sea while climbing onto the ship. The crew members tried to rescue him, but a wave dragged him away and we all watched him drown. Nobody talked about it thereafter."

Crossing Oceans

Most of my respondents sailed across the Pacific Ocean to reach Mexico or the U.S. West Coast, though a few ships (like the *Golden Venture*), traveled across the Atlantic Ocean. The media often allege that illegal Chinese immigrants invariably have a nightmarish voyage, and while this was the case for most of my respondents, a few had no unpleasant experiences at all. One thirty-eight-year-old male from Changle had an unusually good voyage:

> The boat I was on was one of the first boats to the United States. The large ship did not stop much on the trip. That's why it was quite comfortable, and even though there were storms, we did not feel the impact. The food was not bad either. We ate three meals a day, and the meals were quite good. The ship was very stable. We lived underneath the deck, and the sailors sent us food regularly. We watched videotapes there. The ship sailed for more than twenty days to reach Mexico.

A fourteen-year-old girl from Changle, although she was seasick, described a generally pleasant passage. "The ship was huge; there was plenty of food. We even had vegetables to eat and mineral water to drink. We also had fish and meat. The captain and crew members treated the female passengers very nicely. We were very happy every day. We had parties on the ship. We sang, we played cards, we were not worried at all."

In general, however, bad weather, unseaworthy ships, poor sanitation, lack of food and water, and physical or sexual abuse made the sea voyage a nightmare for many of my respondents. A thirty-five-year-old factory worker described a terrifying journey aboard a smuggling ship:

> It was an extremely arduous trip. The high seas were formidable. Many people cried because they were scared of the waves and the breakdowns

of the ship. It was like we floated to the United States from China. At one time, it seemed like the ship was about to sink. All the passengers cried out in fear. Some were almost killed on the trip. Some men were so hysterical that they cried out loud: "My wife is young; my children have not grown up yet. Heaven, please come to save us as soon as possible!"

Some said they were not able to eat much throughout the voyage because they threw up whenever their ship was pounded by waves. Other respondents said the poor weather and the waves made them feel very uncomfortable on a ship packed with hundreds of passengers.[4]

U.S. authorities have observed that most Chinese smuggling ships are unsuitable for transporting hundreds of passengers across the ocean. A law enforcement official said of one, "I wouldn't even ride on it from one side of the [San Francisco] Bay to the other. It's rotting. You can grab a handful of the wall, and it crumbles in your hand" (Glover and Daniels 1993: 1). Many of my respondents bore out this observation. One described a ship that had sailed across three oceans and suffered an engine meltdown just before entering U.S. waters: "Everybody panicked because the ship almost turned over. All the passengers helped to keep it afloat by removing water from the ship. After repairs, the ship continued its trip, and it took another twenty days to get to New York City."

Another respondent explained how the ship that transported him to Guatemala broke down near Japan:

> The ship sailed for about two months and arrived at a Japanese island. All of a sudden, the ship broke down and was immobilized. When huge waves banged on the disabled ship, it swirled and almost turned over. At that point, the sailors were about to abandon us and leave on a small boat by themselves. They were even planning to dynamite the disabled ship with 279 passengers on it. We were all crying and yelling. We begged them not to do so, and that's why they decided not to discard us. Later on, another ship appeared. It was a small Taiwanese ship. At that point, we used a lottery system to decide who got on that ship first. If someone was fortunate and won the lottery, that person got on the boat first and survived. I was lucky; I was in the first group to be rescued. However, later, all the passengers were able to transfer off the battered mother ship. That small boat brought all of us to Guatemala.

Most smuggling ships were originally designed and constructed as fishing or cargo ships and are usually ill-equipped to accommodate hundreds of passengers. There are rarely enough toilets and passengers have to relieve themselves wherever they can (Mooney and Zyla 1993). A Coast Guard officer who inspected a smuggling ship reported, "It's abominable.... They're living in their own filth. There's vomit, urine and excrement strewn through the decks" (Dobson 1993: 1).Many respondents grumbled about the unsanitary conditions and the lack of food and water. A nineteen-year-old woman from Changle described what it was like to spend almost two months on a ship with little food or water:

> We spent fifty-nine days on the mother ship. During those days, we ate twice daily. There was no water to wash ourselves, so we used seawater to brush our teeth and bathe. When we boarded the ship, every passenger was offered a thick paperboard and that was our bed. Male and female passengers were divided by a wooden wall. The men often fought for food. When we were hungry, we tightened our belts. We did not even have the luxury to fill our stomachs with water when hungry. Many of us were seasick and could not eat much. Most of us lost a lot of weight, and we did not look like human beings.

Because of poor sanitary conditions and lack of water, many passengers developed skin diseases. One man summed up his journey this way:

> On the ship, we ate two meals a day, but there was not enough water to drink. We slept on the corridors, the deck, and the lower deck of the ship. Because there was not enough food, the passengers had to endure hunger. Since there was no water to drink, we drank seawater, which made many people ill. We asked the crew members to give us some water and they refused. Then we stole water. There was a passenger who stole a pack of instant noodles, and he was beaten by the crew members. Many people got sick, and the sailors provided only some pain relievers. There was no water to take a shower, so most of us developed skin irritations.... Those not sick received two small bowls of rice a day and some canned food. The sanitation on the ship was horrible. In brief, we were starving and we were cold.

ABUSES ON BOARD

In the crowded conditions at sea, on ships not designed for carrying passengers, conflicts often erupt. One subject described fights that broke out over food and cigarettes. Another said, "It was always the strong exploiting the weak. Many passengers acted like animals" and got in fist fights over food or water.

Typically snakeheads would hire a small number of passengers to maintain order on the ships. According to many of my respondents, these *ma zhais* (enforcers) often beat other passengers who threatened stability; one subject described beatings with handguns and iron bars. "The whole trip was like a nightmare. The *ma zhais* did not treat the passengers as human beings. They assaulted those they disliked and raped the women passengers at will."

Passengers tried to protect themselves by sticking together according to their native villages; respondents described groups of people from Changle or Tingjiang looking out for each other. A twenty-two-year-old male who headed one of these groups said, "The main purpose of grouping people together was to decide eating arrangements through something like a lottery system. Of course, I tried my best to help my group when the crew distributed food."

People from areas with few immigrants were often left unprotected and had to fend for themselves, and members of large groups sometimes victimized passengers belonging to small groups. A twenty-nine-year-old male from Minhou gave an example: "Because I am from an area that had very few passengers, I . . . was exploited by the large groups from Changle and Tingjiang. We had to listen to them, and we received less food than they did. On the trip, the Changle and Tingjiang groups often got into fights. Once, a Changle male was stabbed several times by people from the Tingjiang group. That stopped because the sailors discharged their guns." Another subject was assaulted after he refused to be victimized: "Those who belonged to a big group noticed that my clothes and luggage were better than others, so they tried to rob me and I resisted. They beat me up. Also, I was often hit over food. Those who belonged to the big group were helpers of the *ma zhais*. They did whatever they wished, like eating, drinking, and exploiting the women. Some were beaten crazy on the ship."

The rape of female immigrants does not usually attract much media or public attention, but it can be ubiquitous, and several of my respondents described being raped by big and little snakeheads, crew, enforcers, guides, and male passengers. One case that *was* widely publicized was that of woman who was gang-raped by the captain and crew of her ship; she committed suicide by jumping overboard (*Sing Tao Daily*, June 22, 1993).

Several of my respondents described terrible scenes of rape aboard the ships. "The sailors raped all eight females on the ship," recalled a thirty-eight-year-old man from Changle.

> The women were crying all the time. At the beginning, the crew refused to give female passengers drinking water. Later, when the women begged the crew for water, the crew placed sleeping pills in the water and raped them. One victim became pregnant, and she had an abortion right after the ship arrived in Guatemala. In Guatemala, we were robbed by a group of bandits, and all the women were raped again.

A thirty-three-year-old female from Tingjiang explained how the crew extorted sex from female passengers by bribing them with food or water:

> Women passengers stayed on the second deck. There was no way we could avoid being sexually harassed by the crew and the *ma zhais*. Once they wanted a woman to have sex with them, it did not matter whether she was a lady or a bitch; there was no way she could protect herself. We had to take care of ourselves on the ship. The crew and the *ma zhais* were all awful people. Sometimes they brought water to us to impress us, but it was like *huang su lung kay chi pai nien* [wolves visiting chickens during the Chinese New Year]; they had something else on their minds.

Another subject, a twenty-year-old male from Changle, explained how vulnerable the women were when they were surrounded by men on board a smuggling ship. Of the ten female passengers on his ship, five were raped by the sailors. The crew threatened them with violence and withheld food to make them submit. Eventually, faced with terrible hunger and thirst, the other five women gave in.

Those who were raped were not likely to be treated with sympathy by other passengers. A twenty-five-year-old female factory worker from Changle told this story:

> There was a Tingjiang woman who traveled along with me. A crew member asked her to sleep with him. She refused. Then he stopped offering her meals. In addition, he harassed her in a variety of ways. Later, she slept with him. She cried often. But later, she got used to it because we spent fifty-five days on the ship. After that, she was provided with nice meals and a comfortable place to stay. Later, that woman got sick. I heard she was pregnant. After arriving here, she was treated the same way as we were by the debt-collectors. Actually, she was discriminated against by the debt-collectors. They considered that woman shameless and often used dirty words when talking to her.

Rape could also lead to violence among men. A twenty-year-old male worker from Changle saw a sailor hit a male passenger after he tried to defend a woman from the advances of a Taiwanese sailor. Sometimes the enforcers and the sailors would get into fist fights over the possession of a female passenger. A nineteen-year-old woman from Changle recalled:

> There was a *ma zhai* on the ship who was also an illegal immigrant. He often verbally or physically abused us. There was a female from Tingjiang who got very close to a sailor, and she "voluntarily" slept with him. I think she really made us women lose face. She had no self-respect at all. That sailor may not have really liked her after all. Also, there was a girl being pursued by another male passenger. And when she refused to be close to him, that guy hit her. Later, the *ma zhai* learned about that, and he beat that guy almost to death.

Robert Perito, former director of the U.S. State Department's division of International Narcotics and Law Enforcement Affairs, said that both male and female passengers aboard the *Jung Sheng,* a smuggling ship discovered near Hawaii in July 1995, were sexually abused by the crew. According to Perito, a sixteen-year-old male passenger was repeatedly forced to masturbate in public. Moreover, two male passengers were forced to perform anal sex in the open. Some of the passengers were so traumatized by the experiences that they tried to commit suicide. According to Perito, these were the worst instances of sexual abuse on smuggling ships detected by U.S. authorities (*Sing Tao Daily,* August 24, 1995).

Arriving in the United States

Once the smuggling ship arrived near U.S. waters, small boats picked up passengers on the high seas, a frightening and dangerous procedure. One nineteen-year-old student from Fuzhou City described a situation in which the two vessels collided and a passenger lost two fingers when his hands were crushed by chains. A few even lose their lives in this difficult and dangerous process. A female factory worker described the fear involved in leaping from a two-story-high mother ship down into a small boat. She watched some of her compatriots fall into the sea. A 23-year-old female from Changle recalled, "I was scared when we transferred from the mother ship to the small boats. It was as if I had to jump to the ground from the top of a tall building. The male on the small boat helped, though."

Passengers were then ferried ashore and transported to their destination by motor vehicle. A twenty one-year-old female teacher described the process:

> After we arrived in international waters near the United States, we remained there for half a month. Later, a small boat came to meet us. We didn't get on the boat in groups; rather, more than two hundred passengers got on the boat simultaneously. The small boat almost sank. The captain of the small boat spoke Mandarin. The small boat traveled for about two days, and we arrived at the shore. We all went ashore quickly. We were not detected by U.S. authorities because we moved after midnight. We were driven to Los Angeles; all this was arranged by the little snakeheads. The truck that picked us up was a huge container truck. All 210 passengers got on the truck, which was driven by a Fujianese. It took about thirteen hours to arrive in Los Angeles.

Sometimes snakeheads transported passengers directly from their point of entry in California or elsewhere to New York City immediately. A thirty-six-year-old male from Fuzhou City recalled, "After the ship arrived in Los Angeles, the snakehead loaded all 160 passengers in four huge trucks to New York City. It took about a week to get there." Another subject explained what he and his traveling companions went through to get to New York:

> When the ship arrived near the United States, a small fishing boat chartered by a group of Fujianese and Vietnamese came to meet us. All 134 passengers boarded the small boat, and it sailed for three days and three nights to arrive in Boston. A car came by every ten to fifteen minutes to pick us up. The cars could carry only six to twelve passengers at a time. The cars drove for about an hour, and we were kept in a private house overnight. The next morning we were put inside a huge container truck and drove for eight hours to get to New York City.

Not all respondents who arrived by boat were as fortunate as the aforementioned interviewees; some were arrested by U.S. authorities. The small boat that came to retrieve them might be part of a government sting operation (Kamen 1991b), or the trucks that were to pick them up on shore might fail to arrive. Still others were discovered before their smuggling ships entered U.S. waters. A twenty-nine-year-old male from Changle told this story:

After sailing for twenty-one days, we arrived off Hawaii. Then our ship was discovered by U.S. authorities. The authorities demanded that our ship not enter U.S. waters. They sent us a message through wireless radio. The captain and the crew members were frightened. They suggested that they would turn the ship back to China or sail to another country. The passengers disagreed. Later, the *ma zhai*s mobilized us to protest the captain and the sailors' idea. So we captured all the crew members, bound them, and locked them up. At that moment, the captain threatened that if we mutinied, he would blow up the ship. We were not scared however, so we locked him up. We were fortunate that there were two passengers who used to work on ships and they knew something about handling a ship at sea. We had a discussion and decided to set the captain and the chief officer free and forced them to sail the ship in the direction of Honolulu. The patrol at the coast constantly sent us signals not to proceed, but our ship forced its way. When the ship entered American waters, the U.S. patrol sent two fast boats and arrested all the passengers.[5]

OTHER FORMS OF SEA SMUGGLING

A small number of my respondents arrived in the United States aboard a cargo ship or a small pleasure craft. Unlike the cargo or fishing vessels that are converted into smuggling ships, these may carry only a small number of smuggled Chinese into the United States while involved in their normal, legitimate operations such as transporting goods or tourists to the United States.

Media and law enforcement reports rarely mention the arrival of illegal immigrants by cargo ship. According to some of my respondents, coming to the United States by well-managed and well-maintained cargo ships was often much to be preferred to the poorly managed and poorly maintained smuggling ships filled with immigrants. A forty-one-year-old Changle male who sailed with six other immigrants in 1989 had no complaints about the twenty-day voyage. "We ate well, and there was plenty of water to take showers. When the ship arrived in California, we were ferried ashore by a small boat managed by an English-speaking captain. After we landed, the captain drove us to a small airport and put us on a plane headed for New York City."

Another respondent, a forty-six-year-old factory worker from Fuzhou City who also arrived in the United States on board a cargo ship, was not as impressed with the trip:

There were altogether sixty illegal immigrants on the ship, including three females. The ship journeyed through several countries, including Egypt. The ship was carrying commodities, and after sailing for three months, it arrived in San Francisco. A small boat handled by Vietnamese and Cantonese ferried us ashore. For me, this trip was like an eternity. I felt like it took a century for me to get to America, especially the three months I spent on the ship. I felt like I was living in another planet, without any sense of life and death. Everyday, I wished I could go home, and at the same time, I hoped to be in the United States soon. I was in a bind, torn apart by mixed feelings and contradictory hopes.

Most of my respondents who were smuggled into the United States by sea suffered terribly on their trips. Many of them broke into tears when asked what it was like to spend months on board a smuggling ship. A thirty-three-year-old woman from Tingjiang who paid $20,000 for the right to board a smuggling vessel cramped with 239 passengers summed up her feelings about the trip: "All those things I experienced on the trip are enough to make me feel bitter for the rest of my life. This is a trip I will never, ever forget. I would not have imagined all these sufferings, even in my worse dreams. If someone paid me $20,000 to do so now, I would not take this dangerous trip again."

Another subject, a Tingjiang teenager transported to Mexico from China, agreed: "I will not do this again for the rest of my life, even if someone is willing to pay me $100,000. It's a dangerous trip. For fifty days, it was like living in a nightmare." A thirty-five-year-old female from Zhejiang who spent more than three months on a smuggling ship to the United States said, "I could not describe this whole trip in words, only my tears could explain everything. The sufferings on the trip are something I will never forget because they are filled with blood and tears."

The conditions my sea-traveling respondents suffered were intolerable and inhumane. Sea smuggling and other methods of transporting illegal immigrants need to be curbed if only to spare these poor passengers. U.S authorities should not underestimate the suffering of people who pay tens of thousands of dollars to be smuggled into the United States. Their experiences on board the ships may have long-lasting effects on their mental health, a subject addressed in Chapter 8.

6   The Land Route

SNAKEHEADS regard the land route as the most reliable way of smuggling immigrants into the United States, and many of my respondents entered the country by crossing the border from Mexico or Canada. The smuggling of Chinese into the United States via Mexico seems to have begun in the late nineteenth century, after the Chinese Exclusion Act denied most Chinese legal entry (Lyman 1974; Samora 1971). Most of my subjects were transported out of China by sea to Central or South America and were later brought into the United States overland by Mexican smugglers. Others flew to Central America or Canada before being smuggled overland into the United States. Although the land route entails fewer risks of discovery, it is still dangerous and full of hardship.

ENTERING THE UNITED STATES VIA MEXICO

Once their smuggling ships approached the Mexican shore, my subjects boarded small boats operated by Mexicans who ferried them to shore. Most of the time, the operation went smoothly, as in the case of a young woman from Changle who crossed the border with a group that made its way to Los Angeles. "Several Mexicans worked as guides. They were very nice to women. They gave us plenty of food. They instructed us to 'be quiet' in Mandarin, and to 'lie low' and 'kneel down' in the Fuzhou dialect."

In a few instances, Mexican or Taiwanese smugglers immediately transported my subjects directly to the U.S.-Mexican border. More often than not, however, the immigrants were stored in safe houses for several days or weeks, waiting for the right time to cross the border. According to my subjects, security within the safe houses was extremely tight. They were provided with enough food to eat but their movement was severely restricted. A thirty-year-old construction worker from Tingjiang recalled:

We stayed in Mexico for a week. We ate very well at a house located in a suburban area. However, we were not allowed to talk to one another or to go outside. Every day, the little snakeheads ordered us to go downstairs to eat in a group. We did not have a chance to go out. Actually, we were not even allowed to go near the gate. Later, we were transported to the U.S.-Mexican border by mid-size buses that carried ten passengers each.

Worse than the heavily guarded confinement, some of my subjects were abused by their Mexican smugglers. A twenty-two-year-old grocery store owner told this story:

When our ship arrived in Mexico, local people picked us up with small boats. They then drove us to a place and ordered us to climb mountains. Whenever there were patrol airplanes hovering around, we hid in sewers or bushes. The Mexicans brought food to us, and it consisted mostly of instant noodles. When we got to the mountain area, the Mexicans searched everybody for weapons. They were concerned that we might start a riot and threaten them. They also took away everybody's watches and physically assaulted some people. That was their way of sending us a message that we'd better obey them.

As on the ships, there were fights among the Chinese when food or water was scarce. For many of my subjects, the temporary stay in Mexican safe houses could be another nightmare after spending several traumatic weeks on a ship. A twenty-year-old male from Changle struggled to survive in a huge "safe house" operation in Mexico:

The Mexicans came to meet us in international waters and brought us ashore on small motor boats in groups of twenty people. They then drove us to foothills, which we climbed. Everybody slept on the ground and ate whatever the local people brought us. At that place, in addition to the 240 passengers from our ship, there were passengers from other ships. There was about eight hundred people altogether. When the trucks arrived with food, the passengers grabbed it as soon as it arrived. Fights broke out. As a result, each ship sent a representative to discuss how to distribute the food. Thereafter, each ship sent a representative to pick up the food. Several days later, there were helicopters hovering around the area, and we spread out and hid.

Crossing the U.S.-Mexican Border

To avoid detection, some smugglers take immigrants over rugged terrain and barbed wire barriers to cross the border into the United States. Others use large trucks. Although most succeed, the trip is dangerous and often terrifying. A thirty-five-year-old driver from Mawei described a narrow escape:

> In order to cross the U.S.-Mexican border, we were hidden inside a huge truck that was used to transport frozen food. We were discovered by Mexican authorities and a chase ensued. The driver drove the truck to a park and ordered us to get out, and he fled on foot. The passengers spread out and ran. With the exception of a few, all were arrested. I escaped by hiding in a Taiwanese restaurant. A week later, I got in touch with the snakehead and he sent somebody to escort me and two others into the United States.

A nineteen-year-old woman from Tingjiang traveled in a similar truck. "Seventy of us entered the United States from Mexico inside a frozen food container. There was very little air inside the container. . . . Throughout the trip, my heart felt like it was hanging in the air. I had no sense of security at all. It was lucky that no one died."

One of my subjects described an unusually unlucky crossing:

> After we arrived in Mexico, we were driven to the border in a car by local snakeheads. On the road, we were discovered by Mexican police, so everybody ran. That's how I got lost. I followed the lights, and we slept in bushes near the border. We met two Mexicans who were on their way to the United States, so we followed them. After we entered the United States, we came across a group of little snakeheads from Changle, and they locked us up for two days. Then they moved us to New York City. They got in touch with our snakehead and asked him to ransom us for $3,000 per person. That money was later added to our smuggling fees.

The majority of my respondents who entered the United States via Mexico crossed the California border, especially if they had come to Mexico by ship, but a few small groups who flew from China or a transit point entered the United States via the Arizona or Texas borders. Once in the United States, my subjects were usually transported to San Diego or Los Angeles and after a few days moved to New York City. Generally Mexican smugglers turned them over to other smugglers in the United States. Like the many Mexican and Caribbean immigrants without documents, many Chinese are arrested immediately after they cross the U.S. border (Mahler 1995). A thirty-five-year-old male from Tingjiang described being arrested by U.S. border patrol officers at a San Diego thruway and detained for twelve hours. "At the detention center, we were almost starved to death. However, the U.S. officers were friendly. They were not prejudiced. We were photographed and finger-printed, and then for reasons we do not know, we were released."

Some respondents reported that their snakeheads bribed U.S. border patrol officers in order to get them across. A thirty-year-old male from Tingjiang told this story:

> We went through checkpoints to get to Los Angeles. The passengers were asked to lie down, and not look out from the bus windows. When the first bus went through a checkpoint in Los Angeles, its passengers were arrested because the snakehead had not bribed the officials. The passengers were fined $2,000 per person. I was on the second bus. After the snakehead paid the officials, when our bus arrived at the checkpoint, there was no one to check us. It took about two hours to reach Los Angeles. The process was painful; my whole body was stiff after remaining motionless for so many hours.

Arriving in Mexico by Air

Some of my subjects who entered the United States via Mexico arrived in Mexico by air. Compared with those who traveled by ship, those who flew were generally less likely to suffer en route. Their experiences with Mexican safe houses and border crossings, however, were not much different from those of immigrants who came by ship. A thirty-four-year-old male from Changle traveled for two and a half months from Fuzhou to South America and then to Mexico, where he and his fellow travelers had little to eat and slept in mosquito-infested banana fields. Although they were not spotted before arriving in Phoenix, he said, "I was so tired that I didn't even want to continue, hoping that I would be arrested."

Another respondent, a forty-one-year-old man from Changle, offered an unusually detailed and poignant account of his journey:

> My snakehead was a Chinese from Hong Kong. The day before my departure, he came to Fujian and gave me a Chinese passport and a Hong Kong visa so I could go to Hong Kong via Shenzhen. After staying in Hong Kong for four days, he gave us [three men and a woman and her ten-year-old son] back the passports with Thai visas attached. We then flew to Thailand. The snakehead traveled to Thailand with us. Six days later, he provided us photo-sub Taiwan passports and Mexican visas. We flew to Mexico via Japan and three other transit points. The snakehead escorted us to Japan.
>
> When we arrived in Mexico, a guide who spoke English and some Mandarin came to meet us at the airport. He put the two males in a car

trunk. The woman and her son were asked to sit in the front seat of another car. We could not move inside the trunk, and there was not enough air. The driver drove very fast, and the heat was unbearable inside the trunk. The engine was right underneath my back, and I could not straighten my feet. The two of us did not even dare to cry. We comforted one another so we could hang on. We almost passed out; we were exhausted.

After driving for quite a while, the cars stopped. After they opened the trunk, they moved us out of the trunk like we were baggage. We were extremely hungry, and we were stiff from the cramped trunk. Later, we went to a private house to eat. After we rested for two hours, the woman and her son arrived. . . .

We continued to climb through the hills. When the boy could not walk, his mother started to cry. The guide said she might have to pay a local Mexican to carry her son. I was very sympathetic to the mother and child. The woman was concerned that if she hired someone to carry her son, she and her son might be separated by accident. Later, I discussed this with a friend of mine who was with us and we decided we would take turns carrying her son. At that time, we were strangers, but we had a strong feeling that we were all from the same area.

The boy was very nice; he did exactly what we told him to. That lovely boy made us think of our families back in China. In fact, we endure this simply because we want to give our children a better life.

After we walked for a few days, there was little water left, but we kept most of it for the boy. The mother was very appreciative. Her husband was already in the United States, and that's why she came with her son. She probably had no idea about all the hardships she would face on the trip.

After we arrived at the border, we crossed the fence at night. I helped the boy over the fence. His mother crossed the fence with trembling feet. At the U.S. side, we checked into a hotel with the aid of a guide waiting for us there. At midnight, someone came to tell us to flee. The two of us jumped down from a window. The woman and her son stood in front of the window and dared not jump. Actually, it was only about seven feet to the ground. We walked over to underneath the window and signaled to her that we would catch her after she jumped. The boy was very smart; he jumped first, and we got him. His mother also jumped, and we caught her. We hid in a bush underneath a tree. The police knocked on the door of the hotel and then departed. We then came out of the bush and went back to our rooms. Later, we were driven to an airport to catch a flight to New York.

A twenty-year-old woman recalled how much she and two female companions had to endure throughout their clandestine trip. Her experiences are typical of those my respondents who entered the United States across the U.S.-Mexican border:

We, four men and three women, went to Thailand via Shenzhen and Hong Kong with Chinese passports and Colombian export labor visas. We stayed in Thailand for forty-five days and flew to Colombia. A Cantonese-speaking male met us at the airport and checked us into a relatively decent hotel. Later, he gave us documents so we could board a ship. The ship sailed for many days before it arrived in Guatemala. Once there, two men came and picked us up in a truck. The truck headed for the Guatemala-Mexico border. We females were very tired, but we were lucky the accompanying males took care of us. At the border, the guides arranged for us to stay at a farmer's house. At two o'clock in the morning, we entered Mexico on a small boat. There was a car waiting for us in Mexico, and it transported us to a house in a remote area.

At that point, all of us were very tired and hungry. We were also covered with dirt. After staying there for twenty days, we were transported to the U.S.-Mexican border on a fruit truck. The truck traveled for twelve hours and then stopped. When we got off the truck, we could barely move, but the guide urged us to climb a hill right away. The females climbed slowly, and the guide was anxious for us to move faster. He yelled and pushed us. After walking for seven to eight hours, we arrived at the border.

All of a sudden, there were police officers yelling at us. We did not know what to do, so everybody started to run in all directions. The guides ran the fastest, and the males followed them. The females could not run fast, and within half a minute, we [three females] lost the guides and the males. We began to cry, but we did not dare to cry out loud.

It was getting dark, and after we explored the area, we found that there were lights at the foot of the hill. We were very hungry, and the three of us tried to cheer one another up. We decided we could not spend the night in the hills because there might be bandits or wild beasts. We were hoping the authorities could find us and save our lives. We began to go down the mountain and headed in the direction of the lights. We fell down often, and our arms and legs were bleeding. However, we had no time to be concerned with ourselves.

After we got to the foot of the hill, we walked along a road without knowing where we were going. We later bumped into two police officers, but they did not arrest us. We thought they were joking. They looked at us with curiosity. At that point, I saw "U.S.A." on the police officers' badges. I told the other two that we had reached the United States. When we tried to approach the police officers, they were gone. Then we decided not to stray away from this road and continued to walk along it.

Later, a car passed by and stopped. There were two Hispanic males inside the car, and they appeared to be very friendly. They offered us a ride, and we thought they might have been sent by the snakehead. We got in the car, and they took us to their home where we met their wives.

They treated us very nice. Later, the Mexican guides found out where we were, and they showed up with a Taiwanese and took us with them after they paid the two Hispanics $1,500.

Among those I studied, a twenty-two-year-old female factory worker from Changle took one of the most arduous routes. She left China via Myanmar overland, traveled from Thailand to Mexico by ship, and then crossed the Mexican border into the United States. She had to endure adversity not only in the remote area of the China-Myanmar border but also on the high seas and in Mexico. On the ship, she recalled,

> There was a *ma zhai* who asked me to "talk heart" [have sex] with him. I refused his request several times, and he burned my face with cigarettes. . . .
>
> Later, the ship arrived in Mexico, and a Mexican fishing boat transported all of us ashore. The fishing boat sailed for about four hours, and we got to shore. There was a large truck waiting for us, and it drove about twenty-four hours before arriving at a farmhouse. We were offered a lot of food. The next day, we started to climb mountains. There were four guides, and we were divided into four groups of twelve people each.
>
> After we arrived at the U.S.-Mexican border, we were first asked to hide behind bushes. Twenty minutes later, the guides asked us to get past a sewer and sneak inside the United States through a hole in a fence. There were two cars waiting for us, driven by people who spoke the dialects of both Fuzhou and Guangdong. They did not say much, but they were armed. We arrived in Los Angeles, and after staying there for four hours, we flew to New York.
>
> On the whole trip, it was like we were members of the Red Army. We felt like we were being chased all the time. It was all right on the ship, but after we got to Mexico, I came to know what it means to be hungry. The fifteen days I spent in the safe house [in New York City] were the darkest hours of my life.[1]

Some of my respondents traveled by sea or air to Guatemala and then entered the United States via Mexico. Conditions in Guatemala were much the same as in Mexico and my subjects described horrific treks through the jungle, long periods without food, and ill treatment. Many who took this route suffered enormously, especially if they were apprehended by Mexican or Guatemalan authorities.

A thirty-one-year-old woman from Changle provided a detailed account of the frustrations and dangers she encountered passing through Guatemala and Mexico:

When we arrived in Guatemala in January 1992, we were arrested by Guatemalan authorities and locked up for a month. In jail, the living arrangements were extremely poor and the food was awful. Later, our snakehead bailed us out, group by group. The snakehead transported us to a large, dilapidated house in a remote area in Guatemala. Every day, we received only biscuits and a bottle of water. We stayed there for about a month, and then we were transferred to a mountainous area where we waited for the arrival of a huge container truck that was used to transport bananas. Fifty of us were stacked into the container. There was a small hole for ventilation. All of us carried a small amount of water.

The truck drove for thirty-six hours, and then we got out. We climbed mountains, and we crossed rivers. We either ran or hid. Some people passed out for a while and then continued the trip. When people were too tired to move, the Mexican guides beat them up. Some people fell down cliffs, and we helped them to get back. We traveled for more than ten hours, and we crossed the Guatemala-Mexico border.

In Mexico, we traveled in cars. Later on, when the cars broke down, we got out and hid in the jungle. The three groups hid separately in the mountains. One group was discovered by the Mexican police and arrested. We remained in the jungle for five days. During these five days, we all drank mountain water to fill our stomachs. Sometimes we ate the wild fruits we found. Some people went down the mountain and brought some sugarcane back. One day, we were accosted by a group of bandits. They robbed us clean. They took all the women away and searched us thoroughly. In the process, they sexually abused the women.

Later, we were told that we had to move on, so we all went down the mountain and got into a number of cars. The cars drove for more than an hour, and then we were ordered to dash across several main roads. We subsequently climbed across barbed wire and entered the United States. At the border, the debt-collectors were waiting for us. They all spoke the Fuzhou dialect. It took me six months to complete the trip.

A forty-five-year-old male from Changle had a similar experience:

As soon as our ship arrived in Guatemala, a group of Taiwanese living there ferried us to shore by boat. Then we were transported to a remote area by car. After staying there for three days, we were dispatched to Mexico in the evening by car. We were arrested in Mexico and detained for twenty-five days; then Mexican authorities released us in a jungle near the Guatemala-Mexico border. We wandered in the jungle for three days without food or a place to sleep. We were arrested by Guatemalan police and locked up for eighteen days. We were then brought back to the jungle near Mexico and set free.

I was very weak. I had to crawl to find some water. I gave my jacket to a local person in exchange for food. After I filled my stomach, I was arrested again by the Guatemalan authorities. After being detained for three days, the snakehead bailed me out and kept me in a place for about two weeks. After recovering my strength, I continued on the trip to Mexico. I was hidden in the cover of an empty truck. The truck drove for six to seven days to get to Mexico. There were altogether forty immigrants in the truck, including seventeen females. We were kept in a remote area in Mexico. We rested for two days, then climbed the barbed wire along the border and entered the United States. In San Diego, we were discovered by U.S. authorities. We were detained for twenty-four days before our snakehead hired a lawyer and bailed us out. It cost him $3,000 per person. The expense was later added to the smuggling fee.

Some subjects were arrested repeatedly. One twenty-six-year-old male from Changle who attempted to enter Mexico from Guatemala concluded that neither the Mexican nor the Guatemalan authorities knew what to do with him:

While attempting to cross the Guatemala-Mexico border, I was arrested in Mexico and detained for seven days. Then the process of being dumped into the jungles at the border by both Mexican and Guatemalan authorities began. After being incarcerated for seven days, the Mexican officials took me to the border with Guatemala and released me. Immediately, I was arrested by Guatemalan officials and detained for ten days before they ditched me near the Mexican border. Altogether I was incarcerated four times in Mexico and three times in Guatemala. Finally, I found a Chinese snakehead in Guatemala, and he helped me to get to the United States via Mexico.

As journalists have suggested, Central America plays an important role in the Chinese human trade for several reasons (Farah 1995; DeStefano 1997). As Farah put it, "With coasts on the Atlantic and Pacific oceans and a long tradition of corruption, the region is attractive because Central Americans have, over two decades, developed sophisticated smuggling networks of their own to enter the United States illegally.... And Central America is popular for another reason. It is not a crime in any country in the region to transport illegal aliens, meaning that if a person is caught, the migrants can be deported but the transporter faces at most a misdemeanor fine" (1995: A1).

ENTERING THE UNITED STATES VIA CANADA

According to Canadian authorities, Canada is becoming a major destination or transit point for smuggled Chinese (Yates 1997), and some of my respondents entered the United States by that route. A twenty-seven-year-old male from Lianjiang explained how:

> We flew to Canada from Beijing via Hong Kong, Thailand, France, and England with photo-sub foreign passports. An English-speaking Chinese from Shanghai escorted us along the way. Once we arrived in Canada, the guide took our passports to a school to obtain Canadian student visas. It cost about $3,000 per person. We then crossed the U.S.-Canadian border and arrived in Seattle. A Vietnamese transported us from Canada to the United States by car. We did not encounter any problem at the checkpoint. From Seattle, we flew to New York City.

Others came to the United States after they had spent some time in Canada as refugees, like this twenty-eight-year-old woman who owned a store in China:

> After we obtained our Chinese passports, we went to the Bolivian embassy in Beijing and applied for visas to go to Bolivia. We knew that there were people from our town working as snakeheads in Bolivia. We also knew that they could help us to go to the United States. We flew to Bolivia from Shanghai and stayed there for two months. The five of us, two males and three females, went out to look for a snakehead. Later, we found a Taiwanese who said he would help us to go to Canada. He gave us Argentinean passports so we could fly to Canada. We were arrested in Canada because we entered the country without documents.[2] After we applied for refugee status, we were released.
>
> I found a friend who was living in Canada, and he found me a job in a garment factory. I earned about $1,000. Later, we learned that the U.S. government was offering permanent resident status to all Chinese living in the United States because of the June 4 incident [1989 student protest in Tiananmen Square]. So we decided to go to the United States. We went to the U.S.-Canadian border to find a driver who could transport us to the United States. Afterward, we met someone who said his boss was a native Canadian. The driver was a Mandarin-speaking Taiwanese. He promised to take us to the United States for $3,000 per person. Two days later, the driver hid us inside a huge truck filled with timber. The truck drove for ten hours and stopped. The driver announced that we were in the United States.

My data suggest that there were Canadian smuggling rings operating at the U.S.-Canadian border. A forty-three-year-old male from Lianjiang claimed to have flown with a photo-sub passport from Hong Kong to Canada, where he worked for four months in a restaurant. Eventually a Canadian snakehead transported him across the U.S.

border in the back of a truck and bought him a bus ticket to New York City.

Another respondent, a forty-year-old man from Mawei who slipped into the United States via Canada, did not intend to come to the United States when he left China.

> I left China with a genuine Chinese passport and a Bolivian tourist visa. At that time, there was a woman from the Fuzhou region who worked for the Bolivian embassy [in Beijing] and she helped a lot of people from Fuzhou obtain Bolivian visas. When I left China for Bolivia, I wasn't thinking about going to the United States. However, while I was in Bolivia, the Tiananmen Square incident occurred and I didn't want to go back to China. So I found a snakehead in Bolivia who helped me to come to the United States for $18,000. I first flew to Canada and then crossed the U.S.-Canadian border by hiding inside a bus.

Some entered the United States from Canada after they left China as students. A chemistry teacher from Lianjiang explained how he went to Australia as a student in 1989 and there found someone to transport him to the United States via Canada:

> I went to Australia as a student. The snakehead [in China] charged me $5,000 and asked me to find another snakehead to smuggle me to America from Australia. I was informed by the Chinese snakehead that the fees for going to the United States from Australia would be about $15,000. I stayed in Australia for three months. While I was there, I found a job in a factory that paid about $1,200 a month. Later, I found a snakehead who helped me get a hold of a visitor's visa to Canada. He also sent a person along with me to Canada. That person later brought me across the border to the United States.

VICTIMIZATION OF ILLEGAL IMMIGRANTS

As we have seen, Chinese illegal immigrants, regardless of their route to the United States, are vulnerable to many forms of abuse and victimization. Their lack of proper documents, language barriers, and need to avoid capture by authorities prevent them from seeking help and make them easy prey to all manner of exploitation. My respondents recounted many instances of extortion by authorities in transit points and robbery by local criminals.

A forty-four-year-old construction worker described being robbed by police in a Peruvian airport. Another respondent said that Thai police officers extorted money from him at a transit point in Bangkok. Others were robbed in the streets of Bangkok by local thugs. A thirty-year-old Tingjiang male recalled, "While we were in Thailand, we were robbed on the streets. The robbers pointed their guns at us and took away everything, including our Chinese passports."

Some were physically or verbally abused by authorities in transit points. According to a thirty-two-year-old male from Changle, his group was abused by Russian police. Those who resisted demands for their money were assaulted. Sometimes the very snakeheads and guides who were supposed to protect them exploited my respondents. An eighteen-year-old youth from Changle was devastated by his experience en route to the United States:

> Throughout the trip, I had to endure all kinds of humiliations. Whatever was said in China by the snakehead about the trip was completely different from our experience. Once we arrived in Thailand, they [the smugglers] called us "little duck." When we arrived in America, they called us "little pig." I suffered a lot throughout the journey. My sense of personal dignity was badly ruined. Initially, the snakehead in China said he would help me to get to Canada. When I arrived in Thailand, I was sold to another snakehead, and he wanted me to go to the United States. I refused the offer, and he threatened me. I had no choice but to come here instead.

Others were robbed by little snakeheads. A forty-two-year-old construction worker from Tingjiang remembered how his group was shaken down. "When seven other Chinese immigrants and I were in Thailand, local *ma zhai*s knew that we were the newly arrived 'ducks.' So they took away our new clothes, watches, gold rings, and other stuff. They said they would mail our belongings to us after we arrived in the United States. They insisted that these items would not be safe with us."

As on the ships, women were especially prone to sexual violence and abuse at various transit points, especially in Bangkok. A thirty-year-old male from Guantou recalled:

> When we were in Thailand, we were kept in a "duck house."[3] The wooden house, located on a hill, was originally a place for addicts to take drugs. We were forced to stay in Thailand for four months. As a result of the unexpectedly lengthy stay, there was no money left to buy food and other stuff. Finally, the *ma zhai*s beat those who did not have money with them and forced them to find money. One female was unable to come up with any money. The *ma zhai*s stripped her naked and allowed people who stayed there to have sex with her. The *ma zhai*s then collected money from

those people to cover her daily expenses. One of them was a relative of that woman, so he refused to sleep with her. He was beaten by the *ma zhais*.

Often these women were forced to provide sex in exchange for a discount on their smuggling fees. A twenty-four-year-old woman from Fuzhou City wept as she described how she was sexually abused for ten days by her captor in a Bolivian hotel and later in New York City. She eventually became a prostitute, much to her shame.

If I agreed [to sleep with my snakehead], he promised to reduce the amount of money I owed him. If I disagreed, he demanded that I come up with the whole payment within a week. Otherwise, he threatened to sell me to a massage parlor. The debt-collectors started to treat me nicely when they found out that the snakehead was interested in me. Later, I moved into the snakehead's house.

I worked in a garment factory for a while, but later started to work in a beauty [massage] parlor. . . . When I worked, I was doing things I could not explain to you. I am making $4,000 a month now. I knew I became a very low-life human being, but I could not get out of this predicament. I have relatives here, but I rarely get in touch with them. It was my decision not to be affiliated with them. Later, the friends of the snakehead sexually harassed me, but I didn't think I should report it to the police because of who I am.

Another respondent recounted how a snakehead pressured a female immigrant for sexual favors:

Our group included a woman from Shanghai and three males from Fuzhou. When we arrived in Holland, local Chinese snakeheads took care of us. One evening, the woman from Shanghai was asked to visit the snakeheads' room. A deal was struck between the woman and the snakeheads. She would sleep with them, and they would deduct between $200 to $400 from the smuggling fees for every night she slept with them. We all knew what was going on. In fact, we were wishing that the woman would do her best to please the local snakeheads, hoping that this might lead them to treat the whole group well and help the group have an early departure for the United States. From what I know, the woman eventually was allowed to deduct about $3,000 from her smuggling fees.

A COMPARISON OF VARIOUS SMUGGLING ROUTES

Each of the methods used to smuggle Chinese illegals into the United States has its advantages and disadvantages. The methods vary as to expense, length of time, travel documents needed, risk factors, and so on (see Appendix B, Table 6).

The air route was probably the least demanding route for the undocumented Chinese in this study, yet it cost only slightly more than the other two routes. Subjects who flew to the United States made the highest down payment, however, while those who came by ship tended to make the lowest down payment.

Respondents who entered the United States by air had to wait an average of seventy-four days to be smuggled out of China, while those who came by sea waited, on average, less than a month, primarily because fewer travel documents were needed. The average amount of time spent en route was almost three months, with air travel being the slowest route, with an average of 107 days. This irony is explained by the need for reliable travel documents and by the greater number of transit points typical of air smuggling. Immigrants were often "sold" by their original snakeheads to snakeheads in transit countries and long delays were common. Those who came to the United States by ship spent an average of sixty-four days en route.

The choice of smuggling route also depends in part on the number of people waiting to be transported. Air travel is appropriate for small groups of around ten, while larger groups tend to travel by sea. Smugglers also tend to be less demanding in their requirements of immigrants smuggled into the United States by boat. About 38 percent of those in my sample smuggled by air were required to pay a down payment *and* obtain a guarantor; only 11 percent of those smuggled by sea had to do the same.

U.S. authorities were less likely to detect those entering the United States overland than they were those entering by sea or by air. Although the average detection rate for the whole sample was 37 percent, only 11 percent of those who crossed the U.S. border overland were discovered by U.S. border patrol officials, whereas as many as 64 percent of those who flew into the United States were detected by U.S. authorities at their point of entry.

There is also a close association between smuggling route and the chance of being detained by debt-collectors in New York City and elsewhere. Although about half of my respondents who flew into the United States were locked up by debt collectors, 83 percent who entered by sea were confined by smugglers upon their arrival. Appendix B, Table 6 shows that the probability of being abused on the trip is highest for those who entered the United States overland or by boat. Those who flew into the United States were least likely to be victimized.

Like the respondents who came to the United States by air or by sea, those who entered overland from Mexico or Canada endured a variety of risks and hardships. The majority had traveled to Mexico or Guatemala by sea and suffered a variety of hardships both during the voyage and crossing the border. Nevertheless, their passage fees were as high as those who flew or sailed to North America.

A snakehead I interviewed in Fuzhou said that the land route via Mexico is the most "reliable" route, the surest way to enter the United States illegally, a conclusion that is borne out by my data, which show that respondents who took the land route had the lowest detection rate. No doubt this smuggling route will continue to play an important role in facilitating the movement of illegal Chinese immigrants into the United States, despite the dramatic increase in the number of border patrol officers along the U.S.-Mexican border since 1993 (Ayres 1994; Mydans 1995).

III. CLIMBING THE MOUNTAIN OF GOLD

7   Safe Houses

It APPEARS TO BE a common practice among human traffickers from all ethnic groups to detain illegal immigrants upon their arrival in the United States until the immigrants' families and friends pay their smuggling fees. As Mahler has written, in a study of smuggled Salvadorans in New York, "Safe houses are used to sequester immigrants and hold them until their sponsors send the second portion of the trip's price to the coyote [smuggler]" (1995: 65).

In May 1993, two journalists reported that immigration officials had discovered sixty-one smuggled Chinese in an auto repair garage in Jersey City, New Jersey (Finnegan and Chan 1993), and a year later sixty-three illegal Chinese immigrants were found at a house in the small, rural community of Mitcheville in Prince George's County, Maryland (Jeter and Thomas 1994). According to news reports, between 1993 and 1994 law enforcement and immigration authorities in Los Angeles and New York City raided at least a dozen safe houses for smuggled Chinese, and were stunned to find so many people crowded into tiny basements or rooms that were poorly maintained.

As U.S. authorities became aware of the "safe house" phenomenon, they also learned of the prevalence of rape, gang rape, and other sexual abuse of female immigrants. During a raid of a safe house in New York, police discovered two young immigrants who had been sexually abused by their captors (*Sing Tao Daily,* November 18, 1993).[1] There were also reports of female immigrants being forced to work as prostitutes to pay their smuggling debts (*New York Times,* July 23, 1993). In 1995, when a female immigrant was gang-raped, had a finger cut off, was hit over the head with a television set and finally strangled in a safe house, authorities and the public were shocked and outraged (Faison 1995).

Portions of this chapter are reprinted with permission from Paul J. Smith (ed.), *Human Smuggling: Chinese Migrant Trafficking and the Challenge to America's Immigration Tradition* (Washington, D.C.: The CSIS Press, 1997). © 1997 by The Center for Strategic and International Studies.

There are no reliable data on how many safe houses exist in the New York metropolitan area. In 1993 police estimated that in Queens alone there might have been as many as two or three hundred (*World Journal,* June 30, 1993).

KIDNAPPING OF SMUGGLED CHINESE

As we saw in Chapter 6, respondents who entered the United States aboard sea vessels or overland were significantly more likely to be picked up by debt collectors than were subjects who arrived on commercial airplanes. Of the three hundred immigrants I interviewed, 257 said they were "greeted" at their port of entry into the United States by *ma zhai*s or people who were working for their snakeheads.

Once smuggled to their final destination, they were obliged to pay their snakeheads the remaining smuggling fee immediately. To ensure prompt collection, most snakeheads denied their clients freedom of movement. Debt collectors kept watch over the new arrivals until the balance was paid, something that happened only after family members in China had spoken to the immigrant by telephone.

Because smuggled immigrants are worth as much as $30,000 apiece to snakeheads, outside kidnappers sometimes abduct them and then demand ransom, which snakeheads usually pay. The media have reported the kidnapping of new immigrants at John F. Kennedy International Airport (Faison 1993c; Y. Chan 1995) and from safe houses in New York City (*Sing Tao Daily,* December 2, 1997). According to my respondents, kidnapping also occurred in Los Angeles. A thirty-seven-year-old male respondent from Minhou told this story:

> After we arrived in Los Angeles, our snakehead checked us into a hotel. Two days later, we were kidnapped by another group of debt collectors who spoke the Fuzhou dialect. They transported us to New York City, locked us up, and forced us to pay. The next day, they moved us to another place. They beat us every day. Some of us were beaten badly. Sometimes they stuck a gun to my head. Finally, they called the snakehead who smuggled us to the United States and demanded ransom money. Later, our snakehead bought us out for $10,000 per person. There were altogether twelve of us.

Immigrants were not always detained in safe houses upon arrival in the United States but occasionally were delivered to their families there with the understanding that payment would be made reasonably soon. If payment was not forthcoming, the snakeheads themselves kidnapped the immigrants. In fact, the first reported case of a Chinese smuggling-related kidnapping involved a male immigrant who was abducted because he and his relatives had failed to pay the balance of his fee on time (Strom 1991: B3). Since then there have been other reports of Chinese illegals being abducted by their snakeheads from the streets of New York's Chinatown (Daniels 1991; Kifner 1991).

When subjects were detained by U.S. authorities at the point of entry, the snakehead hired a lawyer to bail them out before demanding payment. Some were released without bail, however, and tried to evade their snakeheads, risking capture and punishment by the snakehead's enforcers. One male immigrant hid for several months before being kidnapped by a group of youths working for his snakehead when he appeared at an employment agency in New York's Chinatown looking for work. A determined young man, he was taken to a safe house and managed to escape again after wresting a gun from one of his captors (Lii 1995a).

Newspapers have reported a number of unaccompanied minors being smuggled into the United States, most of them detained by U.S. immigration authorities and placed in foster care. In spite of efforts to maintain the secrecy of their location, snakeheads' enforcers sometimes travel across the country to track down and kidnap teenage immigrants (Dunn 1995).

In 1992, authorities in New York reported that kidnapping among the Chinese was becoming a major problem and that it sometimes triggered smuggling-related murders in the streets of New York City's Chinatown (*Sing Tao Daily*, May 23, 1992). They estimated one or two kidnappings per week in the Chinese community, many of them unreported. According to a detective from Queens, almost half of all kidnappings in New York in 1995 were committed by Chinese offenders, invariably against Chinese victims (*Sing Tao Daily*, October 16, 1995). In addition to indebted immigrants, smuggled Chinese who had paid their smuggling fees were also being kidnapped by gang members who saw them as easy prey (Y. Chan 1993b; Faison 1993c; Hevesi 1993).

Moreover, some of those kidnapped at JFK airport were not even illegal immigrants but included naturalized Chinese (U.S. citizens) and legal Chinese immigrants who arrived in New York from Los Angeles or were passengers on flights returning from China. Nonetheless, the kidnappers, after realizing their mistake, went ahead and demanded ransom from the victims' families (Y. Chan 1995).

DETENTION BY DEBT COLLECTORS

Of the three hundred survey subjects, 191 (64 percent) were locked up in a safe house after their arrival in the United States. A respondent's sex, marital status, region of origin, education, and so forth had little to do with whether he or she was confined in a safe house—only age seemed to be a factor, with younger subjects being more likely than older ones to be detained (see Appendix B, Table 7).

On the other hand, smuggling-related variables—method of departing China, method of entering the United States, year of arrival, method of finding a snakehead, whether or not a down payment was made— did affect a newcomer's chance of being detained by debt collectors. Fewer than half of the subjects who left China by air were detained in safe houses, whereas 89 percent who left China on boats were confined by debt collectors (see Appendix B, Table 8).

Year of arrival is one of the most important smuggling-related variables associated with the likelihood of detention. Only four out of ten respondents who arrived in 1988 or before were confined, but by 1993, more than eight out of ten subjects were locked up upon their arrival in the United States. Even after controlling for smuggling method, the relationship between year of arrival and detention rate remains strong.

Another factor associated with the risk of detention is the way a subject found his or her snakehead. Those who found foreign-based snakeheads through friends and relatives abroad were less likely to be detained than those who were approached by China-based snakeheads. About nine out of ten respondents recruited by this method were later confined in safe houses.

Contrary to the assumption of U.S. authorities, immigrants who paid more for their trips were more likely to be confined than those who paid less. My data also suggest that although immigrants who were detained generally made a smaller down payment, the difference is not statistically significant.

LENGTH OF CONFINEMENT

The average stay in a safe house for my respondents was eleven days, and 62 percent of those detained were released within a week. Those who arrived by air spent an average of seven days in safe houses, compares to ten days for those who came by sea and fifteen for those who arrived overland. Respondents who had made a down payment spent less time in confinement than those who had not. Whether subjects had relatives in the United States affected the length of confinement, probably because nearby relatives were more likely to make a timely payment of smuggling fees. Subjects with relatives in the United States were detained for an average of ten days, as compared to fifteen days for those without.

As we shall see, the longer a subject was held in a safe house, the more likely he or she was to be seriously and frequently abused by the safe house operators.

METHODS OF PAYMENT

Little is known about how human traffickers are paid for their services. U.S. authorities assume that illegal immigrants need not pay their smugglers in advance or upon their arrival but can gradually pay down their debt once they have found work. Authorities and some researchers often refer to undocumented Chinese as "indentured slaves" or "indentured servants" (U.S. Senate 1992; Kwong 1994).

My interviews with smuggled Chinese suggest otherwise. Human traffickers were unwilling to collect smuggling fees from their customers on a monthly basis and demanded immediate payment of the entire fee. Even respondents who were related to their snakeheads by blood were expected to pay at once and in full, although they were sometimes set free with a small debt still outstanding.

Of the 288 smuggled Chinese who owed the balance of their smuggling fee upon arrival, 110 (38 percent) said their entire balances were paid by family members in the United States. Another 107 (37 percent) stated that their families in China made the final payment. Forty-seven (16 percent) said their balances were paid partly in China and partly in the United States. The rest (twenty-four subjects, or 8 percent) made payment elsewhere, usually at a transit point in Hong Kong, Thailand, Singapore, or Bolivia.[2]

The method of payment appears to be changing, however. Of my subjects who arrived in 1988 or before, more than 75 percent paid the balance of their smuggling fee in the United States; by 1993, this figure had dropped to 25 percent. Another 50 percent who arrived in 1993 paid the full fee in China, and the remainder made payments in both China and the United States. The subject's region of origin also affected the method of payment, with the majority of respondents from Tingjiang and Lianjiang paying the balance in the United States and those from Changle paying in China.[3]

As we have seen, many of my subjects relied on their families in the United States to pay for their passage. A restaurant owner from the Fuzhou region who has lived here since 1980 told me that he had so far paid for the delivery of three relatives but could afford no more and had changed his phone number. Another man, who helped his nephew get out of a safe house, reported in detail how he paid the enforcers:

Four days ago, my nephew arrived in New York City from Romania. I was at a clinic in Chinatown when the smugglers called and informed me of my nephew's arrival. The caller spoke the Fuzhou dialect. He sounded very rude. He said, "You'd better come and pick up your relative as soon as possible. Otherwise, we are going to charge you $100 a day for keeping him. If you don't come fast, you may end up collecting his corpse." I was furious. I said, "Why should I pay you $100 a day for holding my nephew? What the hell are you talking about?" The caller hung up the phone on me.

This morning, I came to Chinatown with a friend. I was prepared for the worst. We met at the rear of [a specified] restaurant. A van arrived, and inside the van there were two males, a driver, and my nephew. I told them that there were too many people around. One of the guys said, "Come into our car. We'll go somewhere else." My friend and I got into their car and drove to a nearby place. I saw one of the guys had a gun. I was not afraid because I was sitting behind him. I know I could attack him from behind if he pointed the gun at me.

I asked my nephew, "Did they hurt you?" He said no. I paid them $21,000 in cash. They seemed to be very cautious because they counted the money. I know other smugglers do not count. If you pay them that much money, they just take a look at it because they are sure that you know that if you cheat, they'll come after you. After they counted the money, one of the guys ordered me to pay them an additional $300 because they kept my nephew for three days that they were not supposed to. To that I replied, "Look, if you are asking for tea money, I'll pay you $100, that's it." They agreed. The driver was nicely dressed in a suit, so I told him, "I am surprised to see such a decent guy like you. Over the phone, you guys sounded so obnoxious." He smiled.

The guys who detained my nephew were not the smugglers. They were simply hired by the smugglers to keep an eye on the newly arrived illegal immigrants and collect the money. A smuggler I know told me that he has to have seven to eight guys who can help him to hold the immigrants and collect the money.

Only thirty-nine of my three hundred subjects were allowed to pay off their balance in two installments rather than all at once. Only thirteen of these were allowed to have an outstanding balance for several months. According to a thirty-five-year-old construction worker:

> My snakehead is an American citizen who came from China. He is rich and very well connected. His clients feel safe because he has a very good reputation. He is not like other little snakeheads who "walk *jiang hu*" [are small-time opportunists]. After meeting the snakehead, it was understood that I would be leaving in a month by ship; when the ship arrived in international waters, I agreed to pay the snakehead $1,000. The total fee was $30,000; I could owe the snakehead $10,000 after my arrival in the United States and I would repay the balance within a year. If I decided to pay the entire balance upon my arrival, I would get a discount of $1,000.

GENERAL TACTICS OF THE DEBT COLLECTORS

Debt collectors or enforcers hired by snakeheads to operate the safe houses and collect money oversee a variety of operations. They rent a house or an apartment to function as a safe house; pick up illegal immigrants at airports and other points of entry; put newcomers in touch with friends and relatives who can pay their fees; oversee the release of immigrants once the payments are made; arrange meetings for the payment of fees; and feed immigrants while they are in custody (Hurtado 1993).

Immigrants who can guarantee payment on time tend to be treated fairly well by these enforcers. A twenty-three-year-old male from Changle stated:

> I was detained for eight days in a safe house. More than thirty immigrants were locked up in a basement. Two other immigrants and I were allowed to live on the second floor because the smugglers were confident that we would pay promptly. We had newspapers to read and TV to watch. However, I was nervous. During the days I was there, I saw five

people being either beaten or kicked because they were having problems coming up with the money.

Usually, however, there is no way to be certain who will be able to pay promptly. Assuming that most illegal immigrants must be coerced into paying on time, enforcers make life in the safe houses as unpleasant as possible. For one thing, according to my subjects, they charge exorbitant prices for phone calls—typically $100 for an international and $20 for a local call. They charge additional fees if immigrants overstay their grace period, the mutually agreed upon time within which payment must be made, normally three to seven days. Debt collectors charged my respondents $100 a day for each day over the grace period.

Debt collectors are also stingy with food and sometimes withhold food and water. In general, they try to create as frightening and unpleasant an atmosphere as possible, using threats and intimidation to force their captives to come up with the money on time. A female respondent from Guantou who arrived in New York at age fifteen was told that she and the other females in her safe house would be sold to massage parlors. "When the girls heard that, they all cried uncontrollably. Sometimes, the debt collectors walked around holding guns to scare us."

Sexual harassment of women is common in the safe houses, and immigrants of both sexes are often beaten. A twenty-one-year-old female elementary school teacher from Changle described how an immigrant could be punished for making a mistake:

> After we came to New York, we were locked up in a safe house not far from Chinatown. I guess it was about a ten-minute drive from the safe house to Chinatown. Later, they moved us to another place which was also not far from Chinatown. Living conditions and the food were fine. We all [ten females] shared one bedroom. There was a TV for us. However, the debt collectors were not nice. At the very beginning, they seemed all right. Later, I often heard people being beaten or threatened. They told one woman that if she could not come up with the balance soon, she would be sold to a house of prostitution. Another woman used the telephone without their permission. She was so badly beaten that she was unconscious for several hours.

It is not clear whether these brutal tactics persuaded my subjects' families to pay smuggling fees any sooner than they would have otherwise. Payment schedules are subject to factors and pressures beyond the control of these families. Twenty-seven thousand dollars, the average balance due, is an extremely large sum of money for most families in China—the equivalent of twenty years' income for an average wage earner. Although very few of my subjects had that much money in the bank before leaving China, they came ahead in the knowledge or belief that their extended families and close friends would help them, after arrival, with loans and gifts of money.

Once a subject's family in China hears from the immigrant in the United States, it immediately begins collecting the money pledged by other family members and friends. This usually takes a few days, as most financial transactions in China are made both in cash and in person through a series of door-to-door visits, and in most cases this means many visits. A few people, in addition, usually renege on their promises for one reason or another.

Even when the family can collect the money easily, disputes between the family and the snakehead may cause a delay in payment. Additional charges, such as legal fees, bail money, and expenses for overseas phone calls, may be added to the balance, without the family's knowledge. And even a family pays a China-based snakehead promptly, the snakehead must then inform his counterpart in the United States before the immigrant is released. With such a large number of immigrants involved in any given snakehead's dealings, crossed wires and other mistakes can delay release.

Some of my respondents avoided harsh treatment at the hands of debt collectors by calling their families while still at their last transit point, just before boarding the plane. In this way a few were able to avoid detention in a safe house altogether. One man recalled phoning his family in China just before boarding the U.S.-bound plane in Thailand. "When we arrived in New York, our friends, not the debt collectors, were there to pick us up." Most of my subjects, however, were unwilling to pay the full amount until they reached their final destination.

LIFE INSIDE THE SAFE HOUSES

As I said, immigrants were treated differently by their captors depending on how long it took them to pay their fees. My subjects fell into five groups: those who paid within a day of their arrival in the United States; those who paid within the grace period of three to seven days; those who missed the deadline but paid soon thereafter; those who could not pay for a month or more after the grace period expired; and those who paid only several months after the grace period had elapsed.

Respondents who paid their smuggling fees within hours went unharmed and were sometimes even commended for their punctuality. One man received the compliment from his snakehead that he was a *haojiao* [literally: good feet, meaning reliable]. Debt collectors treated financially well-to-do respondents rather cordially.

Relatively few of my respondents had this option, however, and those who did not often suffered even when they paid the balance of the fees within the grace period. A thirty-five-year-old truck driver from Mawei who paid on time recalled:

> I was kept in a relatively clean basement. About fifty people were locked inside the three rooms located in the basement. Ventilation was poor, and we were not provided enough food. Almost everyone was beaten daily. It was like hell. I was very scared. The debt collectors were very nasty. I didn't know where the snakehead was hiding; he never showed up. The debt collectors often verbally or physically assaulted us. They also threatened us with guns and iron bars.

Some were severely beaten. In the words of a forty-year-old man from Fuzhou City:

> The place I was kept was hell. We ate, lived, and urinated in the same place. More than a dozen people were confined in a room. We were starving all the time. The air was awful. Often, people cried in their sleep. The debt collectors treated me poorly; others who were there longer than I were treated even worse. They yelled at or beat us whenever they wished. Often, people were beaten until they were bloody. There was one person I think who didn't come out alive.

A thirty-two-year-old male from Changle confirmed that this kind of treatment was common:

> The food they fed us was awful. You could say they did that intentionally to force us to pay as soon as possible. We were locked in a basement without any sunlight. I don't know what hell is like, but the basement was like the hell I have seen in the movies. The debt collectors often used various methods to force us to pay promptly. Some were soaked with cold water when the weather was very cold. Some were shackled to prevent them from moving. Some were asked to move heavy objects, and so on.

Once an immigrant has overstayed the grace period, his or her relationship with the debt collectors may change dramatically, as debt collectors intensify their abuse. Some of my subjects were made to do house work or were deprived of adequate food and water. Others were handcuffed to heavy furniture to prevent free movement. Police raids of safe houses have uncovered evidence of shackling captives to metal bed frames and other heavy objects (U.S. Senate 1992).

As punishment for overdue payment, some debt collectors poured cold water on the immigrants and left them to shiver in the cold. A respondent was told that this would "clear my mind so that I would able to think of a way to pay." Debt collectors threatened to kill some of my male subjects and to send some female subjects to work as prostitutes. Most of my female subjects came from rural areas where traditional Chinese norms and values prevailed. For women who probably had not even dated, the thought of being forced to work as a prostitute was terrifying. According to a twenty-year-old female subject from Changle, the enforcers threatened not only her but her parents:

> Whenever I talked to my mother over the phone, she asked me in tears how I was doing. Because I was scared, I cried. At that moment, the debt collectors yelled at me and threatened that if my family did not come up with the balance soon they would sell me to a house of prostitution. When my family heard the threat over the phone, they panicked. Later, my family went all out to borrow money from loan sharks. The debt collectors spend all their time talking dirty to the women.

In fact, beating immigrants during their phone calls with family members was a common practice. A thirty-five-year-old male from Changle recalled one such attack:

> The debt collectors were very tough with me. Every day, they demanded that I pay the smuggling fee. But they did not hit me. Some who were there for a few months were beaten and their faces were covered with blood. They also forced them to call home to China. While they were talking to their family and relatives, the *ma zhai* hit them so that their relatives in China could hear their screaming over the phone. This way, the people in China would come up with the money sooner. I was scared to death watching these incidents.

Almost everyone in my sample witnessed at least one beating incident in the safe houses. "During the eight days I was there," said one, "I saw five people being either beaten or kicked because they had problems coming up with the money." Some were beaten so severely that they required hospitalization, something their captors usually forbade.

Describing the fate of immigrants who had "overstayed their welcome" in safe houses, one respondent said, "You could see their bones through their wounds, but the snakehead would not allow them to see a doctor. He only gave them some Chinese medicine and asked them to take care of their wounds themselves. Some were beaten so badly that they could not even move."

Sometimes the enforcers tried to prevent a smuggled immigrant from bleeding by putting a book on top of his head before striking it with a hammer. One subject described how beatings were carried out in the safe house where he was detained:

> In general, whenever debt collectors were about to punish the male immigrants, they first shackled the immigrants so they wouldn't be able to put up any resistance. It was like restraining a victim in a cross and then beating him with sticks. At first, I did not dare to watch, but later I got used to it. I saw their wounds all over their bodies. After the beating, they were half-conscious and could barely crawl back to their places. The enforcers beat up people one by one, and the place was like hell. These male immigrants later got so used to these beatings that it became an everyday routine.

Sometimes the captors forced immigrants to beat other immigrants, as happened with this twenty-two-year-old male from Changle:

> We were confined in the basement of a single-family house. The windows of the basement were all tightly closed. Because I paid the balance late, I was often beaten. They struck us with iron bars while we were talking to our family members over the phone, so that our families would hear us crying in pain. I was beaten really badly. It was like being in a prison. Everybody in the safe house was quite aware of what was going to happen in a certain day. If we thought that they were going to punish us soon, we would wash the toilet so that we could drink our own urine to cure our wounds. According to traditional Chinese medicine, urine can cure wounds. We tried to protect our bodies so that we could endure the hard work awaiting us after our release. Later, the enforcers instructed me to punish other immigrants who hadn't paid their fees. Under those circumstances, even though I was reluctant, I had to obey their order. Otherwise, I would be the first to be assaulted. To avoid revengeful acts from the people I punished, I hit them with very little force. I also told them that it was coming and to be prepared. When I was asked to soak the immigrants with water, I mixed in some warm water. After the punishment, I massaged them or provided other help. In fact, as time passed by, they preferred to have me to carry out the punishment because I hurt them

significantly less than the enforcers. They were quite appreciative of how I treated them. Only heaven knows how painful it was for me to do that to them!

A few of my respondents spent several horrible months in safe houses when their families, for whatever reason, could not make the payment. Immigrants were sometimes deceived by their little snakeheads in China, told they could work off their smuggling debt once in the United States, only to discover the hard truth upon arrival. A thirty-year-old farmer from Changle explained how he was tricked in this way and paid the consequences:

> Back in China, my snakehead told me that I would be charged a little more than $20,000 for the trip. Besides, he said I don't have to pay the money immediately after my arrival in the United States. That is, I could pay him after I started making money in the United States. However, once I arrived in New York, they [the snakeheads in the United States] said I had to pay right away. On top of this, the total smuggling fee was increased to $31,000. I was locked up for three to four months. And when I told them what the snakehead told me back in China, they struck me.

Although I found no evidence that women were smuggled from China in order to work as prostitutes in the United States, as some authorities have speculated, they sometimes fell into prostitution after their arrival as a way of paying off their debts. A twenty-year-old female subject was allowed to work and pay off her smuggling fee on a monthly basis, but with the catch was that the work was prostitution in her snakehead's massage parlor. One newspaper reported the case of a young woman from Changle forced to work as a prostitute for two years to pay off her smuggling fee. Her snakehead gave her $1,000 a month to live on and kept the rest (*Sing Tao Daily,* June 11, 1993).

Respondents who were punished regularly over time said they became accustomed to it and their sense of fear disappeared. A nineteen-year-old male from Tingjiang described this process:

> I was locked up for five months in a safe house located in a suburban area. Thirteen people were confined there. We did not have enough food or enough clothes. Even now, whenever I think about my experience in that safe house, I become frightened. I was beaten about once a week because my family was having a hard time coming up with the money. In fact, I was lucky; others were beaten every other day. They beat us with sticks. Those who were locked up together could not help one another. That's

why we just let them do whatever they wanted to do. I can't really describe what kinds of people they were. After being there for a period of time, I had no sense of fear anymore because being punished became a daily routine.

Several of my respondents attested that, like other forms of physical and psychological terrorizing, rape is condoned as a method of motivating immigrants to pay their smuggling fees. I heard many accounts of rape and sexual abuse from my respondents. Some were subjected to gang rape as well. As with beatings, rape during phone calls with horrified family members was not uncommon. It is not clear what percentage of smuggled Chinese women are sexually abused in safe houses, but one thing is certain: the longer a woman remains in a safe house, the more vulnerable she is to sexual assault.

After enduring much suffering throughout their journey, many respondents in this study arrived in the United States only to discover that the worst was yet to come. I do not know how severely these immigrants are marred by their traumatic experiences in the safe houses, but it is probably safe to assume that those who are repeatedly abused and tortured over a period of weeks or months may suffer permanent psychological damage. One respondent told me of a man who became mentally unbalanced and verbally disorganized after repeated beatings. Another subject told of a female immigrant who was raped and beaten by her captors for months on end. When her family finally paid her fee and she was released, she was paralyzed and could not work to fulfil her American dream, the dream that led her to make the illegal voyage from China in the first place. Certainly, many would-be immigrants knew in advance what they were likely to confront if they could not come up with their smuggling fees quickly—but probably none of them imagined that they would be subjected to such inhuman treatment in a place they thought of as the Beautiful Country.

8   Life in the Mountain of Gold

SINCE THE MID-NINETEENTH CENTURY, hundreds of thousands of Chinese have immigrated to the United States (Tsai 1986). Many think of the country as *Jinshan,* or the Mountain of Gold (Sung 1967), a place where the streets are paved with gold, and they believe that everyone who makes it there will make a fortune. Almost all of the Chinese immigrants I interviewed had fantasized about living in the United States. Many of them had dreamed of coming to the United States since they were teens and did everything they could to achieve this goal. All of the respondents in my sample were convinced that they could not possibly lose by going to the United States.

CHINATOWN AND THE FUJIANESE COMMUNITY

New York City's Chinatown is the largest Chinese community in North America (Zhou 1992). It was established in the late nineteenth century by Cantonese immigrants who came from the Taishan area of Guangdong Province (B. Wong 1982). Initially the community consisted of only three blocks. Today it is an ethnic enclave that covers more than twenty blocks of the lower east side of Manhattan (Kinkead 1992).

Most Fujianese come to live in New York's Chinatown and Fujianese businesses and residents now dominate East Broadway, Eldridge, Allen, Forsyth, Delancey, Grand, Hester, and Broome streets. The entrances to the Triple Eight Palace restaurant and the Bank of China, both on East Broadway, are major gathering places for Fujianese. Most of the employment agencies that cater to Fujianese are located on East Broadway or on the corner of Eldridge and Forsyth streets.

As the number of Fujianese in New York City increased in the early 1990s, the political economy of Chinatown changed dramatically

This chapter is reprinted from *Illegal Immigration in America,* David W. Haines and Karen R. Rosenblum. Copyright © 1999 by David W. Haines and Karen R. Rosenblum. Reproduced with permission of Greenwood Publishing Group, Inc., Westport, Connecticut.

(Kwong 1997). Until then, the largest community associations in China-town were mostly controlled by Cantonese from the Guangdong Province. These associations were predominantly supportive of the nationalist government in Taiwan and were vehemently anti-communist (Lyman 1974). The few pro-communist organizations that existed were ostracized and occupied only a marginal role in community affairs. Every year, Chinatown celebrated the national holiday (October 10) of the nationalist government. The communist national holiday, October 1, was never celebrated there (Kwong 1987).

All of this changed in the early 1990s, when tens of thousands of both legal and illegal immigrants from mainland China began to pour into Chinatown and develop their own community associations. Currently, there are four Fujianese umbrella organizations—the United Chinese Associations of New York, the Fukien American Association, the United Fujianese of American Association, and the American Fujian Association of Commerce and Industry. These organizations represent a dozen or so smaller Fujianese groups.

These newer community organizations are ardently pro-communist, though members may privately criticize the Chinese government. As the number of pro-communist community organizations began to grow, the first-ever celebration of the communist national holiday was held in Chinatown in 1994 (*New York Times*, September 26, 1994). Since then, the Cantonese celebrate the nationalist holiday in their territory, primarily Mott and Bayard streets, and the Fujianese celebrate the October 1 holiday, mainly on East Broadway. The Bowery is considered the dividing line between the Cantonese and Fujianese territories.

The economics of Chinatown have also changed. Before the late 1980s, Chinatown's economy was under the firm control of the Cantonese (Kleinfield 1986). While many Fujianese arrived in the mid-1980s, they lacked the capital at first to start their own businesses. Many Cantonese business owners resented the arrival of large numbers of Fujianese (Tsao 1993), but for economic reasons had to change their business practices to attract Fujianese customers.

By the early 1990s, the Fujianese had begun to start their own businesses. Many opened take-out restaurants and in a few years the whole Chinese fast-food industry had come under their control. There was a correspondingly dramatic increase in the number of Fujianese-owned businesses related to the take-out restaurant industry—food wholesalers, renovation companies, accounting firms, real estate companies, and law firms (*World Journal*, January 10, 1998).

Fujianese-owned garment factories also began to appear. Already-established garment factories in Chinatown were owned by investors from Hong Kong and Taiwan, and women from the Fuzhou region went to work in them (Gargan 1981; Reid 1986). As the Fujianese became familiar with the operations of the garment industry, some of them used their savings to open their own businesses and there is now a strong Fujianese presence in Chinatown's garment industry. Of the approximately six hundred garment factories in Chinatown, 150 were believed to be owned by Fujianese by 1997 (*Sing Tao Daily*, October 27, 1997).

As the Fujianese began to flex their economic muscle, other businesses developed to meet the needs of Fujianese workers and business people—employment agencies, florists, barber shops, clinics, immigration consultant offices, and driving schools. Even illegal enterprises such as massage parlors and gambling dens have grown to accommodate the needs of Fujianese immigrants (Chin 1996).

ADJUSTING TO A NEW LAND

When asked about their main problems in the United States, almost all of my respondents emphasized their inability to communicate in English. Because most worked long hours side by side with other Chinese and had only one day off per week, they did not have time to learn English. Homesickness was another common theme. A substantial number of my respondents missed their families in China, especially when they were sick and during Chinese holidays and festivals. They were lonely and talked about how shallow their existence in the United States was. "Life has no meaning for me now," said one man, "because I am so far away from my family and relatives. Every time I call home, my wife cries." A forty-four-year-old man from Changle described his existence in the United States this way:

> Work in America is tough. I work in a restaurant for more than twelve hours a day and rarely have a chance to see the sunlight. It's like I am a cow or a horse. That's why America for me is like a prison. Besides, I am all by myself here, with no family or relatives. If I get sick, only my family and relatives will look after me. Who else will come see me? Also, people

here care only about their own business. This is a utilitarian society where people have no compassion.

The third most often-mentioned problem involved the nature of work in New York—the difficulty in finding a job (especially a permanent or satisfying one), long hours, low wages, hardships at work, and abusive employers. Subjects felt constantly at risk of being fired because there was an abundance of cheap labor waiting to take their places. This type of pressure was overwhelming for most of my subjects, who were accustomed to *chidaguofan* (literally: eating food from a huge bowl, a reference to the socialist system), or to *tiefanwan* (literally: an iron rice bowl, or government job). The freewheeling, cutthroat business of hiring and firing, especially in ethnic enclaves, was a shock to people from China, where most people work for the government and most government jobs are easy and secure.

A number of my respondents were under enormous financial pressure. Some had to repay their debts to family and friends who had sponsored their trip; others were paying loan sharks exorbitant interest charges. Even after these debts were paid, many respondents still felt pressure to send money to their families in China.

Other problems were dissatisfaction with living accommodations and the difficulty of adjusting to a new physical and cultural environment. One respondent said, "You have to come see our apartment yourself to really understand how bad our living conditions are. If you look at the apartments in Chinatown from the streets, they may appear to be all right. But if you step into one of these apartments, they are like pigsties: small, filthy, and overcrowded."

Another respondent explained his difficulty adjusting to his new life and expressed a strong desire to return to China:

> For me, the most formidable obstacle is finding a stable job. Keep in mind that the main reason I am here is to make money. I like U.S. dollars. They're worth much more than Chinese yuan. Besides U.S. dollars, there's nothing I like about the United States. The living environment here is not as good as in Fuzhou. Actually, it is much worse than there. I was relatively rich back in China; I owned two business stores. After I got here, my family became a *meiguoke's* [a guest from the Beautiful Country's] family, and of course they are very happy. Since I can't adjust here, I wish that after I clear my debts and save $10,000 to $20,000, I would return home. I regret I came. In China, I did not need to hustle for a living. Here, I cannot afford to stay idle even for a day. After all, I agree with the saying

among the Fujianese, "After you see the whole world, you'll find that Fuzhou is the best place on earth."

The vast majority of my respondents answered "U.S. dollars" when asked what they liked about the United States, and more than half said dollars were the only thing they liked. "Freedom" came in second after dollars. A substantial number of respondents spoke about the opportunities available in the United States. Here, they believed, there were more and better opportunities, and more equality and fair competition in the workplace. Some were impressed with the transportation networks and facilities and the overall quality of the environment. In contrast to the Changlenese man quoted above, some respondents found the American people civilized, polite, and very nice to women. They believed they were surrounded by people of a higher quality than they had been in China. Some liked the democratic political system and its protection of human rights. Several subjects said they liked the casinos and shopping malls. Others liked the stability of U.S. government policies and the fact that it is ability, rather than connections or political ideology, that matters.

WORK AND INCOME

At the time these interviews were conducted, most of my respondents were working either full- or part-time (see Appendix B, Table 9). Most had been employed either full-time or most of the time since coming to the United States. Of the thirty-four subjects who were unemployed, only one was female.[1]

Occupation

Immigration scholars have noted that most illegal immigrants in the United States work primarily in low-wage, low-prestige occupations (North and Houstoun 1976; Chiswick 1988; Mahler 1995). My respondents were mainly employed in the food, garment, and construction businesses (see Appendix B, Table 10).

Although I did not ask those who worked in restaurants what kind of restaurants these were, most were probably take-out restaurants, which are smaller then eat-in restaurants and more likely to cater to cost-conscious customers. In the tri-state area of New York, New Jersey, and Connecticut, there has been a dramatic increase in the number of

Chinese take-out restaurants since the late 1980s, when so many Fujianese began to arrive. More than a thousand Chinese take-out restaurants were in operation in the New York metropolitan area in the early 1990s, almost 90 percent of them owned by Fujianese, by some accounts (*World Journal,* January 10, 1998). Table 10 shows that almost 60 percent of my male subjects worked in restaurants, though that trend appears to be changing. While 70 percent of those who came in 1988 or before worked in restaurants, only 26 percent of those who came in 1993 do.

This decrease has been offset by an increase in employment in the garment industry. Seventy-seven percent of my female subjects who were employed worked in garment factories, where work conditions are notoriously poor (Kwong 1997). In the words of one journalist, "In these [sweat]shops, holes in warping floors are covered by plywood boards. Sprinkler systems, unmaintained, no longer work. Electrical wiring dangles dangerously overhead . . . fire exits are covered by metal gates that are padlocked" (Finder 1995: B4).

Chinese restaurants in the tri-state area change hands quite frequently and new owners invariably make some renovations or at least rename their new restaurants. As a result, there is a strong demand for renovation/construction services and many small construction, renovation, and signboard companies, also dominated by the Fujianese, have sprung up to meet this need.

Of my respondents who worked, the great majority worked in one of these three industries-restaurants, garments, or renovation/construction. Only twenty-eight were employed elsewhere.

Working Hours

Most of my respondents worked long hours. Of the respondents who worked full-time, 63 percent worked twelve hours or more a day and only sixteen worked eight hours or less. Eighty-five percent of them worked six days a week; only 5 percent worked a normal five-day week or less. For those who worked full-time the average work week was sixty-nine hours.[2]

Most restaurant workers in my sample averaged seventy-two working hours per week in six days. Garment workers, who were paid by the type and quantity of their work, averaged seventy hours per week over six or seven days. Respondents employed by renovation/construction firms worked only fifty-two hours per week. Subjects who

worked in other industries averaged fifty-six working hours per week
(see Appendix B, Table 11).

A fourteen-year-old girl from a relatively rich family in Changle
described her work week:

> I work almost fourteen hours a day. Sometimes, I work from eight in the
> morning to dawn. My mom begged me not to work too hard. However,
> since I had to pay so much money to be smuggled here, I have to make
> money. My mom wants me to eat well, get a green card, and attend school.
> My mom frequently sends me plenty of beautiful clothes. You see, I am
> working in a garment factory almost seven days a week; why do I need
> all these nice clothes?

Income

Because no systematic study has ever been conducted to determine the
wages of smuggled Chinese, policy makers rely on anecdotal evidence
from the media and the law enforcement community for estimates.
These accounts may be misleading, however. For example, a *New York
Times* reporter who conducted a field study by working in a garment
factory for two weeks said she made about sixty-five cents an hour in
the sweatshop (Lii 1995b). Law enforcement authorities have also suggested that illegal Chinese are getting paid far below the minimum
wage and conclude that many immigrants may never be able to repay
their smuggling fees (U.S. Senate 1992). This conclusion raises several
questions. Why would so many immigrants come to the United States
to enter a life resembling indentured servitude? How are illegal immigrants able to send money to their families in China and indirectly
encourage others to emigrate?

My data do not support the contention that smuggled Chinese make
very little money in the United States. The average monthly salary of
the 234 full-time workers in my sample was $1,359 (see Appendix B,
Table 11). Of workers in the three main occupation categories, those in
the renovation and construction business had the highest average
monthly salary ($1,740), followed by restaurant workers ($1,520) and
garment industry workers ($1,252). At the time of my study, the U.S.
minimum wage was $4.25 per hour, or $731 per month under the legally
mandated maximum of forty working hours per week.

To determine whether my respondents made a decent income simply because they worked many more hours than a minimum-wage

American worker, I calculated their hourly wage by types of occupation[3] and found that the Chinese in my survey, in all occupations, made more than the 1993 minimum wage, which is consistent with Chiswick's research on illegal Mexican immigrants, which concluded that "the average hourly wages for aliens are substantially in excess of the federal legal minimum wage.... To the extent that exploitation is defined as payment of a wage below the federal minimum wage, it appears to be rare or nonexistent in these data" (Chiswick 1993: 98). These wages are actually worth more in real dollars because the American minimum-wage earner is also subject to taxes whereas illegals are not.[4]

It is clear, nevertheless, that most workers, especially those in the garment and restaurant industry, make a relatively decent income mainly because they work long hours. As with all jobs, though, wages vary within industries. In the restaurant business, the average hourly wage was higher for waiters and waitresses ($6.12) than for cooks ($5.35), food delivery workers ($4.00), kitchen helpers ($3.65), and dishwashers ($2.38). Likewise, in the garment industry, pressers (mostly male) averaged two dollars more per hour than seamstresses (mostly female). Table 12 presents a detailed list of positions within the various industries and their corresponding wages.

Debt

Given their need to repay their smuggling debt, I asked my respondents how they managed to repay the debt. Although fewer than half said they had borrowed money to make the down payment, 90 percent said they had borrowed to pay the balance of the smuggling fee and were therefore in debt when they first sought employment in the United States.

Contrary to the popular belief that smuggled Chinese immigrants are exploited by loan sharks who charge them an exorbitant interest rate, most respondents said they borrowed money from either relatives or friends. Of the 264 subjects who borrowed to finance their passage, 164 borrowed from relatives in China, 147 from relatives in the United States, and 53 from friends in one country or the other.[5] Only eleven respondents said they borrowed all or part of their smuggling fee from loan sharks in China. Only 30 percent were charged interest by relatives and friends, at an average rate of 2 percent per month. Loan sharks typically charge 3 or 4 percent in monthly interest.

Assuming an average, interest-free loan of $24,000 (as was the case with 70 percent of my respondents who borrowed from friend or family), how long would it take to repay the debt? Based on the false assumptions we have already examined, media and government reports erroneously conclude that many illegal Chinese immigrants may never be able to clear their debt (Hood 1993a). According to a senior INS official, "They can work in a dishwasher job for the rest of their lives to pay off that debt" (Glaberson 1989: B3). Again, however, my data refute this conclusion.

At the time of the interviews, 105 respondents, or about one third, said they had repaid their smuggling debts. Most were able to repay the debts within two years, although some took as little as six months and others as long as four years—on average, twenty-six months. Though these claims may strain belief given the amount of debt, the average income of illegal immigrants, and the cost of living in the most expensive city in the United States, most illegal immigrants economize by crowding large numbers into small apartments, eating in the restaurants where they work, and living frugally in other ways. Regardless of whether they were still in debt, most (86 percent) said they had not encountered any problem in fulfilling their financial obligations.

Eighty-six percent of respondents said they were sending money home to China—either through the Bank of China, the underground banking industry of Chinatown, or through friends and relatives returning to China—whether to repay smuggling fees or simply help out with living expenses.

According to a manager of the Changle branch of the Bank of China, more than $2 million in overseas remittances were deposited to the branch in 1991. Deposits skyrocketed to $24 million the following year. He projected that in 1993 deposits from overseas would total more than $30 million and estimated that 96 percent of this money came from the United States (*Tai Kung Pao*, June 15, 1993).

Impact on the Local Economy

What impact do illegal immigrants have on the U.S. labor market and especially on vulnerable native groups such as youths, women, and African American men, who may compete with illegals for jobs? In a 1964 study, the Urban Institute found that immigrants in southern California, far from taking jobs away from other minorities, provided industries with more manpower, thus enabling them to produce higher profits and lower prices. During the 1970s, when southern California took in more immigrants than any other part of the country, it also led the nation in the creation of new jobs and enjoyed an above-average increase in per capita income.

Wayne Cornelius, an authority on international migration, has claimed that "there is simply not enough credible evidence to establish the existence of a cause-and-effect relationship—even an indirect one— between illegal migration and domestic unemployment" (Cornelius 1978: 60). A 1982 study by the Rand Corporation similarly concluded that, at current levels of immigration, immigrants will have little effect on the overall national economy. And summarizing several studies of illegal immigration, *Business Week* concluded that "on balance, the nation benefits more from the increased economic growth and lower inflation stemming from illegal immigration than it loses in jobs, lower wages and welfare costs" (Dowty 1987: 242).

Little is known about the impact of illegal Chinese on New York City's economy. Because most of the respondents in this study worked in Chinese-owned businesses, however, it is unlikely that they take jobs away from non-Chinese minorities or women. I do think, though, that wages and job prospects for legal Chinese immigrants may suffer from the influx of illegal Chinese, and many people, notably the Cantonese of New York's Chinatown, blame the large numbers of Fujianese illegals for a drop in wages. According to one media report, the average monthly wage for garment workers in Chinatown was $2,000 in 1992, but it had fallen to between $1,600 and $1,500 by 1994 (*World Journal*, September 10, 1994). In 1995, one of the largest restaurants in Chinatown became involved in a labor dispute when its owner replaced Cantonese with Fujianese workers after the Cantonese employees protested unfair practices such as withholding a portion of the waiters' tips. The firing of Cantonese employees resulted in a major strike that continued for months and split the community into pro-immigration and anti-immigration forces (Jia 1995; Lii 1995c).

In addition to taking jobs away from natives and suppressing wages, illegal immigrants are also thought to have cost their host society dearly in costs for detention, health care, education, and so forth (Padavan 1994; Clark et al. 1995).[6] According to the U.S. General Accounting Office (1993), for example, California, Texas, New York, Illinois, and Florida estimated $2.9 billion in annual federal, state, and local costs for illegal aliens and their citizen children.

According to Cornelius (1989), the illegal immigrants in California most likely to use state health and education services are spouses and children of the 1.1 million immigrants who won legal status under the SAW (Special Agricultural Worker) program. Their wives and children were not covered under this program, however, and retained their illegal status. According to a study conducted by the Urban Institute, welfare dependence among working-age (15 to 64 years), non-refugee immigrants is very low. The major "cost" of immigrants involves the education of their children.

Most of the smuggled Chinese in this study were married and had children, but these children were in China with their spouses or grandparents. I do not know how many Chinese illegals nationwide have children in the United States and thus cannot gauge the cost to the U.S. education system. Only one of my respondents said she had received state benefits, in her case Medicaid. Lacking a random sample, I cannot estimate the potential financial impact of smuggled Chinese on the wider community. My data, however, suggest that respondents kept to themselves and did not use health or educational services available to legal immigrants and citizens. I can only guess that this is common practice among smuggled Chinese.

MENTAL HEALTH

Social workers in Chinatown have been alarmed by the increase in the number of smuggled Chinese who develop mental disorders (*World Journal*, February 27, 1990).[7] Faced with the difficulties of adjusting to a new environment, language barriers, and stressful working conditions, and often still suffering from the traumas of the voyage, many develop depression, somatic problems, and sleeping disorders. Some become dependent on alcohol; a few commit suicide. Despite the growing number of psychological disturbances among illegal immigrants, Chinatown has few social service programs that meet their needs.

After working a seventy-hour week, illegal immigrants return to cramped, miserable apartments and collapse in exhaustion. In an effort to economize, immigrants often crowd as many as a dozen people into a one- or two-bedroom apartment.[8] Bunk beds are set up not only in bedrooms but also in living rooms and kitchens. In some apartment buildings one bathroom serves all the tenants on a given floor. Some apartments have makeshift showers constructed in the tiny kitchen area. Most lack air-conditioning, and in winter the heat often does not work.

Many of the young adults in my sample were married and had children but had come to the United States alone. They missed their families and were sometimes traumatized by rumors that their spouses in China were having affairs, as well as by their spouse's suspicions that they themselves were being unfaithful. Smuggled Chinese males separated from their wives sarcastically described their lives in the United States as "living in a world of two *tou*." "During the day, we face the *lutou* [foyer]. At night, we hug our *zhentou* [pillows]" (*World Journal*, January 11, 1998: E1). Some felt that they had no life here and viewed themselves merely as *huojiqi*, or machines made of flesh and blood. A forty-four-year-old sailor from Changle described the experience of his roommate:

> Many people told me America is a prison. Here, human beings are exploited like animals. We have to go to work for more than twenty hours a day and then go home just to sleep. The next day, you go to work again. There is a person who is sharing an apartment with me. When he arrived here, he had a hard time finding a job. After he finally found a job, he got fired quickly. He has been dismissed from work several times. Later, he lost his mind. Now, he verbally and physically assaults people around him. As a result, he was incarcerated in a mental hospital for three months. Now, he appears to be recovering gradually.

Some respondents were overwhelmed with smuggling debts. Others complained of their spouses' insatiable demands for U.S. dollars and worried that they might never satisfy their families back home. The combination of heavy debt and lack of good job opportunities can be an illegal immigrant's undoing. According to a thirty-five-year-old male from Mawei:

> A thirty-three-year-old male from Tingjiang came here with me. Because he had no money to repay his debts and could not find a job, there were enormous pressures from the people he owed money to. Maybe he was overwhelmed; he had a mental breakdown. Also, my wife became very nervous the day I left, and she became mentally ill. The first time I called home, my family told me the bad news. I almost did not know what to do with my life here.

A twenty-nine-year-old Tingjiang male described the plight of another immigrant who was failing badly in the United States:

> There is a person from my village who is twenty-eight years old. After his arrival, he had a hard time finding a job, and his family owed a lot of money. Besides, he could not adjust to the new environment. Now he is out of his mind. He does not work. Every day, he wanders around and comes back to sleep. He can not differentiate between day and night. He is still surviving simply because we are taking care of him. He is not willing to go home, and there is nothing we can do to persuade him to find a job.

Illegal immigrants who had government jobs in China were the least likely to adjust to the capitalist labor market in the United States. Accustomed to the work habits of Chinese government agencies, they were ill-equipped to adapt and often lost their new jobs in Chinatown. Many yearned for the lax working atmosphere that prevails in Chinese bureaucracies. One respondent described a former government official who was unable to make the transition. "He has become like a fool. He wanders in the street everyday and asks anybody he meets for help. He's like a beggar now."

Since most of the Chinese in my sample spoke no English, they were isolated from mainstream society. For them, the Mountain of Gold was Chinatown, an extremely small world indeed. Although no one in my study could be described as mentally ill, many described fellow immigrants who had become deranged as a result of the financial, emotional, and job-related stress to which all of these immigrants are vulnerable. (Because I did not interview these mentally disturbed people, I do not know whether any of them had similar problems before they left China.)

People who cannot cope with the pressure and suffering they face in their new lives sometimes commit suicide. A thirty-four-year-old man from Fuzhou City told me that he knew a young immigrant who committed suicide because he was unemployed and worried about his debts. Another respondent knew someone who killed himself because he could not repay even the interest on his debt. It is likely that many suicides among illegal Chinese immigrants go unreported.

VICTIMIZATION

Studies on clandestine immigration have shown that illegal immigrants are vulnerable to crime in their host countries because of their undocumented status and inability to protect themselves. The media have reported that smuggled Chinese in New York City are often victimized by both Chinese and non-Chinese (*New York Times*, December 3, 1993). Because immigrants who work in restaurants and garment factories tend to leave work late at night, they are likely targets for predators. Their reluctance to report crimes to the police makes them all the more vulnerable (*Sing Tao Daily*, May 7, 1992).

Many of the respondents in this study lived in fear of the Fujianese criminals who kidnap, extort, and rob illegal Chinese immigrants. Many subjects moved frequently, trying to find a place where they felt secure, and changed their phone or beeper numbers often. Of the three hundred subjects in this study, 139 (47 percent) said that they had been victimized at least once since their arrival in America, mostly by thieves. Ninety-seven (32 percent) were robbed at least once in the subway.

Because smuggled Chinese typically have no bank accounts and deal mainly in cash, they tend to keep a substantial amount of cash in their homes (*World Journal*, January 10, 1998). Home-invasion robbery has long been considered the trademark crime of Chinese and Vietnamese gangs (English 1995; Long 1996), and about 10 percent of my respondents were robbed in their homes or apartments.

Few of my respondents suffered other forms of crime, though three said they had been the victims of extortion or sexual harassment. Of those who were robbed or otherwise victimized, only twenty-five (18 percent) contacted police. This reporting rate is substantially lower than that of a national sample of household victims (Bureau of Justice Statistics 1992).

PROSTITUTION

U.S. law enforcement officials have long been concerned about the prevalence of prostitution in the Chinese communities of San Francisco and New York City (U.S. Senate [1877] 1978, 1992). As I mentioned earlier, police have generally presumed that Asian women are smuggled into the United States by members of Chinese crime groups and forced to work as prostitutes (Martin 1977). Authorities believe that some women become prostitutes in order to pay off their smuggling debts, while others choose prostitution over the grueling hours and conditions of Chinese garment factories or restaurants.

It is not clear how many smuggled Chinese have been recruited into the sex industry. Of the sixty-two females in my sample, only one said she was a prostitute. Another respondent, an eighteen-year-old girl from Guantou, said she was urged by her snakehead to become a prostitute but refused, in spite of the snakehead's offer to waive her smuggling fee in return. Five other subjects said they knew someone who became a prostitute after arriving in the United States. A thirty-year-old technician from Fuzhou City described one of them:

> There was a woman on the smuggling ship I was on. Back in China, she was a member of a *chaoshu* [overseas family], so she did not have to work hard to be able to live a comfortable life. That's why here in America she cannot withstand the pressure, nor can she endure hardship. So she went to work in a massage parlor voluntarily. She also hung out with members of the underworld society. She was also seen helping gangsters rob newly arrived immigrants. Because she's a woman, it is easier for her to make her way into the victims' apartments.

Another respondent knew two women who became prostitutes because of debt and marital problems. Some women, in debt to loan sharks, gave up on garment factory work and turned to the more lucrative work of prostitution. A $25,000 loan from a loan shark would accrue up to $750 a month in interest, making it virtually impossible for even the most determined seamstress to stay afloat and make her loan payments.

CRIME

As is often the case with such complex issues, researchers and other observers disagree about the association between crime and immigration, especially illegal immigration (Marshall 1997). Some have argued that immigrants are more likely than non-immigrants to be involved in illegal activities, although they may have different explanations for this. Scholars like Thorsten Sellin (1938) have suggested that immigrants may have a higher crime rate because they have different norms and values from those of their host society. Others, such as Francis Ianni (1974), have suggested that each new wave of immigrants has been responsible for the emergence of ethnic organized crime in the United States in order to establish itself in the host society.

U.S. law enforcement authorities have alleged that immigrants, especially illegal immigrants, are disproportionately represented in correctional facilities (Lyall 1992). Some states have begun to sue the federal government for failing to prevent large numbers of illegal immigrants from entering the country and overwhelming state correctional facilities and have demanded reimbursement for the expense of locking these criminals up (Lyall 1992).

Scholars who disagree argue that the "overwhelming majority of illegal aliens do not engage in violence or crime in the United States, and if they skirt the law because of their status they do not necessarily commit violent acts of lawlessness" (James 1991: 62). Alex Schmid (1995) maintains that illegal immigrants are in fact *less* likely than others to commit crimes because they fear deportation.

The media have reported extensively about the relationship between illegal Chinese immigration and heroin trafficking (Wren 1996), prostitution (Y. Chan 1993a), kidnapping (Burdman 1993d; Faison 1993c; Y. Chan 1995), and murder (Kennedy 1995). Illegals are seen as especially vulnerable to the temptations of crime because of their heavy debts (Glaberson 1989). Alan Lau, former president of the Fukien American Association, agrees, citing the recruitment of debt-laden immigrants as enforcers, debt collectors, gambling den guards, drug couriers, and so on. "Sooner or later," he says, "these people working for the snakeheads would become hard-core criminals. Besides, some of them might have been street thugs in their homeland to begin with" (*Sing Tao Daily,* November 9, 1993: 28).

Most respondents in my sample, however, repaid their smuggling fees through years of hard legal work rather than by criminal activity. Several of them, in fact, thought that passage to America often had the reverse effect. A thirty-seven-year-old male from Fuzhou City explained, "After they have arrived here, only a few turn into criminals. In fact, many of those who were involved in criminal activities back in China became law-abiding people. Why? Because they were isolated and powerless in America, and they, like everybody else, needed to work hard to repay the smuggling fees."

Another respondent also believed that most smuggled Chinese, including those who did not bother to work in China, became industrious after immigrating to the United States: "I observed many people change for the better. For example, many of those who were unwilling to work in China now work very hard because of the dire circumstances they are in now." A former gang member in China supports this view:

[Members of the Fuk Ching] asked me to help them collect smuggling fees after I arrived here. However, when I got here, the Fuk Ching gang was history.[9] That's why I didn't join them. My main problem now is this: "People" [gang members] often come to where I work and look for trouble because of my past gang affiliation. I don't know how they found out where I work. It is very difficult for a person like me to go straight. I stay home and rest when I am not working. Today is the first time I have been in Chinatown since my arrival three months ago. I don't think the United States is better than China. I came here for my future. People like me who have been imprisoned before have no future in China. We were discriminated against everywhere we went. That's why I came here and have tried very hard to change myself into a law-abiding person.

A few subjects in this study did become debt-collectors when they had trouble finding a legitimate job. Few wanted the job but they were desperate. One man earned $1,500 a month for this work but refused to beat anyone. Another subject, a thirty-two-year-old male from Changle, was working as a debt collector for a massage parlor at the time of the interview.

I owned a beauty parlor [house of prostitution] in China, and now I am working as a debt collector for a massage parlor. I make about $1,500 a month. I don't like my job at all because, after a while, I got really sick of it. When I have to go collect money, there are problems. If the person who owes the massage parlor money is one of those powerful people in the society [a gangster], then it's a very challenging task. If I can't collect the money, there will be pressure from my boss. That's why I don't like my job and I am looking for a legitimate job.

Smuggled immigrants who end up working for snakeheads may become the victims of gang warfare in Chinatown. One respondent knew a man who was shot and killed through his association with human smugglers.

I believe that few illegal Chinese immigrants become involved in either violent or property crimes. Because of their illegal status, however, they may fall prey to criminals in their own community, thus reinforcing the vicious cycle of crime and violence. It is also true that the arrival of large numbers of smuggled Chinese has resulted in the creation of an underground economy in which business transactions are not completely legal. Business owners and customers join together in shady business practices simply because it is cheaper or more effective to do so.

FUTURE PROSPECTS

The first wave of Chinese immigrants who came to the United States in the mid-nineteenth century were called "sojourners" because they did not intend to settle here. Their main purpose was to earn enough money to go back to China and live comfortably (Barth 1964). Easy targets for anti-immigration politicians and labor union leaders, they were often portrayed as people who could not be assimilated into American society (Saxton 1971). What about the current wave of illegal Chinese immigrants? Are they, like their predecessors, "sojourners," or are they here to stay?

Of the three hundred immigrants in my sample, 190 (64 percent) said they planned to stay in the United States permanently; eighty-five (29 percent) planned to return to China once they earned enough money. Another twenty (7 percent) were undecided. Thus, the majority of my respondents could not be called "sojourners."

Table 13 in Appendix B shows the characteristics of the respondents who wanted to stay. Subjects who had been in the United States for a relatively long period were more likely to have made up their minds about their future. Younger, more recent arrivals were less sure. Men were more likely than women to say that they planned to return to China, in part because they were more likely to have left wives and children behind. Hondagneu-Sotelo (1994) has suggested that female Mexican immigrants feel "freer" in the United States, where they are less subject to the forms of patriarchal domination prevailing in their homeland. Men, by contrast, lose status through demeaning work. It is possible that a similar dynamic is at work among Chinese immigrants and that the immigration experiences of various ethnic groups are highly gendered.

Respondents still in debt were more likely to want to go home than those who had paid off their debts. Finally, those with full-time jobs were more inclined to stay than those without full-time work. No other variables were statistically associated with a respondent's future plans.

Some of my subjects, notwithstanding their frustration over working conditions or job prospects in the United States, were convinced that America is a better place to live than China. As a somewhat conflicted respondent from Minhou put it:

> I believe America is better than China, no matter how you compare the two countries. America is a free country with plenty of opportunities. Too bad I was fired five times in seven days. And I cannot adjust to the kind of frantic lifestyle here. Moreover, I need to work long hours. Nevertheless, I now realize that in order to be successful, you need to endure this kind of frustration. I am sure I made the right decision in coming here.

Others found solace in the thought that their families in China were enjoying the kind of status only a family with a relative overseas can achieve, like this thirty-six-year-old male from Changle: "Since I came here, my family became rich. My parents are happy because they are respected by others. Now, my family members' sleeves are torn apart by others [i.e., people want to be close to his family]."

A twenty-one-year-old married male from Changle who had worked in a factory in China had made up his mind to stay in the United States. "After all, I think I made the right decision in coming to the United States because there are so many opportunities to make money here. Although there is a lot of hardship, I only need to work a few years to repay the debt and then I can start saving. If I had remained in China, how much money could I have earned for the rest of my life? I wouldn't have had the opportunity to *fanshen* [change one's social status]."

A nineteen-year-old single woman from Changle who was earning $2,000 a month in a garment factory reasoned:

> In general, I do not regret coming here. After all, for a long time, I was determined to improve my family's status, and now I have achieved that. Besides, I like what I am doing now, working as a seamstress in a garment factory. All I hope for is to repay the smuggling debts as soon as possible and then send money home to help my family enjoy a comfortable life. It's no big deal that I myself have to endure some hardship here. If a person's bitterness can bring happiness to so many people, it's worth it. However, once in a while, I feel like this kind of life is boring. You go to work everyday from morning till night, and you can only have one day off.

It is difficult to gauge the level of resolve among the eighty-five respondents (29 percent) who planned to return to China after they earned enough money in the United States. I believe that they were motivated mainly by frustration and that if their conditions improved—especially if they become legal residents—they would be more likely stay.

In some cases, though, there was no doubting the respondents' conviction. A forty-five-year-old fisherman could hardly have had worse luck:

> After I was released from a safe house, I did not have a penny. I didn't have relatives or friends around either. I was wandering in the streets. At night, I slept underneath the vegetable stalls in Chinatown. I had no money to eat. I was starving for two days. Later, a Cantonese woman saw me, and she was very sympathetic. She gave me $10, a cup of coffee, and a Chinese rice cake. She basically saved a hopeless soul. A few hours later, I bumped into a friend, and he took me to his place and offered me food. How bitter it was! I have a never-ending story to tell about my experiences. So far, I haven't found a stable job. I regret that I came here. I am broke now. A lot of people from my neighborhood were sympathetic toward my experiences. I never thought America would be so difficult a place to make money. If you ask me now what happiness is, I will say it's my life back in China. Back there, I had two meals a day, and nothing else, but it was a most fortunate life. Here, people have no compassion. China is the best place to be. I have to cry out loud, "Give me back my wife!" She killed herself last month because she was overwhelmed with the amount of money we owe.

Other respondents were determined to go home because they had discovered that a *meiguoke* did not mean much after all. A thirty-nine-year-old male from Changle described how this "badge of honor" could backfire. "My family is now poorer than ever before. Family members and my children are also getting lazier. Only the label *meiguoke* sounds very good. Whenever there is a new construction project in the village, people will come to us for a donation. Because I am a *meiguoke,* my family must contribute money for all kinds of construction projects."

Another respondent, a thirty-eight-year-old construction worker from Changle earning $1,800 a month as a cook, explained his frustration:

> Since I started to send money home, of course my family lives a much better life. Status? Well, I don't feel it has improved at all. To tell you the truth,

I feel like garbage in the United States; there's no status at all. Besides, in my area, there are so many overseas Chinese, especially *meiguoge,* there's nothing special about being one. Before I came, I had no idea that America would be like this. Here, we sleep on the floor, and we work like slaves. I really regret coming here. At home, I lived and ate well, and work was light. Now, even though I have became a bit used to being here in America, I still want to go back as soon as possible. There's nothing appealing here. Although my job is stable, I see many other people like me having many difficulties. They get fired wherever they go. Those living with me in the same apartment cry all the time. That's why, for three years, I did not apply for any documents. I am going back in a few years; what's the point of applying for anything?

Some respondents had become convinced that money was not the most important thing in life after all. They became philosophical about the shallowness of their existence in the United States, and even though they knew there were many good things about the country, they simply could not see how they could take advantage of its benefits.

Such views capture the basic ambivalence that the Fujianese have about America. On the one hand, few would deny the economic opportunities available here. On the other hand, real access to those opportunities is difficult—if not impossible—for illegal immigrants. Even when those opportunities can be grasped, building a secure, rewarding life, whether in China or the United States, remains an uphill battle.

9 Stemming the Tide

CONTROLLING ILLEGAL IMMIGRATION, especially human smuggling, is a major challenge for immigration and law enforcement officials in receiving, transit, and sending countries for two reasons. First, although human trafficking is a crime in most of the receiving countries, it is not a crime in many sending and transit countries (Interagency Working Group 1995: 2).

Second, even in sending and transit countries where human smuggling is a crime, local authorities are reluctant to intervene (DeStefano 1997). Take China, for example. Many government and law enforcement officials in the Fuzhou area believe that the illegal immigration of Chinese promotes the well-being of their area because the money the immigrants send home improves the local economy (Burdman 1993f). Local authorities in transit countries are also reluctant to intervene because they think the Chinese are "only passing through" (Interagency Working Group 1995). And in the receiving countries, illegal immigrants tend to be supported and protected by their families and relatives who are already there (Seagrave 1995) or by immigration lawyers and human rights advocates (Suro 1994; Fisher 1997). Finally, corruption within immigration agencies in the receiving countries also facilitates the flow of illegal immigrants (Engelberg 1994; Larmer and Liu 1997).

Nevertheless, when illegal immigration is brought to the attention of the international community, it can trigger harsh responses from authorities in both receiving and sending countries (R. Beck 1996). When a sensational incident such as the grounding of the *Golden Venture* is coupled with a depressed economy in the receiving country, controlling illegal immigration may quickly become a top priority among politicians and law enforcement authorities (Brimelow 1995). A "get tough" approach to illegal immigration may generate political capital and win votes, and immigration laws may be reformed to curb not only illegal but also legal immigration as well. For law enforcement authorities, the prevention of illegal immigration can easily be elevated from a domestic problem to a national security issue (Perea 1997).

132

Since 1993, mainly because of the *Golden Venture* incident, U.S. authorities have become more aggressive in preventing the illegal entry of Chinese into the United States (Branigin 1995) by increasing the length of prison sentences for smugglers (Hevesi 1994); stopping smuggled Chinese in transit points and sending them home (Claiborne 1993); tightening border patrols (Ayres 1994); expediting the review of political asylum cases (Faison 1993b); and demanding that governments in China, Taiwan, and other Asian countries cooperate with the United States to curb human trafficking (Burdman 1993e). It is not clear how effective these measures are, however, especially as there is evidence that large numbers of trafficked Chinese continue to arrive (Dunn 1994; Faison 1994a; Farah 1995; Schloss 1996).

In this chapter, I examine the types of measures adopted by China, Taiwan, transit countries, and the United States to prevent Chinese clandestine immigration, discuss some of the problems U.S. authorities face in intercepting and deporting undocumented Chinese, and suggest what China and the United States can do to decrease illegal immigration. As I will discuss in some detail, I believe that such efforts are necessary largely to reduce the human suffering that accompanies this trafficking and that only measures to reduce the desperation in China will have any lasting effect on the problem.

CHINESE ATTEMPTS TO STOP ILLEGAL IMMIGRATION

In the aftermath of the *Golden Venture* incident, authorities in Beijing began to be concerned about the damage to China's reputation caused by the Chinese trade in human beings (Government of the People's Republic of China 1994), and Beijing officials began to pressure authorities in the Fuzhou area to curb illegal immigration (Wei et al. 1995).

Preventive Measures

The Chinese government pursued two basic preventive strategies to prevent illegal immigration—educating the public about the dangers of clandestine immigration and establishing an accountability system that holds local government officials responsible.

PUBLIC EDUCATION. Throughout the history of the Chinese Communist Party, government officials have used community mobilization and public education to deal with social problems (Oi 1989). Because Beijing

officials view unlawful immigration as a manifestation of the exploitation of rural people by greedy foreigners (Government of the People's
Republic of China 1994), they instruct local authorities to educate the
masses about the problems and risks associated with illegal immigration. In these public campaigns, people are urged not to be fooled by
little snakeheads and to stay away from big snakeheads (Wei et al. 1995).

The government adopted three measures to educate the public about
the dire consequences of clandestine immigration. First, under instructions from Beijing, provincial officials ordered local law enforcement
agencies and other government units to put up a large number of banners to discourage people from immigrating unlawfully (Burdman
1993f). Among the most popular slogans were these:

> "Attack the snakeheads, destroy the snake pits, punish the illegal immi-
> grants."
>
> "Anyone participating in illegal immigration must be stringently pun-
> ished according to law."
>
> "Be aware of the risks of clandestine immigration."
>
> "Firmly attack the illegal activities of unlawful immigration."
>
> "We must have determination in controlling unlawful immigration."
>
> "We must intensify our efforts in stopping the pathologic social trend of
> irregular immigration."
>
> "The concepts of law and order must be upheld. We must struggle against
> illegal immigration."
>
> "It is a shame to immigrate illegally, but an honor to get rich through hard
> work."

Although anti-illegal immigration signs and banners have been
prominently displayed on the walls of major thoroughfares in sending
communities, it is doubtful that they have been widely heeded; like
other political slogans of the past, they may be viewed simply as routine government propaganda. Ying Chan, a reporter with the *New York
Daily News,* reports that "Residents privately laugh at calls by the government to turn in any snakeheads" (1993d: 17).

The second type of public education involved special town meetings. Law enforcement authorities in the many so-called "immigration
disaster areas," or "focal areas," sponsored special town meetings where

officers from the Public Security Bureau and other government officials told the audience (most of whom were government employees forced by their superiors to attend), about the perils of illegal immigration. Some townspeople not working for government work units ignored these meetings altogether. A police officer who had organized many of them told me:

> It is really just a show we put on to convince our superiors in Fuzhuo City and Beijing that we are doing something about illegal immigration. Actually, people attend these meetings because they have no choice. These meetings do nothing but to provide the participants with an opportunity to take a nap. All they have to do is to wake up occasionally and clap their hands. The only thing we want from them is not to laugh.

The third preventive measure involved the public denouncement of covert immigration by repatriated Chinese (*Fujian Ribao,* June 17, 1993). For example, after a passenger who had been on board the *East Wood,* the smuggling ship intercepted by the U.S. Coast Guard near the Marshall Islands, was deported to China, Chinese authorities asked him to speak out against his attempt to immigrate illegally:

> Once I learned that I was going to be sent back to China, my immediate reaction was: I will be doomed for the rest of my life. Because I did something that had ruined the reputation of my motherland and my village, my government is not going to forgive me. I was also worried that my family and relatives were going to look down on me for attempting to immigrate illegally. However, I soon found out that all my concerns were simply unnecessary. Four days after my return to China, the village head and other local cadres came to see me. They asked me to stop dreaming about going abroad to dig gold. They said that if I settled down and worked hard, I could get rich too. Within a month of my return, with the aid of the village head, I was able to find a job in a shoe factory. I am making more than 700 yuan [about $90] a month now (*World Journal,* August 30, 1993: A19).

RESPONSIBILITY SYSTEM. Provincial authorities in Fujian have also resorted to the so-called responsibility system, under which local or village cadres are obliged to stop the trend of unlawful immigration (*Wen Wei Pao,* January, 19, 1994). A Public Security Bureau officer informed me that if a village has twenty or fewer people per year leaving China illegally, the annual bonus of the village leaders is forfeited. If more than twenty people per year leave unlawfully, the village leaders are dismissed.

A former village official explained why he was forced to leave his post as deputy secretary of the local Communist Party:

I joined the Community Party when I was seventeen. I was the deputy party secretary of my town for more than ten years. Last year, after my three sons sneaked out of China, someone in the town informed officials in the city [Fuzhou], and they ordered me to give up my job. Not many people in this town go abroad, so I am the only official to have lost his job because of family members who immigrated illegally. There is a town where illegal immigration is so rampant that out of the twenty or so town party leaders, more than a dozen have been dismissed because of their family members who left China illegally.

To prevent people from traveling, officials in some towns demand that townspeople turn in their identification cards, the nationwide ID card for Chinese citizens (Burdman 1993f).

Punitive Measures

Besides educational and administrative measures, the Chinese government is also using increasing coastal and border patrols, dismantling human smuggling organizations, fining and imprisoning deportees and snakeheads, and executing big snakeheads.

Before the *Golden Venture* incident, there had been only one report in the Chinese media about a crackdown on smuggling Chinese to the United States, when authorities in Fuzhou arrested 157 would-be immigrants who were about to board a smuggling ship headed for the United States (*Tai Kung Pao,* April 18, 1993). After the grounding of the *Golden Venture,* the media reported that Chinese authorities had stepped up their border control efforts. In November 1993, authorities in Fuzhou, Guangzhou, and Hangzhou (of Zhejiang Province) captured 151 prospective immigrants and a snakehead (*World Journal,* November 4, 1993), and about a month later thirty-two people were arrested in Guangzhou for unlawful immigration (*World Journal,* December 1, 1993). The Chinese media also reported that between July 1993 and June 1994, Chinese border patrol officers intercepted twenty-three human smuggling vessels, six of which were reportedly headed for the United States and Japan and seventeen for Taiwan (*Tai Kung Pao,* June 11, 1994). (See Appendix B, Table 14 for a list of crackdowns conducted by Chinese authorities).

Before the *Golden Venture* incident, foreign and local snakeheads operated their businesses in China with little interference from Chinese authorities (Chan and Dao 1990c). Only occasionally did the Chinese police make concerted efforts to arrest snakeheads. In May 1991, for example, after authorities in the Fuzhou area adopted an anti-smuggling measure called "Management of Crime and Order in the Coastal Areas," they arrested fourteen snakeheads smuggling Chinese to Taiwan (*World Journal*, May 23, 1991). When the operation was over, more than a thousand suspects had been arrested for smuggling people and goods (*United Daily News*, May 30, 1991).

In the aftermath of the *Golden Venture* incident, authorities in Beijing held an emergency meeting attended by senior officials from the provinces of Fujian, Guangdong, and Zhejiang, and the head of the Public Security Bureau, among others. One central government official suggested that snakeheads who ignored the safety of their clients should be sentenced to death (*World Journal*, August 7, 1993), and under pressure from Beijing, provincial authorities ordered city, county, and village law enforcement authorities to arrest snakeheads. Between July and December 1993, Chinese authorities arrested more than seventy big and little snakeheads (*World Journal*, December 13, 1993) and in June 1994 authorities in Lianjiang, Changle, and Pingtan conducted a highly publicized trial of thirty-one human smugglers (*World Journal*, June 30, 1994).

In March 1994, nine months after the *Golden Venture* incident, the Chinese government promulgated a supplemental provision entitled "Additional Provisions on Severely Punishing Criminals Illegally Organizing and Participating in Trafficking People across the International Border," which called for more severe punishment of human smugglers (Standing Committee of the People's Congress 1994).[1]

Illegal immigrants who are deported back to China from abroad are heavily fined by Chinese authorities (W. Chan 1993; Wallis and Lewis 1993). The amount of the fine differs by locality, though Chinese laws stipulate that it should be between $120 and $550. According to my interviews in China, illegal immigrants returned to Changle, Tingjiang, and Lianjiang were fined up to about $3,000, deportees from Fuqin about $2,000, and from Pingtan approximately $700. Although the fines are intended as a deterrent (Burdman, 1993h), they may actually encourage deportees to embark on another illicit voyage to escape their accumulated debt—the down payment of $1,000 to $3,000 as well as the fine.

IMPRISONMENT. There are two types of secure confinement in China—*laodong jiaoyang* or *laojiao* (re-education through labor) and *laodong giazao* or *laogia* (reform through labor) (Lawyers Committee for Human Rights 1993). People accused of minor offenses such as burglary and fraud are not prosecuted in the criminal court but referred to a *laojiao* institution without a court hearing. This type of punishment, which usually lasts one to three years, is considered an executive or administrative punishment. A person who has served time in a *laojiao* institution is not viewed as an ex-convict and may have little difficulty reintegrating into the community (Yu 1987).

Offenders who commit serious violent or property crimes or engage in counterrevolutionary activities may be sentenced to death (with a two-year postponement of execution), life imprisonment, or long-term confinement and may be sent to a *laogia* (reform through labor) prison. Citizens can be confined to this type of institution only if they are found guilty by a criminal court judge, and their punishment is considered a criminal penalty. A person who has served time in a *laogia* institution is officially an ex-convict with a criminal record, and if he or she commits another crime he or she will be considered a chronic offender and punished more severely (Yu 1987).

Chinese immigrants deported back to China from abroad for the second time may be sentenced to one year of imprisonment in a *laojiao* prison. For Fujianese immigrants this usually means the *Lujian Laodong Jiaoyang Suo* (Lujian Institute of Reeducation through Labor), located in Mawei near Fuzhou City. According to the subjects I interviewed in China, repeat transgressors need not be confined to Lujian if they can pay off local authorities, as this respondent from Pingtan attested:

> If you are deported back to China for the second time, you will be sent to *laojiao* for a year. There, you've got to work everyday and live a bitter life. If you have *guanxi*, you may avoid *laojiao* by paying an additional 10,000 yuan fine. If you don't have this kind of money and are subjected to *laojiao*, you've got to at least spend a few hundred yuan a month bribing the staff at the *laojiao* institution to make sure they treat you well. If you do not know how to take care of this, you will suffer a lot there.

Another subject described his feelings about his brother's confinement at the Lujian Institute in Mawei:

> My brother is now being confined at the *Lujian Laojiao Suo*. He was imprisoned in December last year, so hopefully he will be out by this October.

We can visit him twice a month, on the 5th and 20th of every month. They allow us to stay for about two hours per visit. Last time when I visited him, my god, I don't think anybody could hold back tears when he or she sees what's going on in there. There are thousands of people locked up, mostly illegal immigrants, but some are criminals. That is a huge institution; it's like a small town.

When my brother just got in, he was assigned to work in a unit that produces plastic flowers. Everyday, he had to work from early in the morning until late into the night. Sometimes when he could not finish the assigned work, he had to continue to work until two or three in the morning. My brother told me it was really, really tough to be in there. He had to sit and work for more than ten hours a day, and he felt like he is going to be paralyzed soon. When I heard that, I was very sad. So I found a "friend" [someone who is in a position to help the subject], and told him my brother is an illegal immigrant, not a criminal, and he should not be punished so severely. My "friend" was sympathetic, and he transferred my brother to work in the kitchen. At least now he can move around while he works. My brother's wife had some forms of mental disorder before her husband entered *laojiao*, but now she is so traumatized that she is like a lunatic.

I interviewed another man in his thirties who had just been released from Lujian who explained in detail what it was like to spend several months in this type of institution:

When I was deported back to China for the second time, the local Public Security Bureau sent me to *laojiao*. There were more than two thousand inmates inside Lujian, predominantly illegal immigrants. Some were criminals who may have had to stay there for up to three years. Immigrants like us only had to serve one year. If we behaved or gave them some money, then our sentence would be reduced—for instance, we have to serve only about twenty days instead of a month. In this way, those who were lucky could be released within seven months instead of a year. I followed their orders and also bribed them with more than two thousand yuan, so I got out after a little more than seven months.

You can buy almost anything in there. You can smoke, and you can even eat the food brought to you by your family. You can walk around freely, you can speak loudly, but you have to finish your daily work assignments. For example, if you are asked to produce five hundred plastic flowers a day, you have no choice but to do it. You cannot go to sleep before you fulfil your work. Our monthly wage was three yuan (about thirty cents). All these plastic flowers are exported. Some who served time at Lujian immigrated illegally again. There's really no deterrent effect. A relative of mine was at the *laojiao*—so what, he sneaked out of the country again.

Very often snakeheads, especially little snakeheads, are also sentenced to *laojiao*. For example, in 1991, when the local authorities in Pingtan arrested fourteen snakeheads for smuggling Chinese to Taiwan, six were sent to a labor reeducation camp (*World Journal,* May 23, 1991).

DEATH PENALTY. Since the early 1980s, in order to control the increasing crime rate, Chinese authorities have executed those who have committed serious or violent crimes (Kristof 1991).[2] On many occasions, dozens of defendants in one jurisdiction have been sentenced to death on the same day and publicly executed as a general deterrent to crime (Yueng 1993). Before Chinese began to emigrate illegally in massive numbers, however, most offenders sentenced to death were violent criminals, drug traffickers, or corrupt officials (J. Wong 1994).

Soon after the *Golden Venture* incident, the death penalty was extended to people involved in the human smuggling trade. For example, three border control inspectors stationed at the Beijing airport and one snakehead were executed in December 1993 for transporting more than 120 Chinese out of China. Over a period of three years, the inspectors had received more than 1.6 million yuan (about $200,000) in bribes from the snakehead for their cooperation in the smuggling business (*World Journal,* December 5, 1993). Judging from the level of human smuggling still going on, however, the death penalty does not seem to be having its intended deterrent effect.

THE ROLE OF TAIWAN

Taiwan, like many other receiving countries of illegal immigrants, is greatly affected by the presence of large numbers of illegal Chinese immigrants in its territory (Chang 1995). Although Taiwan is not a major transit point for illegal Chinese immigrants headed for the United States, sea vessels owned by Taiwanese, passports issued by Taiwan's government, and citizens of Taiwan all play a major role in the Chinese human trade (Myers 1992, 1994, 1996). Thus it is important to examine what Taiwan can do to prevent Chinese from clandestinely immigrating to the United States.

Sea Smuggling

As we saw in Chapter 5, most smuggling ships are registered in Taiwan or owned by Taiwanese and are manned, more often than not, by captains and crews from Taiwan. Naturally, U.S. authorities are concerned about the prominent role played by Taiwanese ships and citizens in sea smuggling (*South China Morning Post,* August 28, 1993: 7).

Up until a little more than a decade ago, people in China and Taiwan were prohibited by their respective governments from contact with each other. After Chinese officials adopted a market-oriented economic policy in the 1980s, however, they began developing special economic zones in Guangdong and Fujian provinces to attract manufacturers and investors from Taiwan (van Kemenade 1997). In 1987, ending a policy established in 1949, Taiwan began to allow its citizens to visit China. As interactions between people across the Taiwan Strait began to increase, so did informal trade between merchants from China and Taiwan. Traders from both countries rendezvoused in international waters, exchanging all kinds of commodities on shipboard that were then smuggled into China or Taiwan for resale (Sun 1992; Tyler 1995). Thus the involvement of Taiwanese ships in illegal trade across the Taiwan straight apparently laid the groundwork for their later involvement in smuggling Chinese to the United States (Chang 1995).

A change in high seas fishing regulations also encouraged ships from Taiwan to engage in the human trade. According to Yann-huei Song, an international law scholar, drift-net fishing boats, under pressure from the United States, were prohibited from the Pacific Ocean because they "were the main cause for the decline in the number of salmon and steelhead trout returning to spawn in U.S. waters" and "killed a large number of marine mammals, sea turtles, sea-birds, and other marine living resources in the North Pacific as a result of incidental catch and 'ghost-netting,' which threatened the marine ecosystem of the Pacific Ocean" (1992: 67). Put out of the fishing business, some of these boats came to be used by smugglers to transport illegal immigrants across the Pacific Ocean.

Why was it so difficult for Taiwanese authorities to prevent Taiwanese ships from being used in the human smuggling trade? One reason is that Taiwan's laws do not prohibit the conversion of a ship to a smuggling vessel if the ship does not violate other laws of Taiwan (*World Journal,* June 14b, 1993). Another is that there was no legal basis for the punishment of Taiwanese ship owners, captains, and crew members who were involved in human trafficking (Chang 1995). As a result, after the captain and crew of a smuggling ship from Taiwan were flown back to Taiwan by U.S. authorities, Taiwan officials could not charge them with a crime and had no choice but to release them (*World Journal,* December 29, 1994). Furthermore, authorities have no jurisdiction over Taiwanese-owned smuggling ships registered in other countries or their activities in international waters.

Inefficiency at the Agricultural Affairs Council of Taiwan was another impediment to controlling smugglers (Chang 1995). According to Taiwan officials, some of the boats prohibited from drift-net fishing that were bought by the Taiwan government and slated for destruction turned up in international waters transporting illegal Chinese immigrants (*World Journal,* July 14, 1993).

Corruption among immigration and customs officials in Kaoshiung, an international seaport located in southern Taiwan, was another factor. A news article alleged that port officials received NT$1 million (about $40,000) every time a smuggling ship left port (*World Journal,* May 4, 1995). At the height of ocean-going smuggling activity in the early 1990s, twenty Kaoshiung-based ships were reported to be involved in human smuggling.

Under pressure from the United States, the Taiwan government took action to control its ships' and citizens' involvement in the human trade. After much delay the law regulating interactions between people living across the Taiwan Strait was supplemented in 1997 with a bill calling for the punishment of ship owners, users, and captains involved in the smuggling of illegal Chinese immigrants—a maximum three-year prison term and fines ranging from $37,000 to $550,000 (*World Journal,* January 11, 1996). To prevent ship owners from getting away with crime, the bill also stipulates that Taiwanese who own smuggling ships will be punished regardless of the ship's registry.

Air Smuggling

Taiwan is also involved in the smuggling of Chinese to the United States by air, a method involving Taiwanese passports. Because Chinese and Taiwanese are similar in appearance and speak the same language, illegal Chinese immigrants with Taiwan passports are less likely to be suspected or detected by immigration officers in transit and receiving countries than those with passports from other countries. Now that citizens of Taiwan can more easily obtain U.S. visas, including multiple entry visas valid for five years, human smugglers use a variety of methods to obtain Taiwan passports.

One obvious method is theft, and since the trade in Chinese illegal immigrants has soared, many Taiwan passports have been reported stolen. In one incident, about 250 Taiwan passports were stolen from a travel agency in Taipei (*World Journal*, October 6, 1994); some of them, many with valid U.S. visas, were later intercepted by Taiwanese authorities checking postal packages destined for Bangkok (*Sing Tao Daily*, October 11, 1994).

Some of the Taiwan passports used to transport smuggled Chinese were not stolen but sold to smugglers by the passport holders. Some Taiwanese apply for a U.S. visa in Taipei, then travel to Bangkok and sell their passports and visas to human smugglers. They then report the passport stolen at the Taiwanese government office in Bangkok and apply for a new one (*United Daily News*, June 28, 1994). In 1994, the Department of Foreign Affairs of Taiwan announced that there were 19,891 cases of missing passports in 1993, four times more than in 1987, about 80 percent of them stolen in Taiwan. A Taiwan passport with a valid U.S. visa can sell for approximately $11,000 in the black market in Southeast Asia (*China Times*, June 14, 1994).

In September 1994, the Taiwanese government began replacing the old passports with machine readable passports (MRPs) to prevent smugglers from using them (*China Times*, June 14, 1994). MRP passports are believed to be foolproof because it is almost impossible to replace the photos in them without destroying the passports. The photos are not attached but imprinted directly on a page of the passport.[3] The U.S. consulate in Taiwan also changed its procedures for issuing visas and U.S. visas are no longer printed on a piece of paper attached to the passport but also imprinted directly on a page of the passport and include an imprinted photo of the passport holder.

LAW ENFORCEMENT IN TRANSIT POINTS

As discussed earlier, most of my respondents passed through one or more countries or areas before they entered the United States. This section examines how authorities in the major transit points are dealing with smuggled Chinese passing through their jurisdictions.

Hong Kong

Authorities in Hong Kong have been aggressive in cracking down on smuggling networks responsible for bringing Chinese to Hong Kong illegally. For example, they conducted Operation Closed Door in May 1991, which resulted in the arrests of ninety-five illegal Chinese immigrants and five suspected snakeheads (*Sing Tao Daily,* May 10, 1991). However, the influx of Chinese into Hong Kong continues unabated. Between January and May of 1992, Hong Kong police arrested 11,512 illegal Chinese immigrants, an increase of 42.4 percent over the same period in 1991 (Leung 1992). Another crackdown on illegal immigrants—Operation Champion in 1995—led to the arrest of one hundred illegal immigrants from China (*World Journal,* September 16, 1995). In 1997, authorities in Hong Kong and the United States arrested Hong Kong-based high-ranking INS officials who were working for Chinese smugglers (Larmer and Liu 1997).

To cope with the problem of unlawful immigration, in 1995 Hong Kong authorities increased the fine for snakeheads caught smuggling illegal immigrants from $650,000 to $2.2 million and decreed that snakeheads could be sentenced to life imprisonment. The fine for defendants who aided snakeheads was increased from $25,000 to $64,000, with a possible jail sentence of three to ten years (*World Journal,* September 15, 1995). According to a 1992 media account, one third of the inmates in Hong Kong's prisons at that time were illegal immigrants (Braude 1992).

Because the Hong Kong administration is overwhelmed by the large number of illegal Chinese immigrants in its territory (Sinclair 1993; Vagg 1993), it is not likely to devote much time to controlling those passing through en route to the United States. However, the smuggling of Cantonese from Guangdong to Hong Kong is intricately associated with the smuggling of Fujianese from Fujian to the United States. Since some snakeheads are believed to be involved in smuggling both Cantonese and Fujianese, attempts to control human smuggling activities in Hong Kong will have some impact on the smuggling of Chinese to the United States.

Thailand

There is not much likelihood of effective action against human smuggling in Thailand. Because the Chinese community is well established in Bangkok, illegal Chinese immigrants can easily hide themselves in the cheap hotels of the city's Chinatown (Dao and Chan 1990). Corruption among Thai officials is also a serious problem, and when Thai authorities do attempt to return Chinese to China via Myanmar, they encounter some technical problems. For example, Burmese authorities do not accept illegal immigrants of "non-Burmese" nationality (Charasdamrong and Kheunkaew 1992).

Singapore and Malaysia

A labor shortage in Singapore has created a strong demand for cheap labor from China. Over the past several years, many Chinese workers have been imported to Singapore, and the door is wide open to Chinese who wish to legally travel to Singapore. This naturally provides an opportunity for smuggling, and evidence that ships from Singapore are involved in the human trade is attracting attention among Singapore authorities (*World Journal,* February 21, 1995). In 1996, Singapore officials sentenced a snakehead to twelve years in prison for producing counterfeit Singapore passports (*Sing Tao Daily,* May 1, 1996).

Other Asian nations have recently adopted stringent measures against illegal immigration. To prevent smugglers from using Malaysian passports to transport Chinese, the Malaysian government announced that it will not replace lost passports and in 1996 increased the penalty for human smuggling. People caught with fraudulent passports will be sentenced to two to five years in prison and a maximum of six lashes (*World Journal,* January 23, 1996).

Europe

European countries such as Germany, England, France, Italy, and Spain have reacted to the growth of illegal Chinese immigrants in their territories by stepping up prevention efforts. After five Chinese were murdered, Spanish authorities conducted an investigation of all Chinese living in Madrid in order to screen out illegal Chinese immigrants. According to a news report, officials in Spain believed that human smugglers were using the documents of dead people to bring in more illegal immigrants from China (Dobson and Daswani 1994).

Since the beginning of the 1990s, the question of unlawful immigration and human trafficking has been on the agenda of many international organizations in Europe, including the International Organisation for Migration, the European Union Third Pillar structures, the Berlin-Vienna-Budapest Process, the International Center for Migration Policy Development, and the Inter-governmental Consultations on Asylum,

Refugee and Migration Policies in Europe, North America and Australia (Siemens 1996).

Central America

According to the Interagency Working Group in Washington, D.C. (1995: 4), "Central America is a major conduit and source of illegal migrants entering the United States. In addition to being the source of 200,000 to 300,000 illegal aliens who attempt to enter the U.S., it has emerged as a transit route for some 100,000 aliens from outside the region (primarily Chinese, South Americans and South Asians). . . . Several smuggling rings and hundreds of independent smugglers operate in Central America, including travel agents, guides, and support personnel who run hotels and provide documents. Alien smuggling is not illegal (except in Honduras) so smugglers operate openly and are regarded as 'businessmen' and not criminals."

Even in Honduras, where alien smuggling is illegal, government officials are reportedly actively involved in the human trade. For example, a Honduran-based senior INS official was arrested in Hong Kong in August 1996 for delivering blank Honduran passports containing a seal and a signature to the Honduran Consul-General in Hong Kong (Chow and Schloss 1996).

U.S. POLICIES

The primary focus of the 1992 U.S. Senate hearings on Chinese organized crime was Chinese involvement in extortion, violent crimes, and heroin trafficking, but government officials also began to take notice of the problem of Chinese human smuggling (U.S. Senate 1992). As discussed in Chapter 5, a year after the Senate hearings and immediately after the *Golden Venture* incident, U.S. law enforcement authorities significantly intensified their prevention efforts, with emphasis on detecting and detaining illegal immigrants, controlling borders, sanctioning employers of undocumented workers, deporting illegal immigrants, and waging assaults on Chinese human smuggling groups.

Detection and Detention

Of the three hundred smuggled Chinese interviewed for this study, 111 (37 percent) were detected by U.S. authorities at the port of entry or at the border. My analysis showed no association between the detection rate and the subjects' personal characteristics (see Appendix B, Table 15), but there is a connection between detection and smuggling routes and patterns (see Appendix B, Table 16). For example, as mentioned earlier, respondents who arrived in 1988 or before were unlikely to be apprehended by U.S. officials; of the twenty-three respondents who came in 1988 or before, only one was arrested. Among the forty-three subjects who arrived in 1989, only seven were caught. Beginning in 1990, the detection rate increased, especially for respondents who came by air. For my sample, however, detection rates for 1992 and 1993 dropped from a high of about 50 percent in 1990 and 1991.

As explained in Chapter 6, of the three methods of entry into the United States, the land route, via either Mexico or Canada, was the "safest" for my subjects—the detection rate was only about 11 percent. Detection rate for those who took the sea route was also relatively low, about 20 percent, compared with the detection rate of almost 64 percent for those who took the air route. According to my survey data, the detection rate for New York City (71 percent) was higher than for Los Angeles (39 percent). Although authorities at the Miami and Honolulu airports were relatively successful in catching my subjects, these two cities were rarely used by my respondents (data not shown). Respondents who entered the United States without a guide had a detection rate of 62 percent, compared to 26 percent for subjects who were escorted.

The detection rate increased with the size of the group being smuggled by sea or land. For subjects who flew in, the longer it took to get here, the greater the chance of discovery by U.S. authorities at their port of entry. As we saw earlier, detection by U.S. authorities meant a short confinement for my subjects who were released for reasons of limited detention space, political asylum application, and bail posting by snakeheads.[4]

Border Patrol

The 1996 budget for the INS was $2.6 billion, 24 percent more than the previous year and a 72 percent increase from 1993 (*Sing Tao Daily*, February 9, 1996). In 1997, 3.1 billion was allotted to the INS, most of it for more border patrol officers and sophisticated equipment.

Border patrol is the major component of the Clinton administration's strategy to curb unlawful immigration. On October 1, 1994, the INS launched an ambitious program called Operation Gatekeeper on the U.S.-Mexican border near San Diego (Ayres 1994: D21). Some skeptics argue that stepped-up enforcement measures do not deter clandestine immigration, and it is not clear how effective this operation has been. According to Wayne Cornelius, an authority on the irregular migration of Mexicans, "There is no evidence that pushing illegal immigrants into areas where there are more physical obstacles to crossing will deter more than a small minority from trying repeatedly to gain entry until they succeed." Others contend that a crackdown in one area only diverts border-crossing activities to other, less enforced areas (Mydans 1995: A16).

U.S. immigration authorities launched two additional border patrol operations, in Tucson, Arizona (Operation Safeguard) and El Paso, Texas (Operation Hold-the-Line).

Employer Sanctions

Many immigration scholars have suggested that employment is one of the major pull factors of unlawful immigration (Mahler 1995; Kwong 1997). Under the Immigration Reform and Control Act (IRCA), enacted in 1986, employers were held responsible for checking the immigration status of prospective employees. Alejandro Portes and Ruben Rumbaut (1990: 236) have suggested that the new law might have only made illegal workers more vulnerable because it could "drive the process further underground as both workers and employers seek ways to bypass the new regulations."

Nevertheless, after eight years of IRCA enforcement with mixed results, the U.S. Commission on Immigration Reform (1994) again emphasized the importance of employer sanctions as a tool in curbing illegal immigration and the Clinton administration, on its advice, began cracking down on employers who hire undocumented workers. To make this strategy more effective, President Clinton proposed that an additional 570 agents be assigned to enforce the rule (370 agents for INS and 200 agents for the Labor Department) (*World Journal*, February 6, 1995).

Crackdowns on employers who hired illegal immigrants began in earnest in mid-1995. Many garment factories in Los Angeles and New York City were raided by INS agents looking for illegal workers, and some, like a cleaning business in New York State fined

$1.5 million for hiring illegal immigrants, were heavily penalized (Dugger 1996a).

It is not clear, however, what impact, if any, these raids have had on deterring illegal employment. According to a front-page *New York Times* report, "Most of the workers are released the same day and are usually not deported. Some go back to the very factories where they were picked up. Many move to other factories and sweatshops, or to industries in which there is no crackdown" (Dugger 1996b: A1).

Deportation

The first massive deportation from the United States was carried out in January 1994, eight months after the *Golden Venture* incident, when 150 illegal Chinese were deported back to China (*Sing Tao Daily,* January 18, 1994). This was followed in May by the deportation of eighty-four more Chinese and another eighty-one in September (*World Journal,* September 16, 1994).

In addition, those intercepted in international waters were sent back to China (Devroy and Kamen 1993). On June 18, 1993, two weeks after the *Golden Venture* foundered, President Clinton pledged to allow the U.S. Coast Guard wide leeway to go into international waters and board ships suspected of carrying illegal Chinese, presumably to avoid any lengthy asylum claims once the immigrants landed (Dobson 1994). When the U.S. Coast Guard discovered three Chinese smuggling ships near Baja California (in Mexico), the ships were escorted to a Mexican seaport and all the Chinese passengers were repatriated to China (DePalma 1993). Since then, the U.S. Coast Guard has steered several Chinese smuggling ships to Mexico, Guatemala, Honduras, and the Guantanamo Air Force base in Cuba, whence the passengers were deported to China (*World Journal,* May 7, 1994; *United Daily News,* June 20, 1994).

Even so, there is ample evidence to suggest that only a small proportion of smuggled Chinese who make it to the United States is actually deported. Given that the majority of my subjects entered the United States either by air or overland, the stepped-up patrol of U.S. waters by the U.S. Coast Guard is unlikely to have a significant impact on the level of illegal immigration by Chinese, and most illegal Chinese already in the United States are unlikely to be arrested and deported. Although the U.S. government did on three occasions repatriate a number of smuggled Chinese, the practice stopped once publicity about the *Golden Venture* incident faded away.

Assaults on the Big Snakeheads

Because most big snakeheads use others to help them recruit and transport customers and collect smuggling fees, they cannot be easily identified, and the use of legitimate businesses as fronts for smuggling activities makes big snakeheads even harder to catch (Glaberson 1989; W. Chan 1993). With the exception of a few well-known big snakeheads, I believe most big snakeheads are able to remain hidden and beyond the reach of law enforcement.

Since the development of clandestine immigration by Chinese in the late 1980s, only a handful of big snakeheads have been arrested and prosecuted by U.S. authorities. One of the most significant cases involving human traffickers was a sixteen-month investigation known as Operation Snakeheads that allowed authorities to penetrate simultaneously a number of Chinese smuggling rings (DeStefano 1994). Altogether thirteen snakeheads who belonged to five different smuggling groups were indicted in New York.

Another high-profile case was the indictment of those responsible for the *Golden Venture* incident. After the ship was grounded near New York City, the captain, crew, enforcers, and the U.S.-based big snakehead were arrested and convicted (Faison 1994c).[5] The leader of the Fuk Ching gang who was alleged to be partially responsible for the incident was arrested in Hong Kong and extradited to the United States (Faison 1994b). U.S. authorities also conducted a worldwide manhunt and finally arrested the man behind the operation in Bangkok (Stout 1995). Because the defendant had dual Thai-U.S. citizenship, the Thai government was reluctant to extradite him to the United States, but after extensive negotiations he was eventually extradited to stand trial (*World Journal*, October 7, 1997).

U.S. authorities have also successfully prosecuted two big snakeheads responsible for bringing Chinese to the United States on board a smuggling ship, sentencing both to five years in prison and fining them $25,000 each (*World Journal*, July 16, 1993). Snakeheads found guilty of confining illegal immigrants in safe houses may also draw harsh sentences. Two snakeheads indicted after authorities found a large number of Chinese being kept in a house in Mitchellville, Maryland, were sentenced to fourteen and seventeen years in prison, respectively (S. Beck 1995). (See Appendix B, Table 17 for a list of arrests of big snakeheads in the United States.)

In the recognition that lenient punishment failed to deter smugglers, the U.S. Congress passed the Violent Crime Control and Law Enforcement Act of 1994, which dramatically increased the penalties for human trafficking: "Persons who knowingly bring illegals into the U.S. are subject to a possible imprisonment term of ten years (and/or fines) per illegal.... The maximum penalty is increased to twenty years per alien when bodily injury occurs or life is placed in jeopardy in connection with the smuggling offense. Additionally, when death results, the death penalty or life imprisonment is allowed" (U.S. Commission on Immigration Reform 1994: 48). The U.S. Senate also passed the Foreigners Alien Smuggling Act in 1995, and the first RICO (Racketeering-Influenced and Corrupt Organizations) case against a Chinese smuggling organization occurred in Newark, New Jersey that same year. Fourteen defendants were indicted for bringing illegal Chinese to the United States between 1992 and 1994 (Gold 1995).

Federal and local authorities in the tri-state area also began to crack down on safe houses in the mid-1990s. Since U.S. courts consider the confinement of Chinese immigrants kidnapping, debt collectors tend to receive severe punishment when convicted. In a 1991 incident, for example, an enforcer in New York City was sentenced to twenty-five years to life for kidnapping a Chinese immigrant (*World Journal*, December 26, 1991).

These efforts were reinforced by an all-out attack on Chinese gangs and their affiliated adult organizations. In the three years after the *Golden Venture* incident, eleven Chinese gangs and organized crime groups—almost all the major Chinese gangs in the United States—were indicted on racketeering charges (see Appendix B, Table 18).

PROBLEMS IN COMBATING HUMAN SMUGGLING

Many new anti-smuggling measures are now being discussed either on a regional or international level (Siemens 1996), but it is doubtful that they will be able to stop the illegal flow of Chinese immigrants.

Illegal Immigration as "Sometimes a Crime"

Jon Vagg (1993), a scholar on clandestine immigration from China to
Hong Kong, has suggested that unlawful immigration is only "sometimes a crime," and it is true that human smuggling is different from
transnational criminal activities like heroin and arms trafficking. Many
people do not consider it a crime and some of those who do consider it
a victimless crime. While the U.S. public was horrified by the arrival of
hundreds of Chinese onboard the *Golden Venture*, A. M. Rosenthal, a *New
York Times* columnist, suggested that the United States should treat the
Golden Venture passengers not as criminals but as heroes.

Although the human trade is an extremely lucrative business, it is
normally considered a minor crime and often draws relatively light sentences. In the United States, the maximum federal penalty for alien
smuggling is ten years in prison, but few convicted defendants receive
the maximum sentence (*World Journal,* November 27, 1997). The same
is true in Taiwan, where the maximum sentence for smuggling Chinese
to the United States is three years. Many local Chinese officials view the
immigration of Chinese to the United States as beneficial to their economy and see those involved as patriotic, compassionate people rather
than as greedy criminals (Burdman 1993g: A14).

An official in the Fuzhou suggested the mixed feelings many authorities bring to the issue:

> Frankly, we have an ambivalent attitude towards illegal immigration. On
> the one hand, we hope our villagers will have an opportunity to go abroad
> and make money because this will solve our high unemployment rate.
> Also, money sent back by immigrants helps us to construct the local infra-
> structure. On the other hand, since immigration without proper docu-
> ments is against our law, we must carry out the orders from above and
> stop illegal immigration. Consequently, when it comes to dealing with ille-
> gal immigration, we usually keep one eye open and close the other.

Chinatowns Worldwide

Chinese smuggling networks are deeply embedded not only in the sending communities in China but also in well-connected Chinese communities around the world (Seagrave 1995). As discussed in Chapter 3,
Willard Myers has suggested that smuggling among the Chinese is an
ethnic enterprise. The Chinese smuggling network has been in existence

for centuries, and its power, connections, and flexibility make law enforcement measures largely ineffective.

Regulation of the Airline Industry

Curbing illegal immigration also involves the public regulation of a private industry (International Civil Aviation Organization 1994). Because many illegal Chinese enter the United States by air, preventive measures adopted by government agencies must be supported by private companies that are normally ill-equipped or unwilling to regulate the flow of international travel.

Currently, airlines are liable for all detention costs of their passengers who arrive in the United States without documents and apply for political asylum (Kamen 1992a; Lorch 1992), but it is not clear that the airline industry is capable of policing the illegal movement of people. As a service industry trying to survive in a highly competitive international business, it is not likely that airline staff will give priority to curbing illegal immigration over profits, safety, and customer satisfaction.

Regulation of the Shipping and Fishing Industries

Regulation of the shipping and fishing industries is easier said then done (Kamen 1992b). As one U.S. official indicated, "Other than maritime regulations, it's not illegal to be floating around the Pacific with 500 people on your ship. . . . We could not do anything unless we could prove some sort of conspiracy to violate US immigration laws, and even that could involve some tricky extradition proceedings" (Torode 1993b: 2).

Burdman (1993e: A16) has also reported how difficult it is for U.S. authorities to intercept smuggling ships in international waters: "In most cases, the U.S. government cannot legally board a ship on the high seas even if agents know it is smuggling people. . . . Even a vessel sailing through U.S. waters has not committed a crime until undocumented immigrants disembark." "There are vessels on their way now," said Wayne R. McKenna, the coordinator of a Federal Chinese smuggling task force. "But what can I do? What can I do to possibly stop these vessel on the seas?" (Faison 1993a: A1).

The U.S. Coast Guard simply lacks the manpower to patrol the vast areas involved effectively. A *U.S. News and World Report* article concluded that "The oceans are too vast . . . to catch most of the smuggling ships. The U.S. Coast Guard district in Long Beach, Calif., for instance, is required to monitor a stretch of ocean extending 700 miles offshore from the Mexican border north to Oregon" (1993: 28). U.S. authorities are not in a position to stop sea smuggling by themselves. They need the cooperation of authorities in countries in which the ships are registered and remodeled (Bell and Chan 1993: 23).

Ineffectiveness of Employer Sanctions

There are two reasons why employer sanctions are unlikely to deter Chinese from coming to the United States illegally. For one thing, most Chinese employers, especially owners of small take-out restaurants, prefer to hire relatives or people from their hometown, and that usually means illegal immigrants. Given their informal hiring methods, it is unlikely that these employers will ask their prospective employees to produce documents. In general, the benefits of hiring their own people far outweigh the costs of being caught by immigration authorities, especially given the slim chance that they will actually be raided by the INS or Labor Department.

In addition, as we know, most illegal Chinese immigrants apply for political asylum upon their arrival in the United States and are issued a C-8 card authorizing them to work while their cases are pending (Ignatius 1993). This convenient circumstance makes employer sanctions doubly irrelevant.

Problems in Detecting and Deporting Smuggled Chinese

There are many problems associated with deporting smuggled Chinese. The INS is notoriously ill-equipped to lock up all illegals—in 1993, the agency had one hundred beds in Queens, New York, at a time when 15,000 illegal immigrants were stopped each year at JFK airport alone (*New York Times,* August 17, 1993). In addition, the deportation process is easily disrupted if deportees will not cooperate, and Chinese iillegals often put up quite a fight. In 1993, hundreds of Chinese immigrants overpowered Mexican authorities in Mexicali on the eve of their deportation and escaped (*New York Times,* May 16, 1993). Also in 1993, more than two hundred smuggled Chinese being held for deportation in Honduras clashed with the guards. The uprising was put down only after authorities opened fire on the illegal Chinese immigrants, killing one and wounding six (*World Journal,* May 26, 1993). Violent incidents associated with Chinese deportation have also been reported in France and Spain (*World Journal*, June 19, 1993; October 2, 1995).

There is also the matter of expense. The interception and escorting of the *Jung Sheng* human cargo ship out of U.S. waters cost the U.S. Coast Guard approximately $4 million. The Department of Defense spent another $2.5 million to create a temporary facility to hold the *Jung Sheng* passengers. Sending tens of thousands of illegal immigrants back to China is also very costly. The Organization of International Migration spent about $1 million to fly 528 smuggled Chinese from the Marshall Islands back to China (Woolrich 1993a). Who should pay these bills?

In a few cases, the U.S. government was able to pressure the Taiwanese government into paying for deportation expenses because Taiwan-registered ships were involved (Kamen 1993; *United Daily News*, June 20, 1994). When the Taiwanese people learned of this, they were outraged, and the officials involved were lambasted in the press (*World Journal*, June 20, 1994).

Lenient Punishment

Up until 1993, under U.S. federal sentencing guidelines, a first-time human smuggling offender faced a maximum prison sentence of six months (Kamen 1991a). After the captain and senior crew members of the *Golden Venture* pleaded guilty to human smuggling, their lawyers negotiated with prosecutors for prison terms of only twelve to thirty months. Although the judge rejected the agreement, the defendants were still sentenced to only thirty-six to fifty-four months in prison, a relatively lenient punishment if we compare it to typical jail terms for drug traffickers (Hevesi 1994). Only the key enforcer on board the *Golden Venture* was sentenced to fifteen years in prison and a New York-based big snakehead involved in the operation received a ten-year sentence (*World Journal*, October 14b, 1995). The case received a huge amount of media attention. It is difficult to say whether less widely publicized cases would result in such stiff penalties.

Lack of Law Enforcement Personnel

Even though the INS has dramatically increased the number of border patrol agents along the U.S.-Mexican border, there are still too few patrols to police the entire border. According to one U.S. official, "It's like if you squeeze a balloon, it just pops out around your hand. If we tighten up, they're going to look where there's a weak link" (Dunn 1994: A1). The cleverness and adaptability of smugglers also hampers law enforcement. According to a senior INSINS officer, "Every time we get a handle on what they are doing and how they are doing it, things change" (Mydans 1992: A7).

The lack of Chinese- and especially of Fujianese-speaking agents is another major problem for the INS investigative division. According to one INS agent:

> There are only nine Chinese INS investigative agents (four each in New York City and Los Angeles, one in Newark), and only one of the nine speaks the Fuzhou dialect. Some of them do not even speak Mandarin or are not involved in the investigation of alien smuggling by Chinese. The problem is, even if INS tries to recruit more Chinese agents, the new recruits may not be willing to be involved in the investigation of the Chinese human trade because they do not want to investigate their own people or see this line of work as extremely risky.

The lack of interagency cooperation only increases the difficulty of law enforcement. A federal agent I interviewed said, "The INS is not working closely with other federal agencies in the prevention and investigation of alien smuggling. There are a lot of interagency rivalries. Every agency thinks it can handle the problem by itself and needs no outside help."

The Asylum Program as a Magnet

The political asylum program clearly needs to be reformed; as it stands, it is an open invitation to exploitation by illegal immigrants of all nationalities. One recommendation for revamping the program is to require illegal immigrants to apply for asylum within thirty days after their arrival in the United States, though it is not clear what good this would do (Schmitt 1996). Other approaches involve charging the applicants a fee and delaying the issuing of work permits. Neither anti- nor pro-immigrant groups think that these changes would make a significant difference (Weiner 1994).

The question of whether China's one-child policy constitutes persecution and justifies political asylum has been hotly debated over the past several years. At first, the one-child policy was not considered political persecution. After Tiananmen Square it became the grounds on which many Chinese were granted asylum, but in the wake of the *Golden Venture,*

U.S. policy reversed again. Then in 1997 President Clinton announced that the one-child policy should be considered political persecution (Smith 1997). Clearly, the decision process in asylum cases appears to depend heavily on the public mood toward illegal immigration and U.S.-China relations rather than on how the one-child policy is implemented in China.

Although the U.S. asylum program has been exploited by many smuggled Chinese, Chinese political asylum cases represented less than 5 percent of the total pending cases (i.e., 23,055 of 486,544) as of March 31, 1996 (U.S. Immigration and Naturalization Service 1996). Any changes needed to prevent trafficked Chinese from abusing the program must also take into consideration potentially negative effects on a large number of legitimate applicants.

Problems in Sealing the Border

Many Americans have suggested closing U.S. borders as the best way to stop illegal immigration, but this is not so easy as it seems, as INS Commissioner Doris Meisner points out, "'The border' is a lot bigger than our 2,000-mile frontier with Mexico. Our borders are also the beaches of Florida, the airports and overseas consulates where visas are issued. About 40 percent of the illegal immigrants in this country are people who have overstayed legally issued documents" (Dreifus 1996: 52).

Chinese authorities confront similar problems. China's extensive coastal area, lengthy borders with Myanmar, Vietnam, India, and other countries, as well as China's lack of advanced equipment, defeat government efforts to control illegal crossings.

International Cooperation

There is no question that any effective measure to prevent Chinese illegal immigration requires multinational cooperation involving authorities from sending, transit, and receiving countries. So far, the general lack of trust and the lack of an extradition treaty between China and the United States have been major obstacles to international cooperation in curbing the traffic (Chin 1996; Faison 1996). U.S. authorities do not get much help from government officials in transit countries either. So far, the United States does not have extradition treaties with either Taiwan or Thailand, two major players in Chinese human smuggling. As a result, many big snakeheads wanted by U.S. authorities seek refuge in these and other Asian countries that do not have extradition treaties with the United States. Many such problems combine to make law enforcement problems seem insurmountable. Willard Myers (1994), an expert on illegal Chinese immigration, has concluded that current enforcement strategies have almost no impact.

POLICY RECOMMENDATIONS

My research has convinced me that the flow of illegal Chinese immigrants into the United States can only be curbed if all of the countries involved cooperate in adopting effective policies and each country takes responsibility for its own deficiencies.

China

Instead of blaming foreign-based snakeheads and the U.S. political asylum program for the clandestine immigration of its citizens, the Chinese government should admit that the phenomenon is in large part the result of China's many domestic social ills. It will be difficult for the Chinese government to convince rural Chinese that China is a better place to live and work than the United States. It will take decades and be accomplished only if China continues to improve its economic, legal, and political structures. In the meantime, however, there are many things that can be done.

1. Authorities in Beijing must demand that local authorities in the sending villages get serious about curbing illegal immigration.

If authorities in the Fuzhou area made a genuine effort to control unlawful migration, it would have a significant impact; but because they now view emigration as a good thing, they are not likely to strengthen their efforts to prevent it without pressure from Beijing. Though some observers doubt that Beijing has much control over the provinces (e.g., Smith 1997), I believe that the central government still has tremendous leverage over provincial and city authorities, who in turn have the authority to control county and village authorities.

2. Beijing should closely monitor and control labor-export companies in Fujian, Guangdong, and Zhejiang, the three major sending provinces, through the creation of a permanent special unit designed to prevent these companies from exporting cheap labor illegally.

The unit's main purpose should be to encourage and expand the legal and legitimate export of labor power, for which there is a strong demand in Asia and other parts of the world.

3. China must come up with a comprehensive plan to wipe out official corruption.

Many of China's social problems stem from rampant official corruption. It is so easy for snakeheads to bribe local government and law enforcement officials that they actually brag about it. Pressure from Beijing will not be effective unless it is supplemented with salary increases for these officials.

4. The Chinese government must make a serious effort to educate the public about the risks and costs of illegal immigration.

The red banners, laughable slogans, and town meetings that the people have ignored for years should be abandoned for informative educational materials and programs about the real perils of covert immigration. The Chinese government produced several television programs on the subject, but they were highly charged with patriotism, ethnic pride, and political ideology, which the Chinese people have learned to discount and ignore. The task here may hinge on expanding the freedom of the press to the extent that people can begin to trust what they hear on the news.

5. The Chinese government must speed up its economic and political reform in the sending villages and not focus exclusively on a few coastal urban centers.

Many social factors behind the illegal immigration of Chinese—official corruption, income inequality, lack of freedom and human rights, and so on—need to be addressed. Most Chinese would be reluctant to go abroad if they were happy with what they have and believed that they had a future in China. My subjects were convinced that their lives would not improve in China, no matter how hard they worked. Those who were economically well-off were either dissatisfied with their local government or concerned that China's ever-changing policies might strip them of the fruits of their labor. These goals cannot be achieved overnight, but without them people will continue to seek a better life abroad.

6. The Chinese government should allow its citizens more freedom to travel and emigrate legitimately.

Currently, only the rich, the powerful, the talented, and the well-connected can go abroad legally. Many rural Chinese emigrate illegally simply because they have no legal option. Very few of my subjects had ever been abroad before they set out for the United States, but if they had been able to travel freely and legally, many of them might have been disabused of their fantasies about the "Beautiful Country" and the rest of the outside world. As it is now, once they leave China there is no way back, even if they come to regret their decision bitterly.

Taiwan

As a country deeply troubled by the influx of illegal Chinese immigrants, Taiwan should have no trouble understanding the United States position. Yet authorities in Taiwan have been reluctant to admit that their people, ships, and passports are critical to the Chinese human trade and unwilling to take preventive measures unless repeatedly pressured by the United States. The Taiwanese government and its embassies and consulates in major transit countries need to make a concerted effort to minimize the role of Taiwanese ships and passports in the smuggling of Chinese.

Taiwan must also develop a better way to monitor its fishing and shipping industries. The agency currently responsible for regulating these industries—the Agricultural Affairs Council—is incompetent; either a new unit must be established or the council must be thoroughly restructured. In addition, the 1997 bill criminalizing Taiwanese involvement in smuggling Chinese to the United States should be rigorously enforced. Convicted Taiwanese human smugglers should receive the maximum penalty and, if warranted, smuggling networks should be prosecuted as racketeering enterprises under the newly established organized crime law.

Transit Countries

The U.S. Immigration and Naturalization Service must increase its presence and operation in Hong Kong, Myanmar, Thailand, and Mexico, the four most popular transit points. The regime in Yangon, Myanmar has little control over its border areas, and it will therefore be up to the

Chinese authorities in Yunnan Province to police the China-Myanmar border. If the Myanmar border is adequately policed, Chinese illegals will turn to other neighboring countries, such as Vietnam and Cambodia, as some already do. The question is whether local Chinese authorities have the resources and determination to patrol the vast border area between China and its many adjacent countries, especially when the promotion of border trade is so vital to the economic well-being of the border areas of China.

Because official corruption is rampant in both Thailand and Mexico, I am not sure how much the two governments can do to limit the flow of smuggled Chinese through their territories. The United States (and China) will undoubtedly have to pressure these countries if illegal immigration over their borders is to be curbed.

The United States

The development of U.S. immigration policies has rarely been guided by solid research about the motives and patterns of legal and illegal immigration. In spite of the public furor over the *Golden Venture,* there is very little reliable information on the Chinese human trade. We do not even know for sure how many Chinese are smuggled into the United States every year. Without reliable data, efforts to stop the flow of trafficked Chinese are bound to be miscalculated and ineffective.

Redoubled law enforcement has been the most common approach to stopping illegal immigration. In 1995 the Interagency Working Group proposed that "additional human resources be devoted to combating alien smuggling through expanding our overseas enforcement capability and through expanding our overseas training programs" (1995:1), and the U.S. Commission on Immigration Reform also recommended the "expanded enforcement authorities, such as the Racketeering Influenced and Corrupt Organizations (RICO) enforcement authority provision, wiretap authority, and expanded asset forfeiture for smuggling aliens" and "enhanced intelligence gathering and diplomatic efforts to deter smuggling" (1994: 49-50). The commission also advocated a simpler, more fraud-resistant system for verifying work authorization as an effective way to discourage illegal immigration.

The major problem with U.S. immigration policies has been that they are closely linked to other U.S. foreign policies and to domestic economic conditions. The issue is not only about how much illegal immigration the United States is willing to tolerate, but also when and from where. As I mentioned earlier, smuggled Chinese constitute a relatively small portion of illegal immigrants residing in the United States, and efforts to curb their arrival must consider issues of fairness. I would suggest that the U.S. government consider the following policies:

1. Illegal immigrants who are caught entering the country illegally should be deported.

Most of my subjects were confident that once they set foot on American soil, they had "made it," and for the most part they were right. To erode this confidence, the U.S. government must consistently deport illegal immigrants who have failed the test for political asylum or who have overstayed their visas. The knowledge that they would probably be deported would make illegal Chinese immigrants far less likely to risk the dangerous and expensive trip.

2. The U.S. asylum program must be restructured to prevent abuses.

The testimony of my respondents, informal discussions with lawyers and consultants who prepared their asylum cases, and several visits to the asylum office in Lyndhurst, New Jersey, led me to conclude that the vast majority of asylum claims are fraudulent. Although I support the view that, in a sense, all Chinese are "politically persecuted" under the current government, the U.S. political asylum program is not designed to accommodate such a large population indiscriminately. The good intentions behind the political asylum program must be accompanied by procedures that identify legitimate claims and alternative measures that will encourage the Chinese government to improve its human rights conditions. If the U.S. government were to tighten its asylum policy by screening illegal immigrants to determine their eligibility, speeding up the review process, and expeditiously deporting those who do not qualify, I believe that prospective immigrants might have second thoughts.

3. The best way to attack the smuggling networks is to deprive them of their profits.

The U.S. should encourage illegal Chinese who have been arrested at the border to default on payment to their smugglers. If the U.S. then deports them, smugglers will suffer a huge loss.

4. My subjects came to the United States primarily to make money, most of them through hard work in legitimate jobs. One effective way to discourage them would be to deny them this opportunity.

Currently, the INS and Labor Department lack the manpower to enforce work authorization rules or to sanction employers who hire illegal immigrants, and it is unlikely that this will change anytime soon. But one relatively simple measure could make an impact, and that would be to require anyone who wants to open a restaurant to prove U.S. citizenship or legal resident status. As things stand now, many illegal immigrants operate their own small businesses and this in turn induces more people, especially their relatives, to come. It should not be difficult to implement this small reform, and it could have a disproportionately positive effect on curbing illegal immigration.

5. The U.S. government must step up checks at U.S. customs and immigration offices in airports.

It is imperative that the U.S. government station well-trained Mandarin- or Fujianese-speaking immigration officers at some of the international airports. These officers must be capable of differentiating between Chinese from China, Taiwan, or other Asian countries by their appearance, accent, and language or dialect spoken.

6. U.S. authorities should step up patrol of the U.S.-Mexican and U.S.-Canadian borders.

Entry overland, especially via Mexico, is the most popular and "safest" way to enter the United States because the detection rate is low. The goal of stopping Chinese at these borders must be added to the current border patrol policy, which deals primarily with illegal Mexican immigrants.

7. The U.S. government should deport convicted human smugglers even if they are green card holders or U.S. citizens.

Most undocumented Chinese could not make it to the United States without the assistance of human smugglers. Many snakeheads and their assistants are permanent residents or citizens of the United States, and when they are arrested and convicted they are merely imprisoned, and usually not for long. If the U.S. government would send these convicted smugglers back to China, I believe it would have a major deterrent effect.

Given the exceedingly complex social, political, and economic forces behind the Chinese human trade, when all is said and done, the improvement of human rights in China is more likely to succeed as a deterrent than any bolstering of law enforcement. The conventional strategy of limiting "pull" factors (e.g., American wealth and freedom) has been pursued at the expense of neglecting major "push" factors (e.g., adverse social, economic, and political conditions in China). But in my view the massive emigration of Chinese, both legal and illegal, will subside only when China significantly improves its political and economic conditions.

CONCLUSION

The problem of the Chinese human trade has the potential to grow even worse. According to Wu Pang-guo, the deputy premier of China, 120 million residual laborers or floating migrants were residing in rural areas of China by the mid-1990s, and this population was expected to increase to 200 million by the year 2000. Mr. Wu warns that if the problem is not solved promptly, it will become not only a major economic problem but also a social and political catastrophe (*China Times,* July 27, 1995).

No matter what measures are taken, many Chinese are determined to come illegally to the United States at any cost. On my way back to the United States from China at the conclusion of my research, I passed through Hong Kong and fulfilled a promise to a Fuzhou couple to visit their son, who was being detained at the Lamtau Island prison for attempting to get to the United States with fake documents. I chatted with the young man for about thirty minutes and told him that I would call his family in China once I'd arrived home. When I asked him what he would like me to tell his family, he said:

> Ask my sister to find a snakehead for me right away. Tell her to look for the best snakehead; don't worry about how much it's going to cost. Tell her I will be deported back to China after I've served my sentence here, and that means I should be back home by March 12. Tell her I want to

stay at home for only a couple of days. Ask her to make sure whatever snakehead she finds is able to get me out of China by March 15. I must go to the United States.

Policy makers must be aware that some Chinese will attempt the illegal journey and join the more than 55 million overseas Chinese, no matter what the cost. I am convinced that the outflow of Chinese will stop only after the economic, political, and legal systems of China approach those of the industrialized and democratic countries. In the meantime, the best the world community can do is to create more opportunities for Chinese to emigrate legally, thus decreasing the human suffering associated with clandestine immigration and breaking the unfortunate link between immigration and the trafficking in human beings.

Glossary

CHINESE WORDS AND PHRASES listed here include Mandarin, Fujianese, and Cantonese. Letters in brackets indicate the language or dialect of the words and phrases (M for Mandarin, F for Fujianese, and C for Cantonese) and their English pronunciation. Mandarin words are transliterated in the pinyin style. Since Cantonese have no standardized transliteration style, I adopted the style of Fritz Chang's *A Cantonese-English Dictionary of Cantonese Gang Slang* (unpublished, 1995) and Roy Cowles's *The Cantonese Speaker's Dictionary* (Hong Kong: Hong Kong University Press, 1965).

chaoshu [M: chow-su]: Members of families with overseas connections.

chidaguofan [M: chi-tar-kor-fun]: Eating food from a huge bowl. Referring to the socialist system.

douzheng [M: tote-jen]: To struggle against.

falang [M: far-lung]: Barbershop. In China, some of the houses of prostitution are called falang.

fanshen [M: fun-san]: To restore one's social status.

getihu [M: kirk-tee-hoo]: Private entrepreneur.

guanxi [M: kwan-she]: Connections.

haojiao [F: how-jao]: Good feet, meaning reliable.

haoyong [M: how-jung]: Good to use, worthy.

huang su lung kay chi pai nien [M: huang-su-lung-kay-jee-pie-nien]: Wolves visiting chickens during the Chinese New Year, a phrase similar to the American "fox guarding the chicken coop."

huojiqi [M: hor-ji-chi]: Machines made of flesh and blood.

hutu [M: hoo-tu]: Silly.

jiang hu [M: jiang-hu]: Rivers and lakes, meaning lack of roots. A person who walks *jiang hu* is a small-time opportunist.

Jinshan [M: jin-sun]: Mountain of Gold or the United States.

jueshe [M: jew-sir]: Digging snakes, meaning alien smuggling.

ju jia [M: joo-jia]: Piggies, meaning slave labor or smuggled Chinese immigrants.

kekao [M: ker-kow]: Reliable.

kongshi [C: gong-she]: Business firms.

lakejia [M: la-kirk-jia]: Recruiter.

laodong giazao or *laogia* [M: lau-dong-kia-jau or lau-kia]: Reform through labor.

laodong jiaoyang or *laojiao* [M: lau-dong-jau-young or lau-jau]: Reeducation through labor.

lihai [M: lee-hi]: Shrewd.

Lujian Laodong Jiaoyang Suo [M: lu-jiang-lau-dong-jau-young-sor]: Lujian Institute of Reeducation through Labor.

lutou [M: lu-tow]: Foyer.

ma zhai [C: ma-jia]: Little horse or enforcer.

maiguan [M: my-kwan]: Buying checkpoint by bribing officials.

Meiguo [M: may-kor]: Beautiful Country or the United States.

meiguoke [M: may-kor-kirk]: Guest from the Beautiful Country.

paitou [M: pie-tow]: An aura of wealth.

renshe [M: lan-sir]: Human snakes. Smuggled Chinese are so called for their ability to wiggle through tight border controls.

san chi [M: san-chi]: Arrogance.

shetou [M: sir-tow]: Snakeheads. Human smugglers are so named because of their image of slithering from point to point along clandestine routes.

sidu [M: see-toot]: It means private passage. A person who leaves China with an authentic passport and a valid visa but later uses fake travel documents to enter the United States or other countries from a transit country is guilty of *sidu.*

tian hua luan duo [M: tian-hua-luan-duo]: Flowers dropping from the sky, meaning all very rosy.

tiefanwan [M: ter-fun-won]: An iron rice bowl, meaning a government job in China.

tongzi [M: tung-ji]: Bucket, or ship.

toudu [M: tow-toot]: Stealing passage without travel documents.

xiangzhen chiyeh [M: xiang-jen-chi-yeah]: Village and township enterprises.

xiang [M: xiang]: Township.

yanhong [M: yen-hung]: Eyes turned red with envy.

yazi [M: ya-ji]: Little duck or illegal immigrant.

youbanfa [M: yo-bun-far]: Highly capable.

zhen [M: jen]: Town.

zhentou [M: jen-tow]: Pillows.

Appendix A
Research Methods

THE SURVEY was conducted in a field office located near New York City's Chinatown, which is situated on the lower east side of Manhattan. Interviews were conducted face to face by Fujianese-speaking interviewers.

Utilizing the scant information available about the characteristics of the target population of smuggled Chinese, I adopted a quasi-quota sampling method to generate the sample. According to official and media reports, most unauthorized Chinese in the United States are young, working-class Fujianese males (U.S. Senate 1992). Most came after the June 1989 Tiananmen Square protests. Thus, quotas according to the subjects' sex, age, place of residency (in China), arrival year, and method of entry at the U.S. entry point were established. I sought a total of three hundred illegal Chinese immigrants.

I used two techniques to recruit subjects for this study. First, I developed sources of potential subjects through contacts with friends and interviewers who could provide me with access to smuggled Chinese. Second, I utilized traditional snowball referral methods (Biernacki and Waldorf 1981). That is, subjects who were referred to me by friends and interviewers were asked, after their interviews, to refer colleagues, friends, or relatives who were smuggled into the United States.[1]

My interviewers asked the respondents to provide the following information:

1. Background characteristics: sex, age, place of birth, town of origin, education, occupation in China, occupation in the United States, marital status, number of children (if any), number of years in the United States at the time of the interview.
2. Psychosocial information prior to immigration: reasons for immigrating to the United States, reasons for using illegal means of immigration, level of knowledge of "American society," family reaction to subject's intention to leave China, living and working conditions in China.
3. Migratory process I (the initial stage, in China): method and frequency of contact with "guarantor" in America, initial contacts with human smugglers, preparation for the trip, method used to leave China.
4. Migratory process II (the middle stage, in transit points): number and names of transit cities and countries, means of entering and leaving the transit points, amount of time spent at each transit point, living arrangements at transit points, role of the smugglers at the transit points.

171

5. Migratory process III (the final stage, in the United States): method of entering the United States, point of entry, difficulties (if any) in entering the United States, method used to travel to destination from entry point, roles played by smugglers in the United States.
6. General information about the trip: amount of time it took to arrive in New York City from point of departure, problems encountered throughout the trip, structure of human smuggling operation.
7. Financial and employment aspects: amount of smuggling fee, degree of negotiation with smugglers on smuggling fee (if any), amount of down payment, arrangements made to pay the balance, method used to repay the debt to friends and relatives who paid the fee, amount of time needed to repay the debt, monthly income in the United States, employment history in the United States, purpose and frequency of remitting money back to China.
8. Social and emotional adjustment: problems of adjusting to a new environment.
9. Work and leisure: general working conditions, number of working hours per week, degree and frequency of unemployment and underemployment, type of work normally sought, type of leisure activities.
10. Crime and victimization: degree of involvement in criminal activities (if any), type of illegal behavior, exploitation by employers, other types of victimization by both non-Asians and Asians.

The questionnaire was originally written in English, translated into Chinese, pre-tested, and revised to assure validity and reliability. Some open-ended questions were coded by a bilingual research assistant prior to data entry. A reliability check was conducted to ensure accuracy and consistency in coding.

Interviewer training involved the following: explaining the purpose and sponsorship of the research, explaining how to phrase questions in an appropriately anonymous and non-threatening manner, and how to ensure subjects' confidentiality. Procedures for protecting subjects interviewed for this research were reviewed by the Institutional Review Board of Rutgers University.

The following procedures were adopted to ensure the cooperation and comfort of respondents when being interviewed:

1. Each subject was paid $40 cash after the interview.[2]
2. No information that could identify the subject was collected.
3. The field office where the interviews were conducted was close to Chinatown for the convenience of the subjects, but was located somewhat away from the community so that the subjects did not have to worry about being seen talking to "outsiders."
4. Almost all the interviews were conducted in the Fuzhou dialect, the dialect of the smuggled immigrants.

Using a standardized questionnaire, my interviewers interviewed three hundred smuggled Chinese immigrants. Appendix B, Table 1 shows the personal characteristics of my subjects. According to Liang (1998), the Chinese government conducted a 1 percent population sample survey in 1995 to collect background information on people who have left China. Liang compared the characteristics of the 361 immigrants from Fujian with my subjects and found the two samples to be remarkably similar in terms of sex, age, marital status, and education.

KEY INFORMANTS

I collected the second set of data from fifteen community leaders, activists, and social workers closely associated with unauthorized Chinese to cross-validate the data collected from the illegal immigrants. The sampling of community informants relied heavily on my personal knowledge acquired during prior studies in New York's Chinatown (Chin 1990, 1996).

FIELD RESEARCH

I performed observations in the Chinese community to record daily activities of illegal immigrants and collect field data. I visited restaurants, garment factories, employment agencies, and community associations where unauthorized Chinese congregated and talked to anyone who was willing to engage in a conversation with me. I also spent many hours hanging out in a Fujianese friend's clinic and chatting with her patients, who were predominantly smuggled immigrants from Fujian. I also accompanied many Chinese asylum seekers to the asylum office in Lyndhurst, New Jersey, and acted as their translator in the interviews.

RESEARCH TRIPS TO CHINA

In my attempt to understand why so many Chinese want to immigrate and are willing to suffer so much both on their journeys and after their arrival in their host countries, I needed to examine what it means to be an overseas Chinese. In doing so, I looked not only at the experiences of the Chinese in their new environment but also at the social meaning of illegal immigration for people in the sending communities. For this reason, I took two research trips to China to visit some of the major sending villages in Fujian Province.

The purpose of the research trips was to interview family members of illegal migrants, human smugglers, and villagers who were planning to come to the United States unlawfully. I also frequented well-known temples where family members of migrants go to pray for the safe arrival and good fortune of their loved ones who have left home for the United States. I also attended ceremonies sponsored by families of illegal migrants to celebrate their family members' settlement in the United States.

In December 1993, during my stay in the Fuzhou area, I visited a number of villages under the guidance of a Fujianese research assistant and my father-in-law, who was born and grew up in the area. Twenty subjects were interviewed informally at length, and dozens of others were asked about issues related to the massive outflow of their neighbors.

My research assistant recruited the subjects. Most of them were either her friends or neighbors. She conducted most of the interviews informally at the subjects' homes. Some were interviewed in a restaurant or the lobby of the hotel where I was staying. After the interviews, I wrote down the content of the interviews. I also kept a research diary.

I did not pay the subjects money. They were willing to be interviewed mainly because they knew my research assistant and were aware that we had interviewed their family members in New York City. Illegal immigration is a fact of life in the Fuzhou area, and not one person I met there was afraid or ashamed of having a family member abroad illegally. For them, going abroad was a good thing to do, and whether a person achieved this goal legally or illegally was insignificant. What mattered was whether a person made it or not: Those who succeeded were praised and those who failed were looked down upon.

I went to Fujian for the second time in July 1995 and stayed there for about a month. This time I spent most of my time in Pingtan, an island county located not far from Fuzhou City. The area is the number one sending community for illegal immigrants to Taiwan and is also a major staging point for immigrants going to the United States by sea (Chang 1995). Again I was accompanied by my father-in-law. I interviewed sixty-three subjects during the trip.

Because I have a large number of in-laws living in Pingtan, I was able to interview more subjects during this trip than on my first. Many of them have family members, friends, or neighbors who were smuggled abroad. I conducted the interviews informally in Mandarin. After the interviews, I wrote down what had been discussed. The subjects were not paid for the interviews.

NEWSPAPER AND MAGAZINE REPORTS

I made a concerted effort to collect and analyze all the relevant media reports. Starting in 1986, I have been collecting, categorizing, and analyzing a large number of English and Chinese newspaper and magazine articles on illegal Chinese immigration. I have relied on five major English newspapers: the *New York Times*, the *New York Daily News*, the *New York Post*, the *Washington Post*, and the *South China Morning Post* (Hong Kong). The two major Chinese newspapers I have read are the *World Journal* and the *Sing Tao Daily*, both published in New York City. I also collected news articles on Chinese illegal immigration in Chinese newspapers in China, Taiwan, and Hong Kong, though not exhaustively.

I also read widely in popular weekly magazines such as *Time*, *Newsweek*, *U.S. News and World Report*, *The New Yorker*, and the *Far Eastern Economic Review*. I tried to collect as many articles on the issue as possible from popular Chinese weekly or monthly magazines such as the *World Journal Weekly*, *People and Events*, and the *Asia Weekly Magazine*, among others.[3]

Appendix B
Tables

TABLE 1. Respondents' Personal Characteristics ($N = 300$)

	N	Percentage
Sex[a]		
Male	238	79
Female	62	21
Region of origin		
Changle	146	49
Fuzhou	62	21
Tingjiang	56	19
Lianjiang	23	7
Other[b]	13	4
Education		
Elementary	87	29
Junior high	130	43
Senior high	69	23
College	14	5
Marital status		
Married	205	68
Single	93	31
Widowed	2	1
Number of children[c]		
None	7	3
One	46	22
Two	88	43
Three	47	23
Four or more	19	9
Employed in China?		
Yes	246	82
No	54	18
Occupation in China[d]		
Professional	30	12
Store owner	68	28
Clerical	40	16
Blue-collar worker	85	35
Farming/fishing	23	9

[a]Age in years: mean, 31.8; median, 32; mode, 30.

[b]Seven from Minhou County, one from Fuqin City, and five from Zhejiang Province.

[c]For married and widowed subjects only.

[d]Only for subjects who were employed in China. Their monthly income in yuan: mean, 998; median, 350; mode, 200. The exchange rate was approximately 8.50 yuan = $1 at the time of the interviews.

TABLE 2.   Matching Immigrant-Sending and Immigrant-Receiving Communities or Countries

Sending communities	Main receiving communities
Guangdong Province	Hong Kong
Guangxi Province	Australia

Fujian Province
    Changle City, Tingjiang Township, Mawei District,
    Fuzhou City, and Lianjiang County
	United States

Fuqin City	Japan
Pingtan County	Taiwan
Zhejiang Province	Western Europe

TABLE 3.   Respondents' Reasons for Coming to the United States (N = 300)

Self-reported reason(s)	N	Percentage
Make money	182	61
Make money/avoid one-child policy	28	9
Make money/enjoy freedom	14	5
Make money/reunite with spouse	13	4
Make money/other reasons[a]	8	3
Make money/escape from personal problems	7	2
Make money/under pressure to migrate	5	2
For political freedom	14	5
Envious of others who are living in America	11	4
Want to see the wonderful United States	8	3
Parents' idea	4	1
For religious freedom	3	1
Other	3	1

[a]Other reasons include: unhappiness with official corruption in China, desire to see outside world, desire to find a spouse, and desire to obtain U.S. permanent residency.

TABLE 4.   How Snakeheads Were Contacted, by Year of Arrival in the United States (N = 300) (percentage distribution)

	Year of arrival						
How snakeheads were contacted	1988 and before (%)	1989 (%)	1990 (%)	1991 (%)	1992 (%)	1993 (%)	Total (%)
Through friends/relatives abroad	30	28	6	5	6	12	12
Through friends/relatives in China	57	61	76	82	76	79	74
I found them	9	9	14	13	10	7	10
They approached me	4	2	4	0	8	3	4

TABLE 5.   Average Smuggling Fee by Smuggling Route and by Year of Arrival (in U.S. dollars)

Smuggling route	Year of arrival						Average
	1988 and before	1989	1990	1991	1992	1993	
Air	23,500	27,134	27,459	29,708	30,166	31,230	29,070
Sea	22,000	25,875	27,420	27,250	27,958	28,611	27,560
Land	22,888	23,780	24,756	28,078	28,063	28,472	26,276
Average	22,956	25,017	27,014	29,016	28,857	29,688	27,745

TABLE 6.   Association between Trip Characteristics and Smuggling Routes (N = 298)

	Smuggling routes			
	Air (N = 141)	Sea (N = 35)	Land (N = 122)	Overall mean or %
Average number of days between registration and departure	74	29	46	57
Average number in group	5	133	86	53
Average number of days on trip	107	64	75	89
Average smuggling fee (in US$)	29,070	27,560	26,276	27,745
Average down payment (in US$)	4,044	2,023	2,148	3,069
Average number of transit points	3.1	0.8	2.5	2.6
Percentage required to make down payment and provide sponsor	38	11	36	34
Percentage detected by U.S. authorities at point of entry	64	20	11	37
Percentage detained by smugglers in the U.S.	53	83	72	64
Percentage abused on the trip	11	21	22	17
Percentage who saw others abused on the trip	11	47	39	27

TABLE 7.   Associations between Subject Characteristics and Safe House
Detention Rate ($N = 300$)[a]

	Sample N	Detained N	Percentage
Sex			
Male	236	150	64
Female	62	41	66
Age*			
20 or under	40	31	78
21 to 30	98	68	69
31 to 40	108	66	61
41 or over	52	26	50
Marital status			
Single	93	66	71
Married	205	125	61
Region of origin			
Changle	146	97	66
Fuzhou	61	38	62
Tinjiang	55	36	66
Lianjiang	23	12	52
Other	13	8	62
Education			
Elementary	57	39	68
Junior high	159	104	65
Senior high or above	82	48	59
Relatives in America?			
Yes	208	130	63
No	88	59	67
Safe house detention rate for the entire sample			64

[a]Number of missing observations: age = 2; marital status = 2; region of origin = 2; education = 2; relatives in America? = 4.

*$p < .05$

TABLE 8.   Associations between Smuggling-Related Variables and Safe House Detention Rate ($N = 300$)[a]

	Sample N	Detained N	Percentage
Method of departing China**			
Air	83	34	41
Land	121	73	60
Sea	94	84	89
Method of entering America**			
Air	141	74	53
Land	122	88	72
Sea	35	29	83
Year of arrival**			
1988 or before	23	9	39
1989	42	19	45
1990	49	24	49
1991	61	39	64
1992	62	50	81
1993	61	50	82
Method of finding snakehead*			
Friends/relatives abroad	36	18	50
Friends/relatives in China	222	141	64
Subject initiated the contact	29	22	76
Smuggler initiated the contact	11	10	91
Made a down payment?			
Yes	240	158	66
No	58	33	57
Safe house detention rate for the entire sample			64

[a]Number of missing observations: method of departing China = 2; method of entering America = 2; year of arrival = 2; method of finding snakehead = 2; made a down payment? = 2.

*$p < .05$

**$p < .001$

TABLE 9.   Employment Patterns among Smuggled Chinese in New York City ($N = 300$)

	N	Employed full-time ($N = 234$)	Employed part-time ($N = 32$)	Unemployed ($N = 34$)
		Percentage		
Total sample	300	78	11	11
Sex*				
Male	238	74	12	14
Female	62	93	5	2
Year of arrival				
1988 or before	23	87	0	13
1989	43	84	5	12
1990	50	84	10	6
1991	61	75	13	12
1992	62	84	6	10
1993	61	62	21	17
Route				
Air	143	79	13	8
Sea	35	77	3	20
Land	122	77	11	12
Region of origin				
Changle	146	77	10	13
Fuzhou	62	69	19	11
Tingjiang	56	86	5	9
Lianjiang	23	82	9	9
Other	13	92	0	8

*$p < .01$

TABLE 10. Occupation Patterns among Smuggled Chinese in New York City ($N = 266$)[a]

		Percentage			
	N	Garment factory work ($N = 92$)	Restaurant work ($N = 127$)	Construction work ($N = 19$)	Other types of work ($N = 28$)
Total sample	266	35	48	7	11
Sex**					
Male	205	22	58	9	11
Female	61	77	13	0	10
Year of arrival*					
1988 or before	20	25	70	0	5
1989	38	18	68	3	11
1990	47	36	47	13	4
1991	54	33	48	6	13
1992	56	36	46	5	13
1993	51	49	26	12	14
Region of origin*					
Changle	127	44	37	7	12
Fuzhou	55	24	55	11	11
Tinjiang	51	22	63	4	12
Lianjiang	21	29	62	10	0
Other	12	50	42	0	8

[a]Part-time workers included.
*$p < .05$
**$p < .001$

TABLE 11. Respondents' Average Weekly Working Hours, Monthly Wage, and Hourly Wage by Type of Occupation in 1993 ($N = 226$)[a]

	Garment factory ($N = 84$)	Restaurant ($N = 115$)	Construction ($N = 9$)	Other ($N = 18$)	Average
Work hours/week	70	72	52	56	69
Monthly wage (in US$)	1,252	1,520	1,740	1,387	1,359
Hourly wage[b] (in US$)	4.3	4.7	7.1	5.4	4.7

[a]Part-time employees excluded. Number of missing observations = 8.
[b]The minimum hourly wage in 1993 was $4.25.

TABLE 12. Respondents' Average Hourly and Monthly Wage by Industry and Position in 1993 ($N = 226$)[a]

	N	Hourly wage[b] (US$)	Monthly wage (US$)
Garment factory	84	4.3	1,252
Cloth presser	18	5.9	1,530
Cloth distributor/matcher	1	4.9	1,400
Button installer	3	4.6	1,366
General helper	2	4.2	1,300
Ends sewer	10	4.2	1,200
Seamstress	41	3.7	1,121
Cloth hanger	7	3.5	1,193
Restaurant	115	4.7	1,520
Waiter	6	6.1	1,775
Cook	40	5.4	1,598
Chef	4	5.3	1,725
Food preparer	2	4.5	1,450
Cashier	5	4.4	1,400
Food fryer	6	4.3	1,325
Delivery person	9	4.0	1,272
Kitchen helper	26	3.6	1,146
Dishwasher	2	2.4	800
Renovation/construction	9	7.1	1,740
Other	18	5.4	1,387
Warehouse supervisor	1	8.7	1,500
Food packer	3	6.8	1,066
Delivery driver	2	6.4	1,550
Mover	2	5.3	1,200
Store cashier	2	4.1	1,200
Bakery store worker	1	3.2	900

[a]Part-time employees, business owners, and prostitutes excluded. Number of missing observations = 8.
[b]The minimum hourly wage in 1993 was $4.25.

TABLE 13. Respondents' Future Plans ($N = 295$)

	Plan to stay in America ($N = 190$)	Plan to go back to China ($N = 85$)	Not sure ($N = 20$)
Average age	32	32	27
Length of stay in the U.S. (in months)[a]	31	31	17
Percentage male[b]	73	93	80
Percentage owing money[c]	52	69	80
Percentage employed full-time[d]	84	71	60

[a]Average length of stay: 30 months.
[b]Percentage male: 79 percent.
[c]Percentage owing money: 59 percent.
[d]Percentage employed full-time: 78 percent.

TABLE 14.   Arrests of Snakeheads and Would-Be Migrants by Chinese
Authorities, as Reported in News Media (1991–1994)

Date	Place	No. snakeheads	No. would-be migrants
May '91	Fuzhou	14	Unknown
Apr. '92	Guangzhou	12	150
Nov. '92	Fuzhou	4	62
Apr. '93	Fuzhou	0	157
Jul. '93	Fuzhou	76[a]	Unknown
Aug. '93	Guangdong	12	139
Nov. '93	Fuzhou, Guangzhou, and Hangzhou	1	151
Nov. '93	Guangzhou	0	32
Dec. '93	Lianjiang	1	76
Jun. '94	Fuzhou	31[b]	Unknown
Jun. '94	Wenzhou	0	72

[a]Thirty-two defendants were sentenced to jail for one to five years and forty-four were sent to re-education through labor camps.
[b]Five defendants received prison terms of five years or more, sixteen were sentenced to two to four and a half years, and ten to less than one and a half years.

TABLE 15.   U.S. Official Detection Rate by Subject Characteristics ($N = 300$)[a]

	Sample N	Detected N	Percentage
Sex			
Male	236	92	39
Female	62	19	31
Age			
20 or under	40	11	28
21 to 30	99	42	42
31 to 40	108	43	40
41 or over	53	15	28
Marital status			
Single	93	33	36
Married	205	78	38
Region of origin			
Changle	146	62	43
Fuzhou	62	23	37
Tinjiang	56	14	25
Lianjiang	23	8	35
Other	13	4	31
Education			
Elementary	58	18	31
Junior high	159	58	37
Senior high or above	83	35	42
Average U.S. official detection rate for sample			37

[a]Number of missing observations: age = 2; marital status = 2.

TABLE 16.   U.S. Official Detection Rate by Smuggling-Related Variables
($N = 300$)[a]

	Sample N	Detected N	Percentage
Year of arrival*			
1988 and before	23	1	4
1989	43	7	16
1990	50	25	50
1991	61	30	49
1992	62	23	37
1993	61	25	41
Method of entry*			
Land	122	13	11
Sea	35	7	20
Air	143	91	64
Method of finding snakeheads			
Friends/relatives abroad	36	10	28
Friends/relatives in China	222	84	38
Subject initiated contact	31	12	39
Smuggler initiated contact	11	5	46
Arrived with a guide?*			
Yes	206	53	26
No	93	58	62
Average U.S. official detection rate for sample			37

[a]Number of missing observations: arrived with a guide? = 1.
*$p < .001$

TABLE 17.   Arrests of Big Snakeheads by U.S. Authorities, as Compiled from Media Reports (1985–1996)

Date	Place	No. defendants	Charge
May '85	Los Angeles	4	Air smuggling
May '89	New York City	6	Smuggling via Canada
Jul. '89	New York City	5	Smuggling via Canada
Jun. '90	Mobile, Alabama	2	Smuggling via Panama
Feb. '92	Atlanta	8	Conspiracy to smuggle people into the U.S., bribing INS officials
Nov. '92	New York City	2	Smuggling 150 illegals on board the Ching Wing
May '93	Jersey City, New Jersey	3	Smuggling and kidnapping 57 aliens
Jun. '93	San Francisco	3[a]	Smuggling 180 aliens on board the Angel
Jun. '93	New York City	8[b]	Smuggling and kidnapping 22 aliens
Aug. '93	New York City	3	Smuggling and money laundering
Mar. '94	Mitcheville, Maryland	7[c]	Smuggling and kidnapping
Nov. '94	New York City	9[d]	Conspiracy to smuggle people into the U.S.
Apr. '95	Newark, New Jersey	14	Transporting Chinese into the U.S. on four smuggling ships
Apr. '96	San Francisco	23[e]	Transporting 280 smuggled Chinese by Angel and Pelican boats

[a]Including one Fuk Ching gang member.

[b]All eight defendants were members of the White Tigers gang and were tried and found guilty.

[c]Five of the defendants pled guilty and were sentenced to less than five years in prison. Two went to trial and were convicted.

[d]These arrests were the result of Operation Snakeheads.

[e]These arrests were the result of Operation Sea Dragon.

186   Appendix B

TABLE 18.   RICO Indictments of Chinese Gangs, Tongs, Triads, and Other
Crime Groups, Compiled from Media Reports (1985–1996)

Year	Name	No. defendants	Major charges	Law enforcement agencies involved[a]	Outcome
1985	Ghost Shadows	25	Murder	NYPD and FBI	Convicted
1986	Shih Hsiao Poa	3	Prostitution	INS	Convicted
1986	Bamboo United	9	Drug dealing	NYPD and FBI	Convicted
1990	On Leong	33	Gambling	FBI and IRS	Hung jury
1991	Green Dragons	16	Murder	NYPD and FBI	Convicted
1991	Born-to-Kill	8	Murder	NYPD and ATF	Convicted
1993	Fuk Ching	20	Murder	NYPD and FBI	Convicted
1993	Wo Hop To	19	Arson	SFPD, FBI, ATF, and RHKP	Convicted
1993	Tung On Assoc., Tsung Tsin Assoc., and Tung On Gang	15	Murder	NYPD, DEA, and ATF	Convicted
1993	White Tigers	8	Murder	NYPD and DEA	Pled guilty
1994	Tung On	15	Murder	FBI and DEA	Convicted
1994	Ghost Shadows	21	Murder	FBI and DEA	Pled guilty
1994	Flying Dragons	33	Murder	FBI and DEA	Pled guilty
1995	No name	14	Alien smuggling	INS	Convicted
1996	No name	5	Heroin and alien smuggling	FBI	Convicted
1996	Tung Mun	7	Murder	NYPD	Convicted
1996	Flying Fist	7	Murder	ATF	Convicted
1996	Taiwan Brotherhood	4	Extortion	FBI and NYPD	Convicted
1996	Fujianese Flying Dragons	64[b]	Murder	INS, FBI, and NYPD	Convicted

[a]Agencies: NYPD (New York City Police Department), SFPD (San Francisco Police Department), ATF (Bureau of Alcohol, Tobacco, and Firearms), FBI (Federal Bureau of Investigation), DEA (Drug Enforcement Administration), IRS (Internal Revenue Service), INS (Immigration and Naturalization Service), RHKP (Royal Hong Kong Police).

[b]Twenty-seven defendants escaped, including the gang's two primary leaders, who were believed to have returned to China. The gang was accused of involvement with at least two smuggling ships. One of the gang's primary leaders was later arrested in Lianjiang by Chinese authorities.

Notes

CHAPTER 1

1. I use "China" to refer to the People's Republic of China, and "Chinese," unless otherwise indicated, to denote legal or illegal immigrants from, or citizens of, the People's Republic. "Taiwan" refers to the Republic of China on Taiwan and "Taiwanese" refers to immigrants from, or citizens of, Taiwan.

2. For purposes of this study, people are considered "smuggled" into the United States if they paid fees to a smuggler, even if they arrived with authentic travel documents.

3. The U.S. Immigration and Nationality Act defines a passport as "any travel document issued by competent authority showing the bearer's origin, identity and nationality if any, which is valid for entry of the bearer into a foreign country." If a Chinese passport holder plans to travel to the United States, he or she must apply for a visa or entry permit at the U.S. embassy in Beijing or the U.S. consulates in Shanghai, Guangdong, and Chengdu (in Sichuan Province). Fake travel documents include impostor documents (genuine, unaltered documents used by someone other than the person to whom they were issued); photo-sub passports (passports altered by photo substitution; it is often necessary to alter the biographical and physical data in the original passport as well); counterfeit passports, and fantasy passports (passports not issued by competent authority or issued by a country that does not exist); and "camouflage passports" (passports issued in the name of a country that no longer exists) (Riley 1994).

4. In Chinese communities of America, smuggled Chinese are called *renshe* (human snakes or snake people) for their ability to wiggle through tight border controls. Human smugglers are called *shetou* (snakeheads) because they slither from point to point along clandestine routes. The smuggling activity is known as *jueshe* or "digging snakes" (Han 1993). See the glossary for a list of Chinese terms used in this book.

5. I will use "Fujianese" to refer to people who live in or who are from the Fuzhou area in Fujian Province. These people are also sometimes referred to as "Fuzhounese," "Fukienese," or "Hokienese."

6. To prevent immigrants from abusing the asylum program, the Illegal Immigration Reform and Immigrant Responsibility Act of 1996 (IIRIRA) empowers low-level immigration inspectors at the airport to issue a final and unreviewable order of deportation if they are convinced that an asylum seeker does not have credible fear of persecution in his or her country. Before the enactment of IIRIRA, only federal judges had such power. This new deportation process,

called "expedited removal," has been heavily criticized for its failure to protect genuine refugees (Human Rights Watch 1998; Lawyers Committee for Human Rights 1998).

CHAPTER 2

1. All the materials from the Chinese media presented in this book were translated by me.

2. In China, provinces are geographical areas where citizens speak different dialects and have different customs. Chinese provinces range in geographical size, much as U.S. states do. In China, there are five levels of government—central, provincial, city, county or township (*xiang* or *zhen*), and village (*cun*). For example, Fujian is a province, Fuzhou is a city, Tingjiang is a township, and Sen Mei is a village within Tingjiang. The two most powerful political figures in each level of government are the Chinese Communist Party secretary and the administrative head. Normally, party secretaries are much more influential than administrative heads at all levels of government.

3. When a subject's occupation is given, it is the occupation he or she had in China.

4. During the Cultural Revolution (1966–1976), Chinese leaders encouraged students known as Red Guards to attack the "four old" elements within Chinese society—old customs, old habits, old culture, and old thinking. As a result, thousands of intellectuals, rich people, and anyone who was considered "feudal" or "reactionary" were publicly humiliated, beaten, imprisoned, or killed. Millions were relocated to the countryside to purify themselves through labor (Spence 1990).

5. The Chinese government pampers overseas Chinese investors because China needs both capital and expertise from abroad. Many local Chinese business people consider themselves at a disadvantage when competing with overseas Chinese and have reason to want to emigrate in order to return as overseas Chinese entrepreneurs.

6. According to INS statistics, in 1992 Chinese nationals filed only 3,464 asylum claims. In 1993 that number jumped to 14,485. Asylum applications by Chinese nationals remained high in 1994 (10,871) before dropping to 4,915 in 1995.

7. According to a survey of 421 smuggled Chinese migrants conducted in Taiwan, 51 percent were detected when they entered Taiwan. Those who went undetected stayed in Taiwan for an average of only 131 days before Taiwan authorities arrested them. Once a Chinese migrant is arrested there, he or she is deported. Illegal Chinese immigrants are not allowed to remain in Taiwan under any circumstances (Wang et al. 1997). The detection rate for my respondents, by contrast, was only 37 percent (see Chapter 9).

8. It is not clear what percentage of Chinese asylum claims are frivolous, but it is widely believed that few Chinese applicants have actually been persecuted by the Chinese government. When detained at JFK airport and questioned

about her fake documents, a twenty-three-year-old female respondent reported, "I told him, as instructed by my snakehead, 'I am married. I already have a child, and I am now pregnant. The Chinese government was about to force me to have an abortion,' and so on and so forth. It was really a joke. I was not even married. They took my fingerprints and released me."

9. Recently, due to its own lack of space, the INS has begun to hand asylum seekers over to prisons, where they may be mixed in with accused and convicted criminals. Unlike criminal prisoners, INS detainees have no exact sentence or set date by which they can expect to be released (Human Rights Watch 1998).

10. In China, many so-called *falang* (barbershops) are actually houses of prostitution, though I am not sure what type of barbershop this respondent worked in.

11. Although divorce is unlikely to be condemned in large cities like Beijing and Shanghai, couples in rural areas still view it as a stigma and try hard to prevent it (Kristof and WuDunn 1994).

12. Chinese often speak sarcastically about the relationship between education, job, and *guanxi* in China: "You may be very good at mathematics, physics, and chemistry, but nothing compares to having a 'good' father when it comes to establishing a bright future for yourself."

13. A famine that claimed 20 million lives or more between 1959 and 1962 (Spence 1990).

14. Any Chinese citizen can be labeled "counterrevolutionary" by Chinese government officials if he or she does not follow communist rule. It is a term that has been loosely used by communist party cadres to discredit and punish people for a variety of reasons.

15. The word *douzheng* (struggle against) is loosely and widely used in China. It is, according to the Chinese communists, the ideal way to deal with "enemies," "criminals," and "counterrevolutionaries." When a person or idea is *douzheng*, the masses are mobilized to punish or attack the person or idea without limit.

16. With 1.2 billion people, China is the most populous country in the world. During the 1950s and 1960s the central government encouraged people to have as many children as possible, resulting in a population boom. After Mao Zedong's death, Chinese leaders were convinced that population growth had to be controlled if China wanted to become a developed country and they implemented the one-child policy.

17. The U.S. government has always been critical of human rights conditions in China. In 1994, the U.S. State Department reported that "there continued to be widespread and well-documented human rights abuses in China, in violation of internationally accepted norms, stemming both from the authorities' intolerance of dissent and the inadequacy of legal safeguards for freedom of speech, association, and religion. Abuses include arbitrary and lengthy incommunicado detention, torture and mistreatment of prisoners" (U.S. State Department 1995: 3).

CHAPTER 3

1. The illegal-entry scheme was called the "slot racket." According to Tsai (1986: 99), during visits to China "an American citizen of Chinese extraction who was eligible for reentry to this country, would report the birth of children, usually male, when there had been no such event. He thereby created a 'slot,' which was sold to someone who had no relatives to sponsor his entry into the United States."

2. Chinese triads began as secret societies three centuries ago, formed by patriotic Chinese to fight the Qing dynasty, which they considered oppressive and corrupt. When the Qing government collapsed and the Republic of China was established in 1912, triads degenerated into criminal groups (Morgan 1960). Most triad societies now have their headquarters in Hong Kong, but their criminal operations have no national boundaries (Booth 1991; Black 1992; Chin 1995; Y. Chu 1996). Tongs were established in America as self-help groups by the first wave of Chinese immigrants in the mid-nineteenth century (Dillon 1962). Historically, tongs have been active in gambling, prostitution, extortion, and violence (U.S. Senate [1877] 1978; Chin 1990, 1996).

3. A guarantor is a person who agrees to pay the smuggling fees on behalf of an illegal migrant.

4. Chinese immigrants in the United States can be divided into four groups: (1) U.S. citizens or naturalized Chinese, referred to as Chinese Americans in this book; (2) green card-holders or permanent residents (permanent residents can become U.S. citizens within three to five years, depending on how they obtained their permanent resident status); (3) Chinese of non-immigrant status, such as students with F-1 visas or tourists with B-2 visas; and (4) illegal migrants who are either smuggled into the United States or who enter the country with non-immigrant visas and stay illegally after their visas expire.

5. In China, everyone must have an identification card issued by the Public Security Bureau that is required for many social occasions and transactions and is often shown when purchasing air or train tickets or when seeking a passport.

6. I am not certain how widespread this practice is but it is safe to say that Chinese who are smuggled out of China by sea are significantly less likely to sign a contract than those who leave by air. The following is a sample of the smuggling contract:

Party A (client) would like to go abroad and he/she hereby asks Party B to assist him/her. Based upon the foundation of a common goal, both parties agree to the following terms:

1. Both parties concur that the total fee for Party A to go abroad is US$30,000. Party A will provide Party B with a copy of his/her identification card and an application fee for US$1,000, and US$2,000 after traveling documents are secured (the US$3,000 will be deducted from the US$30,000 total fee after Party A arrives in the United States). Party A will also present Party B with the address and phone number of a

relative in America who will serve as the sponsor. Party B will give Party A the name of a relative in China as the guarantor.

2. Party B will be responsible for obtaining a passport and a visa for Party A (all expenses are included in the US$30,000 fee). If Party A fails to make the trip within three months after the agreement is signed, Party A has the right to terminate this agreement, and Party B should return the application fee to Party A.

3. After Party A leaves China, Party B shall be responsible for all expenses abroad. Party A shall not have to bear any expense until his/her arrival in the United States.

4. If there are accidents on the trip, Party B shall be responsible; however, if the mishaps are the direct result of Party A not following Party B's instructions and arrangements, Party A shall bear the consequences of these accidents.

5. If Party A is arrested, both parties will split the bail money. The bail money is not included in the US$30,000 fee. Half of the bail money has to be paid by Party A or his/her family.

6. If Party A is repatriated back to China and is being fined by the Public Security Bureau, Party B will pay part of the fines out of the US$1,000 application fee. The rest shall be paid by Party A. The US$2,000 down payment will not be returned to Party A by Party B, since this money is needed to cover the expenses for securing travelling documents and buying air tickets.

7. If Party A is sentenced to prison, Party B shall not bear any responsibility. While Party A is on the road, neither party shall terminate this agreement; Party B shall not sell Party A to another smuggler, Party A shall not change snakehead.

8. After Party A has arrived in the United States, his/her sponsor shall be bound by this agreement. If the sponsor fails to do so, Party B has the right to hold Party A as hostage. If the balance is not paid within 7 days after Party A's arrival, Party A will be charged $100 a day to cover meals and lodging.

9. After Party A arrives in the United States, he/she shall not attempt to escape from the control of Party B. If Party A does escape, his/her sponsor and family in China will still need to pay the balance.

10. This agreement becomes valid after both parties sign it. After Party A arrives in the United States, and the balance of the smuggling fee is paid, this agreement is terminated.

Signature of Party A _____

Signature of Party B _____

Date _____

7. A smuggled Chinese who arrived in America in February 1998 told me that his smuggler charged him $45,000 for the trip.

CHAPTER 4

1. For a Chinese citizen to travel abroad, he or she usually needs a Chinese passport, an exit permit issued by the Chinese Public Security Bureau (PSB), a visa (or entry permit) issue by the China-based embassy or consulate of the country of destination, and a second exit permit issued by the PSB. Written permission from the work unit is required before a person may apply for these documents. The purpose of a second permit is to allow the PSB, the work unit, and other "competent authorities" to de-register an exiting immigrant from neighborhood, work unit, and other records (U.S. Department of State 1995). Most countries do not require U.S. passport holders to apply for a visa to enter their territories. As a result, a U.S. passport holder can travel to most countries at will.

2. Even though a substantial number of my respondents arrived in New York via California, few settled in California's three major cities—Los Angeles, San Francisco, and San Diego—probably because none of these cities has a well-established Fujianese community.

3. According to INS statistics, 14,688 people were arrested at JFK airport in 1992 for entering the United States without proper documents. The number of Chinese arrested at JFK Airport increased from 107 in 1990 to 1,233 in 1991 and 3,064 in 1992 (*World Journal*, June 14a, 1993).

4. An advance parole certificate is a document issued by the INS to non-immigrants who are in the process of adjusting their immigration status but need to return to their native countries. The certificate enables the holder to reenter the United States without a visa.

5. Since the *Golden Venture* incident, the INS has expanded its detention capacity by constructing its own facilities, contracting with private corrections corporations, and farming out detainees to county jails.

6. Unlike entry into the United States with fraudulent documents, entry without any documents at all is not a crime, and snakeheads are well aware of this. They therefore instruct their clients to get rid of fake documents once they board U.S.-bound flights (Farah 1995).

7. According to a Chinese government official whom I interviewed, most people from the Fuzhou area who are going abroad for the first time are not allowed to fly out of Fuzhou airport. Instead they must travel to Shenzhen and enter Hong Kong via the Lauhu Bridge Station border checkpoint. Shenzhen, in Guangdong Province, is considered to be the "Hong Kong of China" because it is a special economic zone that Chinese authorities are developing into a commercial center to connect China with Hong Kong and other industrialized countries (van Kemenade 1997).

8. Chinese government officials traveling abroad on government businesses are issued "official passports," also known as "red cover passports." Ordinary Chinese passports are brown.

9. One reason why many of my respondents were not detained for lengthy periods was that they had snakeheads with bail money. Keep in mind, however,

that my sample may be skewed in that only those who "succeeded" at illegal immigration were interviewed.

10. The INS has recently created a legal fiction in claiming that American airports are technically not in the United States, hence thwarting attempts by illegal immigrants (especially travelers without visas) requesting political asylum.

CHAPTER 5

1. Passengers aboard the *Chin Wing* were believed to be allowed to stay in the United States and apply for political asylum.

2. My interviews were conducted between November and December of 1993. Thus my estimations do not include undetected smuggling ships that arrived in the United States, Mexico, or Guatemala after 1993. Moreover, I may have underestimated the actual number of undetected ships because the survey included only a small percentage of the total number of Chinese who were smuggled into the United States before 1993. Or I may have overestimated the number of undetected ships because multiple subjects aboard the same ship may have given different information (e.g., number of passengers, point of departure, point of entry). In that case I might have counted the same boat more than once.

3. Fishing boats are remodeled into smuggling ships in Taiwan or Hong Kong. The most crucial task involves the reconstruction of the hold—a coldroom for the catch—into sleeping quarters for passengers.

4. Many respondents who came by sea stated that their ships almost sank in the high seas, probably because so many people were crowded in poorly maintained ships not designed to transport people. According to a report by the U.S. Coast Guard, "With few exceptions, vessels engaged in the transpacific smuggling of illegal PRC [Chinese] migrants have been in very poor condition and often in danger of sinking. Most have been crudely converted from Asian longline fishing vessels to serve specifically as smuggling platforms. The manner to which migrants are housed on these vessels is reminiscent of the Atlantic slave trade in the 18th and 19th centuries, where large numbers of people were packed into hot, poorly ventilated, and confined spaces. Given the lack of seaworthiness and the large number of people on board, there is a very real potential for a major loss of life at sea" (U.S. Coast Guard, 1996: 2).

5. This respondent was released after he applied for political asylum.

CHAPTER 6

1. It is not clear why the subject made this statement about her safe house, but judging from other interviews it is possible or even likely that she was raped there.

2. The subject and her companions must have destroyed the Argentinean passports before their plane landed in Canada.

3. In Asia, illegal Chinese immigrants are called *yazi,* or little duck, because, in a sense, they are treated like ducks by their snakeheads. That is, the snakeheads move their clients from one place to another quite often, but the people being transported have no idea of where they are going. Consequently, the safe houses for illegal Chinese migrants in Asia are called "duck houses." According to Ted Conover (1987), illegal Mexican migrants are often called *pollo* (chicken) in border slang, and Mexican human smugglers are known as *pollero,* handlers or sellers of chickens.

CHAPTER 7

1. A Chinese newspaper reported the incident as follows: "Two illegal immigrants, a 25-year-old male and a 16-year-old girl, were bailed out by their snakehead from the INS detention centers in Los Angeles and San Diego for $800 each and transported to New York City. In the safe house, the girl was handcuffed and repeatedly raped and sodomized by eight debt collectors while a dozen other immigrants watched. Moreover, the two immigrants were forced to engage in oral and anal sex in front of the debt collectors. The two, with wounds all over their bodies, escaped and screamed for help at a nearby bank. The girl was two months pregnant when the police rescued her" (*Sing Tao Daily,* November 18, 1993: 31).

2. Eight subjects did not say how the second portion of the payment was made.

3. This may be due to the fact that the earlier wave of smuggled Chinese came mainly from Tingjiang and Lianjiang. Therefore, many more trafficked immigrants from these two areas may have a family member or close relative living in the United States. Although there is also a large number of overseas Chinese from Changle, they are more likely to be found in Southeast Asia.

CHAPTER 8

1. Workers in Chinese-owned restaurants and garment factories normally do not have paid—or even unpaid—vacation (Kwong 1997). Most workers are therefore forced to quit their jobs if they need to take a break from work. When they are ready to resume work, they look for another job. During the interviews, respondents who were unemployed said that they were confident they would soon resume work. My multivariate analysis revealed no statistically significant factors about my subjects or their means of entry or length of stay in the United States that could explain unemployment.

2. In New York City, many people work long hours and on weekends, whether they are wage workers or salaried professionals.

3. Before calculating the hourly and monthly wages of full-time workers in my study, I removed six subjects (four restaurant owners, one construction/renovation business owner, and one gambling den owner/operator) from the sample because they were self-employed and their income was substantially

higher than those of wage earners. I also excluded a female subject who was working part-time as a prostitute and earning $4,000 a month.

4. Although I did not ask the respondents whether they paid income tax, it is no secret in the Chinese community that a substantial number of employees in the Chinese business sector are paid in cash by their employers so they can avoid paying taxes. To prevent being audited by the Internal Revenue Service, some employers pay their employees most of their income in cash and a small portion by check. Thus, both the employers and employees pay taxes on only a small portion of their income. When we examined the monthly income of smuggled Chinese, the amount we were considering was their actual take-home pay, on which they probably would not pay taxes.

5. Because of overlap between these three categories, these figures exceed the total of 264.

6. Most illegal Chinese immigrants, however, and some legal ones as well, are denied benefits such as paid leave, health care insurance, and related medical coverage by their Chinese employers.

7. The term "mental illness" as used here should not be taken to mean illness based on medical diagnosis but on the common understanding of my respondents and other lay people.

8. Rent for a two-bedroom apartment in Chinatown may range from $800 to $1,200 a month. Often, a person rents a unit and sublets it to a dozen people, so that each tenant pays only about $100 a month for rent. Landlords are generally reluctant to see so many people living in their properties, but they tolerate it because they know their tenants are unlikely to complain, regardless of the condition of the property.

9. In the aftermath of the *Golden Venture* incident, federal prosecutors in New York City indicted the Fuk Ching gang as a racketeering enterprise. More than a dozen core members of the gang were arrested and most pleaded guilty to the charges against them. The primary leader of the gang was arrested in Hong Kong after he fled the United States. He was extradited back to the United States to stand trial for murder. This is probably why the respondent said the gang "was history," even though the gang is still active in Chinatown.

CHAPTER 9

1. The provision stated that:

To severely punish criminals responsible for organizing human smuggling networks and transporting people illegally across borders, to prevent Chinese citizens from becoming involved in illegal immigration, and to maintain order in the management of border crossings, the following supplemental regulations are appended to our criminal law:

1. Offenders who are involved in organizing the smuggling of people across borders shall be sentenced to prison from two to seven years and fined. Offenders who are: (1) leaders of smuggling groups; (2)

repeated offenders or are involved in the movement of a large number of people; (3) responsible for the serious injury or death of immigrants; (4) guilty of restricting the freedom of immigrants; (5) accused of resorting to violence to resist law enforcement inspection; (6) making huge profits from alien smuggling; or (7) charged with other aggravating circumstances; shall be sentenced to seven years or more, up to life imprisonment, and fined or their assets seized. Moreover, offenders who kill, assault, rape, or sell people, or murder or assault immigration inspectors, shall be sentenced to death.

2. The above rule is equally applicable to the punishment of employees of government-sponsored labor export companies and international trade units who are involved in the human trade.

3. Non-government employees who provide fake or genuine travel documents to human smugglers or prospective immigrants shall be sentenced to five years or less and fined. Serious and chronic offenders shall be sentenced to five years or above and fined.

4. Defendants who are involved in transporting illegal immigrants shall be sentenced to five years or less and fined. If the defendant is: (1) a chronic or repeat offender; (2) utilizes unfit transportation tools; (3) generates a huge amount of illegal gains; or (4) commits the offense under other aggravating circumstances, he or she may have to serve between five to ten years. If the offender's activity results in the death or injury of people, or if he or she resists being inspected by public security or border patrol officers, he or she may be subjected to a confinement of seven years or more and fined. If the offender commits murder, assault, rape, or kidnapping in the process of transporting people, or involves in the killing or assaulting of government officials, he or she will be sentenced to death. If the defendant plays a minor role in this type of crime, he or she will be confined in a police lockup or local jail for 15 days and fine between 5,000 and 50,000 yuan.

5. First-time would-be illegal immigrants will be subjected to confinement in a local police lockup for 15 days and be fined between 1,000 and 5,000 yuan. Repeat offenders may be sentenced to two years or less of imprisonment and fined.

6. Law enforcement authorities who facilitate and provide help to prospective immigrants may be sentenced to three years or less of imprisonment. Serious and chronic offenders can be sentenced to three to ten years of confinement. If an officer conspires with a smuggling group to commit a crime, he or she will be punished according to the above rules no.1 and no.4.

7. Profits from human smuggling activity and transportation equipment used in the activity will be confiscated.

2. According to Amnesty International's estimates, 2,900 criminals were executed worldwide in 1995. Of those, 2,190 executions were carried out in

China (*World Journal,* June 15, 1996). The following year, China reportedly sentenced 6,100 people to death and carried out more than 4,300 executions (Faison 1997).

3. The media report that human smugglers have discovered a way to get around MRP passports. In 1988, Taiwanese smugglers ran a newspaper ad seeking drivers and collected applicants' personal information, including their ID card numbers. The information was then forwarded to Hong Kong-based smugglers, who produced fake Taiwanese ID cards using prospective Chinese immigrants' pictures. Smugglers in Hong Kong then sent the fake IDs back to the Taiwanese smugglers, who applied for Taiwan MRP passports and U.S. visas via travel agencies in Taiwan. In this way, all of the personal information on the MRP passports is bona fide and traceable—except that the pictures of the passport holders are would-be Chinese emigrants. The Taiwan-based smugglers sold the MRP passports to China-based smugglers for $8,000 apiece. When a Taiwan-based smuggler was arrested in Taipei, Taiwan authorities seized twenty-five of these fake MRP passports (*World Journal,* January 8, 1998: A10).

4. In 1992, the INS had only 6,000 beds nationwide, but it arrested more than 1 million undocumented immigrants of all nationalities (*New York Times,* November 21, 1993).

5. The captain of the *Golden Venture* served forty-one months in prison and was subsequently deported. He was arrested near the Washington State coast in December 1997 for attempting to smuggle five thousand pounds of marijuana into the United States (Fried 1997).

APPENDIX A

1. Due to the sensitive nature of the information being collected and the illegal status of the subjects, I anticipated potential problems with subjects' honesty that might affect data reliability and validity. To minimize this potential I hired mostly Fujianese-speaking female interviewers who were themselves illegal immigrants and these interviewers conducted all interviews in a private, natural setting located near the Fujianese community. I also pre-tested the questionnaire with ten illegal immigrants in a pilot study and then revised it, deleting questions that appeared to cause uneasiness among respondents. I was aware that using purposive sampling techniques would limit the generalizability of this study's results in a statistical sense, but because of lack of information about the population of smuggled Chinese in New York City, a random sample was not feasible.

2. I do not think this practice could have significantly affected the randomness of my sample, the honesty of my subjects, or the reliability of my data.

3. I am aware that some of the information in the news media on illegal Chinese immigration is not to be completely trusted, but I have found it useful in helping me understand how the problem is perceived in the public arena and assisting me in developing hypotheses that can be tested with my primary data.

References

IN ENGLISH

Anderson, Eric. 1993. "U.S. bids to curb smuggling of Chinese illegals." *South China Morning Post* May 24: 2.

Arpin, Claude. 1990. "Two investigations launched into illegal smuggling of Chinese citizens." *Gazette Montreal* April 18: 1.

Asimov, Nanette, and Pamela Burdman. 1993. "Baja coast now most convenient back door to U.S." *San Francisco Chronicle* April 29: A9.

Ayres Jr., B. Drummond. 1994. "New border defense stems volume of illegal crossings." *New York Times* October 6: D21.

Barth, Gunther. 1964. *Bitter Strength: A History of Chinese in the United States.* Cambridge: Harvard University Press.

Bean, Frank, George Vernez, and Charles B. Keely. 1989. *Opening and Closing the Doors: Evaluating Immigration Reform and Control.* Washington, D.C.: Urban Institute Press.

Bean, Frank, Barry Edmonston, and Jeffrey Passel, eds. 1990. *Undocumented Migration to the United States.* Washington, D.C.: Urban Institute Press.

Beck, Roy. 1996. *The Case Against Immigration.* New York: Norton.

Beck, Simon. 1995. "No mercy for II smugglers." *South China Morning Post* January 13: 8.

Bell, Bill, and Ying Chan. 1993. "Helpless in Hong Kong: We can't stem the tide, say shipyard officials." *New York Daily News* June 16: 23.

Bernstein, Richard. 1993. "Immigrants both renew and unsettle Chinatown." *New York Times* June 9: B2.

Bian, Yanjie, and John Logan. 1996. "Market transition and the persistence of power: The changing stratification system in urban China." *American Sociological Review* 61: 739–58.

Biernacki, Patrick, and Dan Waldorf. 1981. "Snowball sampling: Problems and techniques of chain referral sampling." *Sociological Methods and Research* 10: 141–63.

Black, David. 1992. *Triad Takeover: A Terrifying Account of the Spread of Triad Crime in the West.* London: Sidgwick and Jackson.

Bolz, Jennifer. 1995. "Chinese organized crime and illegal alien trafficking: Humans as a commodity." *Asian Affairs* 22: 147–58.

Booth, Martin. 1991. *The Triads.* New York: St. Martin's.

Boyd, Alan, and William Barnes. 1992. "Thailand an open door for illegal passages." *South China Morning Post* June 22: 6.

Branigin, William. 1995. "Report to Clinton urges global attack on growing trade in alien-smuggling." *Washington Post* December 28: A1.

———. 1996. "U.S. seeks fugitive Falls Church man after 3-year alien-smuggling probe." *Washington Post* April 21: A12.

Braude, Jonathan. 1992. "China jail for illegals under study." *South China Morning Post* May 30: A2.

Brazil, Eric, Malcolm Glover, and Larry Hatfield. 1993. "Daring smuggler lands 250 in city." *San Francisco Examiner* May 24: A1.

Brimelow, Peter. 1995. *Alien Nation: Common Sense about America's Immigration Disaster.* New York: Random House.

Brinkley, Joel. 1994. "For aliens, a Bahamas cruise is an easy way into the U.S." *New York Times* November 29: A1.

Burdman, Pamela. 1993a. "Huge boom in human smuggling—Inside story of flight from China." *San Francisco Chronicle* April 27: A1.

———. 1993b. "How gangsters cash in on human smuggling." *San Francisco Chronicle* April 28: A1.

———. 1993c. "Web of corruption ensnares officials around the world." *San Francisco Chronicle* April 28: A8.

———. 1993d. "American dream sours in N.Y." *San Francisco Chronicle* April 29: A8.

———. 1993e. "Business of human smuggling tests U.S. immigration policies." *San Francisco Chronicle* April 30: A1.

———. 1993f. "China cracks down on smuggling." *San Francisco Chronicle* November 19: A1.

———. 1993g. "Back home in China, smugglers are revered, feared." *San Francisco Chronicle* November 19: A14.

———. 1993h. "Deportees face harsh penalties." *San Francisco Chronicle* November 24: A1.

———. 1993i. "Desperate dreams of leaving for U.S.; Emigrants ignore Clinton administration smuggling crackdown." *San Francisco Chronicle* December 3: A1.

Bureau of Justice Statistics. 1992. *Criminal Victimization in the United States, 1990.* Washington, D.C.: U.S. Department of Justice.

Chan, Ying. 1993a. "Forced into sex slavery." *New York Daily News* May 17: 7.

———. 1993b. "China ships' unholy cargo." *New York Daily News* May 18: 7.

———. 1993c. "Smugglers spring trap on desperate Chinese." *New York Daily News* June 2: 4.

———. 1993d. "Stop smugglers, China gov't cries." *New York Daily News* June 14: 17.

———. 1995. "JFK gangs prey on Chinese; Victims grabbed for 'easy money.'" *New York Daily News* April 10: 5.

Chan, Ying, and James Dao. 1990a. "A tale of two immigrants." *New York Daily News* September 24: 21.

———. 1990b. "Crime rings snaking." *New York Daily News* September 23: 14.

_____. 1990c. "The official line: A nod and a wink." *New York Daily News* September 23: 15.

_____. 1990d. "Merchants of misery." *New York Daily News* September 24: 7.

Chan, Ying, James Dao, and Kevin McCoy. 1990. "Journey of despair: Out of China, into desperate debt." *New York Daily News* September 23: 4.

Chapman, E. C., Peter Hinton, and Jingrong Tan. 1992. "Cross-border trade between Yunnan and Burma, and the emergence of the Mekong corridor." *Thai-Yunnan Project Newsletter* 19: 15–19.

Charasdamrong, Prasong, and Subin Kheunkaew. 1992. "Smuggling human beings: A lucrative racket that poses a threat to national security." *Bangkok Post* July 19: 10.

Chin, Ko-lin. 1990. *Chinese Subculture and Criminality: Non-traditional Crime Groups in America.* Westport, Conn.: Greenwood Press.

_____. 1995. "Triad societies in Hong Kong." *Transnational Organized Crime* 1 (Spring): 47–64.

_____. 1996. *Chinatown Gangs: Extortion, Enterprise, and Ethnicity.* New York: Oxford University Press.

Chiswick, Barry. 1988. *Illegal Aliens: Their Employment and Employers.* Kalamazoo: Upjohn Institute for Employment Research.

Chow, Magdalen, and Glenn Schloss. 1996. "Jail for fake passports scam." *South China Morning Post* August 17: 1.

Chu, Jeannette. 1994. "Alien smuggling." *The Police Chief* June: 20–27.

Chu, Yiu-kong. 1996. "International triad movements." *Conflict Studies* 291. London: Research Institute for the Study of Conflict and Terrorism.

City of New York Department of City Planning. 1992. "The Newest New Yorkers: An Analysis of Immigration into New York City during the 1980s." New York: City of New York.

_____. 1993. "Estimates of undocumented aliens as of October 1992: Data from the U.S. Immigration and Naturalization Service compiled by the Population Division." New York: City of New York.

Claiborne, William. 1993. "U.S., Mexico end impasse on Chinese; Migrants on ships will be sent home." *Washington Post* July 15: A1.

Clark, Rebecca, Jeffrey Passel, Wendy Zimmermann, and Michael Fix. 1995. *Fiscal Impacts of Undocumented Aliens: Selected Estimates for Seven States.* Washington, D.C.: Urban Institute Press.

Conover, Ted. 1987. *Coyotes: A Journey through the Secret World of America's Illegal Aliens.* London: Heinemann.

_____. 1993. "The United States of asylum." *New York Times Magazine* September 19: 56–57, 74–76, 78.

Cornelius, Wayne. 1978. *Mexican Migration to the United States: Causes, Consequences, and U.S. Responses.* Cambridge: MIT Center for International Studies.

_____. 1989. "Impact of the 1986 US immigration law on emigration from rural Mexican sending communities." *Population and Development Review* 15 (4): 689–705.

Craig, Mark. 1995. "The New Coolie Trade: Organized Illegal Emigration for Chinese and its Implications for Australia." Master's Thesis, Griffith University (Australia).

Daniels, Lee A. 1991. "11 Chinese are arrested in abduction." *New York Times* November 30: 23.

Dao, James, and Ying Chan. 1990. "Thai city hub on smuggle route to U.S." *New York Daily News* September 24: 20.

Delgado, Hector. 1992. *New Immigrants, Old Unions.* Philadelphia: Temple University Press.

DePalma, Anthony. 1993. "Refugees are sent back to China hours after they dock in Mexico." *New York Times* July 18: A1.

DeStefano, Anthony. 1994. "Feds crack 'snakehead' alien smuggling ring." *New York Newsday* November 10: A79.

———. 1997. "Immigrant smuggling through Central America and the Carribean." In *Human Smuggling,* ed. Paul Smith, 134–155. Washington, D.C.: Center for Strategic and International Studies.

DeStefano, Anthony, David Kocieniewski, Kevin McCoy, and Jim Muvaney. 1991. "Smuggling rings victimize clients." *New York Newsday* January 6: 8.

Devroy, Ann, and Al Kamen. 1993. "U.S. asks Mexico to accept 659 Chinese detained at sea." *Washington Post* July 9: A1.

Dillon, Richard. 1962. *The Hatchet Men: The Story of the Tong Wars in San Francisco's Chinatown.* New York: Coward-McCann.

Dobson, Chris. 1993. "Hong Kong ships of shame." *South China Morning Post The Spectrum* February 7: 1.

———. 1994. "U.S. seeks aid to stop boat with illegal immigrants." *South China Morning Post* April 17: 6.

Dobson, Chris, and Kavita Daswani. 1994. "Costa del triads." *South China Morning Post* March 27: 14.

Dowty, Alan. 1987. *Closed Borders: The Contemporary Assault on Freedom of Movement.* New Haven: Yale University Press.

Dreifus, Claudia. 1996. "The worst job in the world?" *New York Times Magazine* October 27: 52–54.

Dubro, James. 1992. *Dragons of Crime: Inside the Asian Underworld.* Markham, Ontario: Octopus Publishing Group.

Duffy, Brian. 1993. "Coming to America." *U.S. News and World Report* June 21: 26–31.

Dugger, Celia. 1996a. "Federal agency fines company a record $1.5 million for hiring illegal immigrants." *New York Times* March 22: L1.

———. 1996b. "A tattered crackdown on illegal workers." *New York Times* June 3: A1.

Dunn, Ashley. 1994. "After crackdown, smugglers of Chinese find new routes." *New York Times* November 1: A1.

———. 1995. "Brooklyn killing is linked to a kidnapping in Seattle." *New York Times* September 7: B3.

Eager, Marita. 1992. "Patten in tough stand against illegals." *South China Morning Post* July 18: 3.

Engelberg, Stephen. 1994. "In immigration labyrinth, corruption comes easily." *New York Times* September 12: A1.

English, T. J. 1991. "Slaving away." *The Smithsonian* February: 10–14.

_____. 1995. *Born to Kill.* New York: William Morrow.

Faison, Seth. 1993a. "Alien-smuggling suspect eluded immigration net." *New York Times* June 10: A1.

_____. 1993b. "U.S. tightens asylum rules for Chinese: Using *Golden Venture* as warning to others." *New York Times* September 5: 45.

_____. 1993c. "Kidnappings tied to fall of a gang." *New York Times* October 5: B1.

_____. 1994a. "U.S. officials fear ship is new smuggling wave." *New York Times* April 7: B3.

_____. 1994b. "Chinatown gang leader to be returned to U.S." *New York Times* April 12: B1.

_____. 1994c. "Major suspect charged in immigrants' fatal voyage." *New York Times* April 14: B3.

_____. 1995. "Brutal end to an immigrant's voyage of hope." *New York Times* October 2: A1.

_____. 1996. "Police try to build bridge to China." *New York Times* June 1: L23.

_____. 1997. "In surge of death sentence, China doomed 6,100 last year." *New York Times* August 26: A4.

Farah, Douglas. 1995. "A free-trade zone in the traffic of humans." *Washington Post* October 23: A1.

Finckenaeur, James, and Elin Waring. 1998. *Russian Mafia in America.* Boston: Northeastern University Press.

Finder, Alan. 1995. "Despite tough laws, sweatshops flourish." *New York Times* February 6: A1.

Finnegan, Mike, and Ying Chan. 1993. "61 Chinese nabbed in N.J. garage 'jail.'" *New York Daily News* May 25: 23.

Fisher, Ian. 1993. "Waves of panic yield to elation of refugees." *New York Times* June 7: A4.

Freedberg, Luis. 1993. "Immigration now a security concern." *San Francisco Chronicle* June 23: A1.

Freedman, Dan. 1991. "Asian gangs turn to smuggling people." *San Francisco Examiner* December 30: A7.

Fried, Joseph. 1993. "Smugglers prey on immigrant detainees, I.N.S. critics say." *New York Times* November 21: 32.

Fritsch, Jane. 1993. "One failed voyage illustrates flow of Chinese immigration." *New York Times* June 7: A1.

Gargan, Edward. 1981. "Asian investors battle for footholds in Chinatown." *New York Times* December 29: A1.

Glaberson, William. 1989. "6 seized in smuggling Asians into New York." *New York Times* May 5: B3.

Gladwell, Malcolm, and Rachel Stassen-Berger. 1993a. "Alien-smuggling ship runs aground." *Washington Post* June 7: A1.

_____. 1993b. "Human cargo is hugely profitable to New York's Chinese underworld." *Washington Post* June 7: A10.

Glover, Malcolm, and Lon Daniels. 1993. "Smuggler main ship hunted on high seas." *San Francisco Examiner* June 3: 1.

Gold, Jeffrey. 1995. "Chinese gang accused of racketeering." *The Record* March 23: A5.

Goldstone, Jack. 1997. "A tsunami on the horizon? The potential for international migration from the People's Republic of China." In *Human Smuggling*, ed. Paul Smith, 48–75. Washington, D.C.: Center for Strategic and International Studies.

Gomez, Rita, and Andy Gilbert. 1993. "Immigration officer charged over passport forgery." *South China Morning Post* October 20: 1.

Government of the People's Republic of China. 1994. "Position of China on the question of illegal migration." Background paper submitted to the International Response to Trafficking in Migrants and the Safeguarding of Migrant Rights, Eleventh IOM Seminar on Migration sponsored by the International Organization for Migration (IOM), Geneva, October 26–28.

Greenhouse, Steven. 1994. "U.S. moves to halt abuses in political asylum program." *New York Times* December 3: 8.

Grinberg, Leon, and Rebecca Grinberg. 1989. *Psychoanalytic Perspectives on Migration and Exile.* New Haven: Yale University Press.

Gurak, Douglas, and Fe Caces. 1992. "Migration networks and the shaping of migration systems." In *International Migration Systems: A Global Approach*, ed. Mary Kritz, Lin Lean Lim, and Hania Zlotnik. Oxford: Clarendon.

Haller, Karen. 1997. "Shadow people." *Connecticut Magazine* June: 54–61.

Harris, J. R., and Michael Todaro. 1970. "Migration, unemployment, and development." *American Economic Review* 60: 126–142.

Hatfield, Larry D. 1989. "Gambling devastates Asia immigrants." *San Francisco Examiner* August 28: A2.

Hevesi, Dennis. 1993. "8 captives are freed in Brooklyn." *New York Times* June 27: 27.

_____. 1994. "Judge rejects a plea bargain for defendants in ship deaths." *New York Times* April 9: B1.

Hondagneu-Sotelo, Pierrette. 1994. *Gendered Transitions: Mexican Experiences of Immigration.* Berkeley: University of California Press.

Hong, Ying, and Henry Vandenburgh. 1995. "Chinese illegal immigration flow to the United States." Unpublished manuscript.

Hood, Marlowe. 1993a. "The new slaves of Chinatown." *South China Morning Post* June 13: 1.

_____. 1993b. "High price of a passport to misery." *South China Morning Post* June 13: 2.

_____. 1993c. "The Taiwan connection." *South China Morning Post* December 27: 11.

Human Rights Watch. 1998. "United States locked away: Immigration detainees in jails in the United States." 10 (1)(G).

Hurtado, Patricia. 1993. "Chinese kidnap suspects detail scheme." *New York Newsday* June 11: 33.

Ianni, Francis. 1974. *Black Mafia: Ethnic Succession in Organized Crime*. New York: Simon and Schuster.

Ignatius, Sarah. 1993. An Assessment of the Asylum Process of the Immigration and Naturalization Service. Cambridge: Harvard Law School.

Interagency Working Group. 1995. "Presidential Initiative to Deter Alien Smuggling: Report of the Interagency Working Group. Summary." Unpublished.

International Civil Aviation Organization (ICAO). 1994. "Sanctions of air companies." Background paper presented at the International Response to Trafficking in Migrants and the Safeguarding of Migrant Rights, Eleventh IOM Seminar on Migration sponsored by the International Organization for Migration (IOM), Geneva, October 26–28.

International Organization for Migration (IOM). 1994. "Trafficking in migrants: Characteristics and trends in different regions of the world." Discussion paper presented at the International Response to Trafficking in Migrants and the Safeguarding of Migrant Rights, Eleventh IOM Seminar on Migration sponsored by the International Organization for Migration (IOM), Geneva, October 26–28.

_____. 1996. "Trafficking in migrants: Some global and regional perspectives." Paper submitted for The Regional Conference on Migration, Puebla, Mexico, March 13-14.

James, Daniel. 1991. *Illegal Immigration—An Unfolding Crisis*. Lanham, Md.: University Press of America.

Jeter, Jon, and Pierre Thomas. 1994. "Chinese hostages found in P.G. house; 63 held." *Washington Post* April 7: A1.

Kamen, Al. 1991a. "A dark road from China to Chinatown: Smugglers bring increasing flow of illegal immigrants to U.S." *Washington Post* June 17: A1.

_____. 1991b. "U.S. seizes illegal aliens from China." *Washington Post* September 5: A5.

_____. 1992a. "'Private prison' holds airline passengers seeking U.S. asylums." *Washington Post* January 19: A1.

_____. 1992b. "The search for the *Lo Sing* No. 3." *Washington Post* March 12: A19.

_____. 1993. "Chinese helping stem flow of illegal immigrants." *Washington Post* November 1: A6.

Kennedy, Randy. 1995. "Five men face charges of murder in a slaying." *New York Times* September 21: B3.

Kifner, John. 1991. "Abducted Chinese illegal aliens rescued." *New York Times* January 8: B3.

Kinkead, Gwen. 1992. *Chinatown: A Portrait of a Closed Society.* New York: Harper Collins.

Kleinfield, N. R. 1986. "Mining Chinatown's 'Mountain of Gold.'" *New York Times* June 1: D1.

Kleinnecht, William. 1996. *The New Ethnic Mobs: The Changing Face of Organized Crime in America.* New York: Free Press.

Kristof, Nicholas. 1991. "Law and order in China means more executions." *New York Times* January 15: A2.

_____. 1993. "Where Chinese yearn for 'beautiful' U.S." *New York Times* June 20: A1.

Kristof, Nicholas, and Sheryl WuDunn. 1994. *China Wakes.* New York: Vintage Books.

Kwong, Peter. 1987. *The New Chinatown.* New York: Hill and Wang.

_____. 1994. "The wages of fear." *Village Voice* April 26: 25–29.

_____. 1997. *Forbidden Workers: Illegal Chinese Immigrants and American Labor.* New York: New Press.

Larmer, Brook, and Melinda Liu. 1997. "Smuggling people." *Newsweek* March 17: 34–36.

Lau, Alan Man S. 1993. "Statement by Alan Man S. Lau, Chairman of Fukien American Association at a press conference held at 125 East Broadway, New York, September 28."

Lavigne, Yves. 1991. *Good Guy, Bad Guy: Drugs and the Changing Face of Organized Crime.* Toronto: Random House.

Lawrence, Susan. 1993. "Smuggling gangs flourish." *New York Daily News* June 12: 6.

Lawyers Committee for Human Rights. 1993. *Criminal Justice with Chinese Characteristics: China's Criminal Process and Violations of Human Rights.* New York: Lawyers Committee for Human Rights.

_____. 1998. *Slamming "The Golden Door": A Year of Expedited Removal.* New York: Lawyers Committee for Human Rights.

Lay, Richard. 1993. "The gangland fiefdom of terror." *South China Morning Post* June 27: 4.

Lee, Adam. 1992. "Macau drive against illegals." *South China Morning Post* September 2: 7.

Leicester, John. 1993. "Dreaming the American dream in Fujian." *The Standard* June 25: 11.

Leung, Jimmy. 1992. "Illegals' policy to stay despite influx." *South China Morning Post* May 29: 4.

Li, Ling. 1997. "Mass migration within China and the implications for Chinese emigration." In *Human Smuggling,* ed. Paul Smith, 23–47. Washington, D.C.: Center for Strategic and International Studies.

Liang, Zai. 1998. "Emigration from Fujian: A sending country perspective." Paper presented at the "International Migration and Transnational Crime" conference, Rutgers University–Newark, May 15.

Lii, Jane. 1995a. "Chinese immigrant flees an Asian smuggling gang a second time." *New York Times* February 23: B1.

_____. 1995b. "Week in sweatshop reveals grim conspiracy of the poor." *New York Times* March 12: 1.

_____. 1995c. "Union and waiters face off at vocal protest in Chinatown." *New York Times* March 13: B3.

Loo, Chalsa. 1991. *Chinatown*. Westport, Conn.: Greenwood Press.

Long, Patrick Du Phuoc. 1996. *The Dream Shattered*. Boston: Northeastern University Press.

Lorch, Donatella. 1991. "Immigrants from China pay dearly to be slaves." *New York Times* January 3: B1.

_____. 1992. "A flood of illegal aliens enters U.S. via Kennedy: Requesting political asylum is usual ploy." *New York Times* March 18: B2.

Lyall, Sarah. 1992. "Albany sues U.S. on aliens held in prison." *New York Times* April 28: B1.

Lyman, Stanford M. 1974. *Chinese Americans*. New York: Random House.

Lyons, Thomas. 1994. "Economic reform in Fujian: Another view from the villages." In *The Economic Transformation of South China*, ed. Thomas Lyons and Victor Nee. Ithaca: Cornell University East Asia Program.

Mahler, Sarah. 1995. *American Dreaming: Immigrant Life on the Margins*. Princeton: Princeton University Press.

Maltz, Michael. 1985. "Defining organized crime." In *Handbook of Organized Crime in the United States*, ed. Robert Kelly, Ko-lin Chin, and Rufus Schatzberg, 21–38. Westport, Conn.: Greenwood Press.

Marshall, Ineke Haen, ed. 1997. *Minorities, Migrants, and Crime*. Thousand Oaks, Calif.: Sage Publications.

Martin, Mildred Crowl. 1977. *Chinatown Angry Angel*. Palo Alto, Calif: Pacific Books.

Massey, Douglas, Joaquin Arango, Graeme Hugo, Ali Kouaouci, Adela Pellegrion, and J. Edward Taylor. 1993. "Theories of international migration: A review and appraisal." *Population and Development Review* 19 (3): 431–66.

Mooney, Paul, and Melana Zyla. 1993. "Bracing the seas and more: Smuggling Chinese into the US means big money." *Far Eastern Economic Review* April 8: 17–19.

Morawska, Ewa. 1990. "The sociology and historiography of immigration." In *Immigration Reconsidered: History, Sociology, and Politics*, ed. Virginia Yans-McLaughlin. New York: Oxford University Press.

Morgan, W. P. 1960. *Triad Societies in Hong Kong*. Hong Kong: Government Press.

Mydans, Seth. 1992. "Chinese smugglers' lucrative cargo: Humans." *New York Times* March 21: A1.

_____. 1995. "Clampdown at border is hailed as success." *New York Times* September 28: A16.

Myers, Willard. 1992. "The United States under Siege: Assault on the Borders: Chinese Smuggling 1983–1992." Unpublished manuscript.

_____. 1994. "Transnational ethnic Chinese organized crime: A global challenge to the security of the United States, Analysis and recommendations." Testimony of Willard Myers, Senate Committee on Foreign Affairs, Subcommittee on Terrorism, Narcotics, and International Operations, April 21.

_____. 1996. "The emerging threat of transnational organized crime from the East." *Crime, Law, and Social Change* 24: 181–222.

_____. 1997. "Of qinging, qinshu, guanxi, and shetou: The dynamic elements of Chinese irregular population movement." In *Human Smuggling*, ed. Paul Smith, 93–133. Washington, D.C.: Center for Strategic and International Studies.

The Nation (Bangkok). 1994. "Former smuggler claims immigration graft." November 9: A2.

New York Times. 1993. "200 Chinese deportees flee Mexican guards." May 16: 29.

_____. 1993. "Voyage to life of shattered dreams." July 23: B1.

_____. 1993. "INS plan for detainees." August 17: B3.

_____. 1993. "Smugglers prey on immigrant detainees, I.N.S. critics say." November 21: 32.

_____. 1993. "An increasing sense of vulnerability: Mourning a murder victim, Chinese express frustration with crimes at restaurants." December 3: B1.

_____. 1994. "Chinatown holds its first parade to mark mainland anniversary." September 26: B3.

North, David, and Marion Houstoun. 1976. *The Characteristics and Role of Illegal Aliens in the U.S. Labor Market: An Exploratory Study.* Washington, D.C.: Linton and Company.

Oi, Jean. 1989. *State and Peasant in Contemporary China: The Political Economy of Village Government.* Berkeley: University of California Press.

Ong, Paul, Edna Bonacich, and Lucie Cheng, eds. 1994. *The New Asian Immigration in Los Angeles and Global Restructuring.* Philadelphia: Temple University Press.

Padavan, Frank. 1994. "Our teeming shore." New York State Senate Committee on Cities.

Pan, Lynn. 1990. *Sons of the Yellow Peril.* Boston: Little, Brown.

Perea, Juan F., ed. 1997. *Immigrants Out!: The New Nativism and the Anti-Immigrant Impulse in the United States.* New York: New York University Press.

Perez, Ramon "Tianguis". 1991. *Diary of an Undocumented Immigrant.* Houston: Arte Publico Press.

Piore, Michael. 1979. *Birds of Passage: Migrant Labor in Industrial Societies.* Cambridge: Cambridge University Press.

Pomfret, John. 1993. "Chinese refugees' new western stop: East Europe." *Washington Post* November 9: A1.

Porter, Doug. 1992. "Trade, drugs and HIV/AIDS in the Shan State border areas." *Thai-Yunnan Project Newsletter* 19: 24–27.

Portes, Alejandro and Ruben Rumbaut. 1990. *Immigrant America: A Portrait.* Berkeley: University of California Press.

Rabinovitz, Jonathan. 1992. "2 men killed in Queens shooting." *New York Times* August 10: B3.

Reid, Alexander. 1986. "New Asian immigrants, new garment center." *New York Times* May 10: A1.

Riley, Peter. 1994. "Passport examination techniques." *The Police Chief* June: 37–39.

Rimer, Sara. 1992. "Crammed in tiny, illegal rooms, tenants at the margins of survival." *New York Times* March 23: A1.

Rotella, Sebastian. 1993. "7 ships being tracked as migrant smugglers." *Los Angeles Times* July 10: 1.

Salyer, Lucy. 1995. *Laws Harsh as Tigers: Chinese Immigrants and the Shaping of Modern Immigration Law.* Chapel Hill: University of North Carolina Press.

Samora, Julina. 1971. *Los Mojados: The Wetback Story.* Notre Dame: University of Notre Dame Press.

Saxton, Alexander. 1971. *The Indispensable Enemy: Labor and the Anti-Chinese Movement in California.* Berkeley: University of California Press.

Schemo, Diana Jean. 1993. "Survivors tell of voyage of little daylight, little food and only hope." *New York Times* June 7: B5.

Schloss, Glenn. 1996. "Kai Tak smuggling racket surge." *South China Morning Post* August 5: 1.

Schmid, Alex, ed. 1996. *Migration and Crime.* Milan: International Scientific and Professional Advisory Council of the United Nations Crime Prevention and Criminal Justice Program.

Schmitt, Eric. 1996. "Senate votes bill to reduce influx of illegal aliens." *New York Times* May 3: A1.

Seagrave, Sterling. 1995. *Lords of the Rim: The Invisible Empire of the Overseas Chinese.* New York: G. P. Putnam's Sons.

Sellin, Thorsten. 1938. *Culture Conflict and Crime.* New York: Social Science Research Council.

Siemens, Maria. 1996. "European responses to the phenomenon of illegal migration: National and international initiatives." Paper presented at the International Conference on Migration and Crime: Global Problems and Responses, Courmayeur Mont Blanc, Italy, October 5–7, 1996, sponsored by International Scientific and Professional Advisory Council of the United Nations Crime Prevention and Criminal Justice Program.

Sinclair, Kevin. 1993. "Life and death in land of illegals." *South China Morning Post* May 22: 5.

Smith, Paul. 1997. "Chinese migrant trafficking: A global challenge." In *Human Smuggling,* ed. Paul Smith. Washington, D.C.: Center for Strategic and International Studies: 1–22.

Song, Yann-huei. 1992. "United States ocean policy: High seas driftnet fisheries in the North Pacific Ocean." *Chinese Yearbook of International Law and Affairs* 11: 64–137.

Sontag, Deborah. 1993. "Reshaping New York City's Golden Door." *New York Times* June 13: A1.

South China Morning Post. 1993. "Taiwan pushed on II problem." August 28: 7.

Spence, Jonathan. 1990. *The Search for Modern China.* New York: Norton.

Stalk, Jeffrey. 1993. "Dutch focus on smuggling of Chinese." *International Herald Tribune* May 7: 1.

Stark, Oded. 1991. *The Migration of Labor.* Cambridge: Basil Blackwell.

Stark, Oded, and David Bloom. 1985. "The new economics of labor migration." *American Economic Review* 75: 173–178.

Storti, Craig. 1991. *Incident at Bitter Creek: The Story of the Rock Springs Chinese Massacre.* Ames: Iowa State University Press.

Stout, David. 1995. "Detention jail called worst than prison." *New York Times* June 19: B5.

Strom, Stephanie. 1991. "13 held in kidnapping of illegal alien." *New York Times* January 2: B3.

Sun, Lena. 1992. "Smuggling of people, goods is big business in China." *Washington Post* March 14: A1.

Sung, Betty Lee. 1967. *Mountain of Gold: The Story of the Chinese in America.* New York: MacMillan.

Superior Court of New Jersey. 1995. *State of New Jersey vs. Dan Xin Lin et al.* Bergen County, Law Division, Indictment No. S-644–94.

Suro, Roberto. 1994. "On immigration, a question of fairness; Advocates for long-detained Chinese allege interference with asylum process." *Washington Post* December 20: A3.

Tam, Bonny. 1992. "198 illegals arrested in Tin Shui Wai." *South China Morning Post* September 8: 2.

Taylor, Edward. 1992. "Remittances and inequality reconsidered: Direct, indirect, and intertemporal effects." *Journal of Policy Modeling* 14: 187–208.

Todaro, Michael. 1976. "Internal Migration in Developing Countries." Geneva: International Labor Office.

Todaro, Michael, and Lydia Maruszko. 1987. "Illegal migration and US immigration reform: A conceptual framework." *Population and Development Review* 13: 101–114.

Torode, Greg. 1993a. "Immigration HQ criticized over illegals." *South China Morning Post* February 10: 3.

_____. 1993b. "United effort to net smuggling gang." *South China Morning Post* February 18: 2.

_____. 1993c. "Triads use HK agency for illegals." *South China Morning Post* March 15: 1.

Torres, Vicki. 1993. "2 men tell of torture at hands of smugglers." *Los Angeles Times* October 3: B1.

Treaster, Joseph. 1993. "Behind immigrants' voyage, long reach of Chinese gang." *New York Times* June 9: A1.

Tsai, Shih-shan Henry. 1986. *The Chinese Experience in America.* Bloomington: Indiana University Press.

Tyler, Patrick. 1995. "For Taiwan's frontier islands, the war is over." *New York Times* October 4: A3.

U.S. Coast Guard. 1996. "Migrant smuggling in the 1990s: The law enforcement perspective." Honolulu: Coast Guard District Fourteen, Law Enforcement Branch.

U.S. Commission on Immigration Reform. 1994. *U.S. Immigration Policy: A Report to Congress.* Washington, D.C.: U.S. Government Printing Office.

———. 1997. *U.S. Refugee Policy: Taking Leadership.* Washington, D.C.: U.S. Commission on Immigration Reform.

U.S. Department of State. 1995. "China—Country conditions and comments on asylum applications." Washington, D.C.: U.S. Department of State.

U.S. General Accounting Office. 1993. *Benefits for Illegal Aliens.* Washington, D.C.: General Accounting Office.

U.S. Immigration and Naturalization Service. 1993. "Vessels that are known to have attempted to smuggle PRC nationals into the United States." Unpublished, August 17.

———. "INS asylum data, FY 1996." Washington, D.C.: Asylum Division of the Immigration and Naturalization Service.

U.S. Senate. [1877] 1978. *Report of the Joint Special Committee to Investigate Chinese Immigration.* Reprint, New York: Arno Press.

———. 1992. "Asian Organized Crime." Hearing before the Permanent Subcommittee on Investigations of the Committee on Governmental Affairs, October 3, November 5–6, 1991. Washington, D.C.: U.S. Government Printing Office.

van Kemenade, Willem. 1997. *China, Hong Kong, Taiwan, Inc.* New York: Knopf.

Vagg, Jon. 1993. "Sometimes a crime: Illegal immigration and Hong Kong." *Crime and Delinquency* 39 (3): 355–372.

Wallis, Belinda, and Tommy Lewis. 1993. "East Wood case discussed." *South China Morning Post* March 15: 2.

Wang, Zheng. 1996. "Ocean-going smuggling of illegal Chinese immigrants: Operation, causation and policy implications." *Transnational Organized Crime* 2 (1) (spring): 49–65.

Weiner, Tim. 1993. "Fixing immigration: New waves of refugees buckle system as cold war policies become obsolete." *New York Times* June 8: B2.

———. 1994. "U.S. to charge immigrants a fee when they seek political asylum." *New York Times* February 17: A1.

Weintraub, Sidney. 1984. "Illegal immigrants in Texas: Impact on social services and related considerations." *International Migration Review* 18 (3): 733–747.

Weng, Junyi. 1994. "Economic growth in Fujian province: A growth center analysis." In *The Economic Transformation of South China,* ed. Thomas Lyons and Victor Nee. Ithaca: Cornell University East Asia Program.

Wong, Bernard. 1982. *Chinatown.* New York: Holt, Rinehart, and Winston.

Wong, Jan. 1994. "The final hour on China's death row." *South China Morning Post* April 22, 1994: 19.

Woolrich, Peter. 1993a. "China slammed over East Wood illegals." *South China Morning Post* March 14: 4.

_____. 1993b. "The town that sells its workers for US$ 15,000 apiece." *South China Morning Post* March 14: 4.

Wren, Christopher. 1996. "Heroin indictments link drugs to smuggling of aliens." *New York Times* March 13: B3.

WuDunn, Sheryl. 1992. "With focus on profits, China revives bias against women." *New York Times* July 28: A1.

Yates, Kenneth. 1997. "Canada's growing role as a human smuggling destination and corridor to the United States." In *Human Smuggling*, ed. Paul Smith, 156–68. Washington, D.C.: Center for Strategic and International Studies.

Yueng, Chris. 1993. "Mass executions held: Drive continues against major crimes." *South China Morning Post* September 29: 8.

Zhang, Sheldon, and Mark Gaylord. 1996. "Bound for the Golden Mountain: The social organization of Chinese alien smuggling." *Crime, Law, and Social Change* 25: 1–16.

Zhou, Min. 1992. *Chinatown: The Socioeconomic Potential of an Urban Enclave.* Philadelphia: Temple University Press.

IN CHINESE

Centre Daily News. 1985. "INS undercover operation crushes a Taiwanese alien smuggling ring." May 9: 3.

Chan, Lun. 1994. *The Encyclopedia of Fuzhou.* Beijing: China Encyclopedia Press.

Chan, Wan-ying. 1993. "The genesis of illegal migration." *Asia Weekly Magazine* July 4: 12–24.

Chang, Jen-liang. 1995. *A Study of the Problem of Illegal Mainland Chinese in Taiwan.* Taipei: San Fung Publisher.

Chao, Joa-ping and Chan Jia-yuan. 1993. *The Geography of Fujian Province.* Fuzhou: Fujian Renmin Press.

Chen, Ping. 1993. "The procreation of Changle human snakes." *China Times* July 2–4: 7.

China Times. 1994. "The number of lost passports quadrupled last year." June 14: 4.

_____. 1995. "By the year 2000, there will be 200 million residual workers in China." July 27: 9.

Fujian Ribao. 1993. "'I'll never want to flee China again': An illegal migrant tells of his experience." June 17: 1.

Gu, Fei-hai. 1993. *Illegal Immigration.* Gu Cheng, Hebei: Inner Mongolia University Press.

Han, Shin. 1993. "People in search of an American dream." *Sing Tao Daily* June 19–28: 29.

Jia, Ling. 1995. "Why must people prey on their own?" *Critical Magazine* No. 14, April: 10–19.

Nyo, Ming-sen. 1993. "Why are so many Chinese illegals coming to the U.S.?" *World Journal Magazine* August 29: S4.

Sing Tao Daily. 1990. "A Chinese social worker discusses his observations of alien smuggling activity in Fujian." July 14: 24.

_____. 1991. "Police arrested 95 II and 5 snakeheads: result of 24-hour 'Operation Closed Door.'" May 10: 40.

_____. 1991. "Dramatic increase in illegal Fujianese now a concern for American authorities." September 18: 27.

_____. 1992. "Many illegal Chinese migrants arrived in the U.S. in Taiwanese fishing boats; Triads are alleged to be behind the illegal operations." March 6: 23.

_____. 1992. "Police chief urges Fujianese immigrants not to be afraid to report crime to authorities." May 7: 28.

_____. 1992. "With the increase in illegal migrants, crime patterns change." May 23: 31.

_____. 1992. "Chinese asylum applicants, citing the one-child policy, are granted asylum in record numbers." September 2: 28.

_____. 1992. "A Chinese merchant is arrested for trafficking heroin and humans." October 10: 32.

_____. 1993. "A bar girl smuggled into the U.S. is working as a prostitute to repay the smuggling fee." June 11: 30.

_____. 1993. "Smuggling ship captain raped a female passenger before she committed suicide." June 22: 27.

_____. 1993. "Alan Lau denies he controlled human smuggling." November 9: 28.

_____. 1993. "Police arrested three men and one woman after Chinese illegals escaped from a safe house; a 16-year-old girl was sexually assaulted and is pregnant." November 18: 31.

_____. 1994. "To curb illegal immigration, INS is preparing to deport a thousand Chinese." January 18: 28.

_____. 1994. "More than 400 stolen passports recovered at the CKS airport." October 11: 59.

_____. 1995. "In the aftermath of the *Golden Venture* incident, the House passed a bill to indict human smuggling organizations with RICO." February 11: 26.

_____. 1995. "Violence and sexual abuse escalate onboard the smuggling ships." August 24: 31.

_____. 1995. "Four human snakes jumped out of a building after being tortured." October 16: 32.

_____. 1996. "INS received an Additional 500 million budget; half of it will be used to enhance border patrol." February 9: 30.

_____. 1996. "Members of an alien smuggling group in Singapore were sentenced to jail." May 1: 55.

_____. 1996. "Chinese human smuggling." December 2: 26.

_____. 1997. The emergence of Fujianese overshadows the Cantonese." October 27: A26.

_____. 1997. "'Iron Bone' plead guilty to kidnapping human snakes." December 2: A23.

Standing Committee of the People's Congress. 1994. A Supplemental Regula-
tion to Crimes Involving Organizing and Transporting People across
National and Regional Borders. Passed at the March 5, 1994 8th People's
Congress.

Tai Kung Pao. 1993. "Fuzhou authorities arrested 157 prospective illegal migrants
to America." April 18: 1.

_____. 1993. "Foreign remittance, foreign language, long-distance phone call."
June 15: 2.

_____. 1994. "Fuzhou deputy party secretary wants to quickly stop illegal
migration." June 11: 1.

Tsao, Chang-ching. 1993. "Illegal migrants had no rights to pursue freedom?"
World Journal Magazine July 25: S8.

United Daily's Mainland China News Center. 1993. *Mainland China Metropolis.*
Taipei: Lien Jin Publishers.

United Daily News. 1989. "Is the Chinese communist government sponsoring
'labor export' to Taiwan?" May 12, 1989: 1.

_____. 1991. "A major crackdown on smuggling activities in Fujian; more
than a thousand were arrested." May 30: 30.

_____. 1994. "Taiwanese government paid the price for mainland Chinese
involvement in illegal immigration." June 20: 2.

_____. 1994. "Illegal migrants are desperate for Taiwan passports." June 28: 40.

Wang, Chi-kun, Ko-lin Chin, and Li-sen Lin. 1997. *The Prevention of the Illegal
Migration of Mainland Chinese to Taiwan.* Taipei: Mainland Affairs Council,
1997.

Wei, Ping-Shung, Auyang Tao, and Wang Shun-kang. 1995. *Crime and Policy in
the Market-Oriented Economy.* Beijing: Public Press.

Wen, Fung. 1992. "Illegal Chinese migrants: Their hearts on fire, eager to go
abroad." *World Journal Weekly Magazine* April 12: 72.

Wen Wei Pao. 1993. "Xian officials fired for receiving bribes from human smugglers." November 6: 1.

Wong, Tse-tun. 1993. "Yellow Earth, new blind mass, and the gold rush." *United
Daily News* July 11–14: 6.

World Journal. 1990. "Chinese restaurant workers suffer from poor working and
living conditions." February 27: 23.

_____. 1991. "Fourteen snakeheads arrested in Fuzhou." May 23: 19.

_____. 1991. "Chen Wei is sentenced to 25 years to life for kidnapping."
December 26: 21.

_____. 1992. "Twelve mainland illegal migrants who are on their way to Amer-
ica arrested in Taipei airport." February 21: 3.

_____. 1993. "Illegal Chinese immigrants in detention attack Honduran
guards; one immigrant was shot to death." May 26: A3.

_____. 1993. "Mainland human snakes leaving China by all means to chase
their dreams." May 31: A3.

_____. 1993. "A 9-year-old Chinese illegal comes looking for his parents."
June 12: A1.

_____. 1993. "Number of Chinese illegals arrested at JFK increase." June 14a: B1.

_____. 1993. "Washington expresses concerns to Taipei over the reconverting of smuggling ships in Taiwan." June 14b: A3.

_____. 1993. "France sent a group of illegal Chinese to jail for resisting deportation." June 19: A3.

_____. 1993. "Authorities believe there are two to three hundred safe houses in Queens." June 30: B1.

_____. 1993. "Mainland snake people and Taiwan smuggling ships." July 14: A1.

_____. 1993. "Two Chinese snakeheads behind the Ching Wing case received 5-year prison term." July 16: A1.

_____. 1993. "An anti-alien smuggling meeting held in Beijing; harsh penalty for snakeheads discussed." August 7: A2.

_____. "Smuggled Chinese escaped from Mexican authorities." August 25: A1.

_____. 1993. "Illegal migrants were aided by government agencies after being deported back to China." August 30: A19.

_____. 1993. "Chinese officials arrested 152 illegal migrants." November 4: A19.

_____. 1993. "Thirty-two Fujianese captured in Guangdong for attempting to migrate to the U.S. illegally." December 1: A19.

_____. 1993. "Three border guards and snakeheads sentenced to death for smuggling more than one hundred people out of China." December 5: A14.

_____. 1993. "Fuzhou officials arrested 70 snakeheads over the past six months." December 13: A20.

_____. 1994. "*Jin Yi* No. 1 arrived in Guatemala; more than one hundred Chinese illegals will be repatriated." May 7: A3.

_____. 1994. "Legislators criticize the government for paying repatriation fees for mainland illegals." June 20: A12.

_____. 1994. "In the war against illegal migration, Fuzhou authorities punish 31 snakeheads." June 30: A21.

_____. 1994. "The existence of sweatshops signifies a new chapter in the history of new migrants." September 10: A4.

_____. 1994. "81 mainland Chinese deported by the INS." September 16: A3.

_____. 1994. "A travel agency burglarized; 250 passports disappeared." October 6: A15.

_____. 1994. "American officials indicate that there will be no repercussion from Washington for Taipei's failure to indict human smugglers." December 29: A15.

_____. 1995. "Tighter Border patrol and workplace enforcement are two measures adopted by the INS to prevent illegal migration." February 6: A3.

_____. 1995. "Taiwan justice officials suggest that Singapore ships replace Taiwan ships in human smuggling." February 21: A13.

_____. 1995. "Port officials of Kaohsiung alleged to have received NT$1 million per smuggling ship in bribe." May 4: A3.

_____. 1995. "Hong Kong authorities to punish snakeheads; fines increase to HK$17 million." September 15: A9.

_____. 1995. "Operation Champion ended with the arrests of nearly 100 illegal Chinese immigrants." September 16: A9.

_____. 1995. "Illegal Chinese migrants fought with security guards aboard an airplane destined for China." October 2: A17.

_____. 1995. "Argentina government smashes an alien smuggling ring; an Argentinean immigration officer was arrested." October 14a: A3.

_____. 1995. "The snakehead behind the *Golden Venture* was sentenced to 10 years." October 14b: A3.

_____. 1996. "The Legislative Yuan to amend relevant laws to punish snakeheads." January 11: A2.

_____. 1996. "Malaysian government plans to punish offenders more harshly for producing fake passports." January 23: A19.

_____. 1996. "China is number one in the world when it comes to executing criminals." June 15: A13.

_____. 1997. "*Golden Venture*'s big snakehead extradited to the U.S." October 7: B1.

_____. 1997. "150 members of the Shenzhen border patrol army were arrested for working for snakeheads." October 17: A13.

_____. 1997. "*Xin Da*'s snakehead sentenced to seven years' imprisonment." November 27: B4.

_____. 1998. "Fujianese dominate the Chinese buffet restaurant industry." January 10: E1.

_____. 1998. "The hefty price of illegal migration." January 11: E1.

_____. 1998. "A Taiwan-based human smuggler arrested for providing fake Taiwan passports to China-based smugglers." January 8: A10.

Wu, Cheng-hsiung. 1988. "Chinese laborers in Cuba in the nineteenth century (1847–1874)." In *Essays in Chinese Maritime History*, ed. Yen-sheng Chang. Vol. 3. Taipei: Academia Sinica.

Yu, Su-tung. 1987. *Principles of Laodong Giazao*. Hebie: Falu Publisher.

Zi, ye. 1993. The doom of the *Golden Venture*. *World Journal Weekly*, August 15: S-5.

Index

Adaptation, 5, 113
Advance parole certificate, 51, 192n. 4
Air smuggling, 50–51, 57–61

Barth, Gunther, 128
Beck, Roy, 132
Bian, Yanjie, 23
Biernacki, Patrick, 171
Big Famine, 24
Big snakeheads: as business owners, 30;
    Canadian, 88; Chinese American, 31;
    convictions of, 150–51; extradition of,
    150; personal characteristics of, 29–30,
    32; as philanthropists, 31; as selfish
    people, 31; Taiwanese, 32, 35, 42, 66, 88.
    See also Little snakeheads; Snakeheads
Black, David, 190n. 2
Bloom, David, 15
Bolz, Jennifer, 7, 38
Booth, Martin, 7, 190n. 2
Border patrol, 147–48, 157
Brimelow, Peter, 132
Burdman, Pamela, 5, 7–9, 11, 33, 35–36,
    42–43, 64, 126, 133, 136–37, 152–53

Caces, Fe, 8
Causes of illegal migration, 3, 10, 24–28.
    See also Theories of international migra-
    tion
Cantonese immigrants, 111
Chan, Ying, 3, 5, 33, 35, 37, 98, 100, 126,
    134
Chin, Ko-lin, 6–7, 113, 157, 173, 190n. 2
China-Myanmar border, 31, 52, 161
Chinatown, New York: brothels and gam-
    bling dens in, 6; as destination, 3; politi-
    cal economy of, 111–12; size of, 111
Chinese Exclusion Act, 28, 79
Chinese gangs, indictments of, 151

Chinese immigrants, 190n. 4
Chinese officials: as big snakeheads, 32,
    45; convictions of, 44; involvement in
    human smuggling, 33, 42
Chinese passports, 192n. 8
Chin Wing (ship), 63
Chiswick, Barry, 115, 118
Chu, Jeannette, 51
Chu, Yiu-kong, 26, 190n. 2
Clark, Rebecca, 120
Conover, Ted, 8, 194n. 3
Controlling illegal immigration: in Cen-
    tral America, 146; Chinese preventive
    measures, 133–36; Chinese punitive
    measures, 136–40; in Europe, 145; in
    Hong Kong, 143–44; in Malaysia, 145;
    problems in, 132, 141–141, 152–53,
    155–58; in Singapore, 145; Taiwanese
    measures, 142; in Thailand, 144–45;
    U.S. policies in, 133, 146
Cornelius, Wayne, 4, 120–21, 148
Corruption: in China, 23, 42, 159; in Tai-
    wan, 142; in transit countries, 45–46,
    58, 161; on the U.S. border, 82;
Counterrevolutionary, 24, 189nn. 14, 15
Crew members, 33
Cultural Revolution, 15, 24, 188n. 4

Debt collectors, 34; the role of, 103; tactics
    of, 103–105. *See also* Enforcers
Deng Xiaoping, 11
Departure points: Beijing, 56, 88; Fuzhou,
    57; Kunming, 53, 55, 59; Putian, 68;
    Shanghai, 56, 88; Shenzhen 51–52,
    57–58, 65, 82, 84, 192n. 7; Xiamen, 56
Deportation: of boat passengers, 64,
    149–50; expense, 155; policy, 162; resist-
    ing, 154–55
DeStefano, Anthony, 40, 42, 45, 150

Detection: rate in the U.S., 146–47, 188n. 7;
by smuggling routes, 92; rate in Taiwan, 188n. 7
Detention, by debt collectors: 98; chance
of 92; factors associated with, 100;
length of, 67, 101
Detention, by U.S. authorities: 81–82,
189n. 9; capacity for, 154, 192n. 5,
197n. 4
Dillon, Richard, 190n. 2
Down payment, 37
Drift-net fishing, 141
Dubro, James, 7

East Wood (ship), 63–64, 135
Employer sanctions, 148–49, 154
Employment. See Work
Enforcers, 33, 52; aboard smuggling ships,
73. See also Debt collectors
English, T. J., 6, 124
Entry points: Arizona, 81; Boston, 39–40;
Chicago, 51; Honolulu (Hawaii), 51, 55,
75; Long Beach, Calif., 38, 63; Los Ange-
les, 35, 43, 50, 56–57, 60–61, 76, 79, 84;
Miami, 51–52; Morehead City, N.C., 63;
New Bedford, Mass., 63; New York, 50,
52, 55, 57–58, 60–61; Phoenix, 82; San
Diego, 63–64; San Francisco, 51, 63–65;
Seattle, 88; Texas, 81
Executive Order (1989), 18
Expedited removal, 187–88n. 6
Exported labors, 65

Faison, Seth, 7, 97–98, 126, 133, 150, 153,
157
Fake traveling documents: 187n. 3,
192n. 6; of Argentina, 88; of China, 51,
58, 60; of Ecuador, 56; of Hong Kong,
52; of Japan, 60; of Liberia, 56; of
Malaysia, 60; of Singapore, 51–52,
58–59; of Taiwan, 51, 53, 55–57, 60, 82;
of the U.S., 58
Financial pressure, 114
Floating migrants, 164
Foreigners Alien Smuggling Act (1995),
151
Fujianese community associations, 112
Fujianese community in New York, 20,
111

Fujianese-owned businesses, 112–13
Fujian Province: 8, 141, 158, 188n. 2;
arable land in, 16; population of, 11
Fuk Ching (gang): indictment of, 127,
150, 195n. 9; involvement in human
smuggling, 39–40
Fukien American Association, 38, 126
Fuzhou area, 11

Gaylord, Mark, 4, 17, 34–35, 42, 66
Golden Triangle, 35
Golden Venture (ship): in the aftermath of,
4, 7, 10, 29, 63, 132, 146, 192n. 5; arrival
of, 62; before the arrival of, 51, 60; the
cost of, 66; and Fuk Ching gang, 39;
impact of, 152, 161; indictment of
people responsible for, 150, 197n. 5
Green Dragons (gang), 39
Grinberg, Leon, 22, 25
Grinberg, Rebecca, 22, 25
Guangdong Province, 26, 141, 158
Guanxi, 23–24, 189n. 12
Guarantor, 5, 37
Guest from the Beautiful Country: mean-
ing of, 9; significance of, 9–10, 114
Guides, 33, 53, 79
Gurak, Douglas, 8

Haines, David, 111
Harris, J. R., 14
Hayes, Jim, 64
Hondagneu-Sotelo, Pierrette, 128
Hood, Marlowe, 9, 20, 42
Houstoun, Marion, 115
Human rights in China, 24, 28, 164,
189n. 17
Human Rights Watch, 188n. 6
Human smugglers. See Big snakeheads;
Human smuggling, group characteris-
tics of; Little snakeheads; Snakeheads
Human smuggling, 187n. 4; Chinese
authorities' involvement in, 42–45; and
Chinese gangs, 39–40; and Chinese offi-
cial delegations, 44; Chinese organized
crime involvement in, 7, 29, 34, 40–41;
as an ethnic enterprise, 152; group characteristics of, 33–35, 41–42; and heroin
trafficking, 8, 29, 35; as an international
trade, 42; as a lucrative business, 4–5, 8;

operational features of, 36–38; penalties for, 151–52, 155; and tongs, 38, 40; and triads, 38, 40. *See also* Illegal Chinese immigration

Human trade. *See* Human smuggling

Ianni, Francis, 126

Ignatius, Sarah, 8, 19, 154

Illegal Chinese immigrants, 187n.1; arrival of, 3; and crime, 125–28; as debt collectors, 127; detention of, 60–61; as exported labors, 43; fining of, 137; as little duck, 194n. 3; number of, arrested, 3; number of, in the U.S., 6, 161; the plight of, 130–31; and the police, 5; predicament of, 6; prospects of, 128–29; and work, 5. *See also* Smuggled Chinese

Illegal Chinese immigration: and Central America, 87; Chinese laws against, 137, 195–96n. 1; Chinese official viewpoint on, 134, 152; cost of, to the host country, 121; in the Fuzhou area, 9; impact on local economy, 120; nineteenth century, 28; the risk of, 7, 55, 69–71, 75; and the "slot racket," 190n. 1; as a threat to national security, 7

Illegal Immigration Reform and Immigrant Responsibility Act (IIRIRA), 187n. 6

I-Mao (ship), 63, 65

Immigration and Nationality Act, 187n. 3

Immigration Reform and Control Act (IRCA), 18, 148

Income. *See* Wages

Interagency Working Group, 6, 11, 46, 146, 161

International Organization for Migration, 145

James, Daniel, 126

Jin Yinn (ship), 64

John F. Kennedy Airport, 51, 59–60, 98, 192n. 3

Jung Sheng (ship), 75

Kamen, Al, 3–4, 9, 63, 76, 153

Kidnapping: causes of, 99; of Chinese Americans, 99–100; of illegal immigrants, 98; prevalence of, 99. *See also* Safe houses

Kinkead, Gwen, 4–6, 9, 20, 111

Kleinnecht, William, 7

Kristof, Nicholas, 3, 17, 20, 140, 189n. 11

Kwong, Peter, 5, 8, 20–21, 28, 43, 101, 112, 116, 148, 194n. 1

Labor export companies, 21, 43, 158

Lamtau Island prison, 164

Land route: via Canada, 87–89; via Guatemala, 85–87; via Mexico, 79–80

Lauhu Bridge Station, 51, 192n. 7

Lavigne, Yves, 7

Lawyers Committee for Human Rights, 138, 188n. 6

Leaving China: by air, 56–57; overland through Hong Kong, 51–52; overland through Myanmar, 52–56; by sea, 62, 68–69. *See also* Departure points

Little snakeheads: contacts with illegal immigrants, 36; as guides, 52; perceptions of, by smuggled Chinese, 32–33; personal characteristics of, 29, 32; recruitment tactics of, 67. *See also* Guides

Living conditions, 114, 121, 195n. 8

Logan, John, 23

Long, Patrick Du Phuoc, 124

Lyman, Stanford, 79, 112

Lyons, Thomas, 11

Mahler, Sarah, 9, 14, 81, 97, 115, 148

Maltz, Michael, 41

Mao Zedong, 189n. 16

Marshall, Ineke Haen, 125

Martin, Mildred Crowl, 28, 125

Maruszko, Lydia, 8

Massey, Douglas S., 8, 16, 20–21

McKenna, Wayne, 153

Meisner, Doris, 157

Mekong River, 60

Mental illness, 121–22, 195n. 7

Mexicali, 45, 154

Minghou, 12

Morawska, Ewa, 8, 16

Morgan, W. P., 190n. 2

Mountain of Gold, 15, 123

Myers, Willard, 5–6, 9, 11, 20, 28–29, 33, 42, 66, 68, 140, 152, 158

North, David, 115

Oi, Jean, 133
One-child policy, 24, 28, 156–57, 189n. 16
Ong, Paul, 16
Operation Gatekeeper, 148
Operation Hold-the-Line, 148
Operation Safeguard, 148
Operation Sea Dragon, 40
Operation Snakeheads, 150
Overseas Chinese, 15, 21, 28, 32, 131,
    188n. 5

Pacific Ocean, 29, 39, 49, 141, 153
Padavan, Frank, 120
Pan, Lynn, 65
Perea, Juan F., 132
Perito, Robert, 75
Piore, Michael, 8, 17
Policy recommendations: for China,
    158–60; for Taiwan, 160; for transit
    countries, 160–61; for the U.S., 161–64
Political asylum: abuse of, 8, 61, 188n. 8;
    claims, 188n. 6; as a magnet, 18–19, 156;
    the need to restructure, 162; protecting,
    63, 187n. 6, 193n. 10
Political persecution, 24
Portes, Alejandro, 148
Pro-democracy movement (1989), 3, 18,
    28, 88–89
Prostitution, 91, 109, 124–25
Public Security Bureau (PSB), 34, 42, 44,
    135, 137, 139, 190n. 5, 192n. 1
Pull factors. See Theories of international
    migration
Push factors. See Theories of international
    migration

Racketeering-Influenced and Corrupt
    Organizations (RICO), 151, 161
Re-education through labor, 138–40
Reform through labor, 138
Refugee Act (1980), 8
Remittances, 119
Rosenblum, Karen, 111
Rumbaut, Ruben, 148

Safe houses: across the U.S., 97; around
    the world, 4; crackdowns on, 151;
depicted as hell, 106; in Mexico, 79–80;
    in Queens, 98; rape in the, 110, 194n. 1;
    violence inside, 97, 107–109
Salyer, Lucy, 28
Samora, Julina, 79
Saxton, Alexander, 28, 128
Schmid, Alex, 7, 126
Seagrave, Sterling, 3, 11, 132, 152
Sea smuggling: and Chinese organized
    crime, 34; crossing oceans, 70; develop-
    ment of, 29, 62–65; other forms of, 77;
    passenger recruitment in, 67; peak of, 4;
    problems in combating, 77
Sellin, Thorsten, 125
Sending communities: Changle, 11–12;
    Fuqin, 13; Fuzhou, 13; Guantou, 13;
    Mawei, 13; Pingtan, 13; Tingjiang, 13
Shaw, Jack, 18
Siemens, Maria, 146, 151
Smith, Paul, 3–4, 6–8, 27, 97, 157–58
Smuggled Chinese: 187nn. 2, 4; disputes
    with snakeheads, 5, 29; estimate of, 6.
    See also Illegal Chinese immigrants
Smuggling contract, 37, 190–91n. 6
Smuggling debt: interest rates on, 118;
    time needed to clear, 119
Smuggling fees: 4; average, 37; methods
    of paying, 101–103, 105; in 1998,
    191n. 7; promptness in paying, 105–106;
    by smuggling routes, 38
Smuggling routes, 4, 49; comparison of,
    92–93. See also Air smuggling; Land
    route; Sea smuggling
Smuggling ships: abuses aboard, 72–73; of
    Australia, 65; boarding, 69; conditions
    of, 71, 193n. 4; detected, 4; lack of food
    on, 72; rape aboard, 73–74; remodeling
    of, 193n. 3; sanitation aboard, 72; suffer-
    ings aboard, 78; of Taiwan, 66; violence
    aboard, 75
Snakeheads, 187n. 4; crackdowns on,
    136–37, 140; execution of, 140; the need
    to deport, 163; personal characteristics
    of, 29. See also Big snakeheads; Little
    snakeheads
Special Agricultural Worker (SAW) pro-
    gram, 121
Spence, Jonathan, 188n. 4, 189n. 13
Stark, Oded, 8, 15

Storti, Craig, 28
Suicide, 123
Sung, Betty Lee, 28, 111
Support personnel, 34

Taiwan: 187n.1; the role of, in the human
    trade, 140–41
Taiwanese passports: abuse of, 197n. 3;
    and air smuggling, 142; machine-read-
    able, 143; missing, 143;
Taiwan Strait, 141
Taylor, Edward, 8, 21
Theories of international migration:
    cumulative effect, 1–22; dual market
    theory, 17–18; neoclassical economic
    theory, 14; network theory, 19–20; new
    economic theory, 15–16; psychoanalytic
    perspective, 22–23; smuggling net-
    works, 21; world systems theory, 16–17.
    See also Causes of illegal migration
Tiananmen Square massacre (1989). See
    Pro-democracy movement
Todaro, Michael, 8, 14
Tong, 38, 40, 190n. 2
Transit points: Algeria, 58; Australia, 50,
    89; Austria, 58; Bangkok, 50, 53; Bolivia,
    4, 60, 88–89; Cambodia, 161; Canada, 4,
    28, 49; Colombia, 57, 59, 84; Czechoslo-
    vakia, 60; Ecuador, 57; England, 88;
    France, 88; Frankfurt, 52; Germany, 43,
    50, 60; Guatemala, 63–65, 71, 74, 84;
    Haiti, 63; Hong Kong, 34, 38, 42, 49,
    51–52, 57–58, 65, 82, 84, 88, 160; Indone-
    sia, 34; Japan, 71, 82; Korea, 61; Macau,
    42; Malaysia, 34, 56; Marshall Islands,
    63; Mauritius, 63; Mexico, 4, 28, 49,
    63–65, 78, 82, 84–85, 160; Morocco, 58;
    Myanmar 49, 52–56, 59–60, 85, 160;
    number of, 50; Panama, 4, 58; Paris, 52;
    Peru, 4; Philippines, 55; Romania, 102;
    Singapore, 43, 51, 56–57; Spain, 58; Tai-
wan, 61; Thailand, 34, 51–52, 55–56, 58,
    60, 65, 82, 84–85, 88, 160; Tokyo, 50, 56;
    Vietnam, 161; Yugoslavia, 60
Transporters, 33
Triad, 7, 38, 40–41, 190n. 2
Tsai, Shih-shan Henry, 28, 111, 190n. 1

U.S. Coast Guard, 7, 63–64, 135, 149,
    153–55, 193n. 4
U.S. Commission on Immigration Reform,
    60, 151, 161
U.S.-Mexican border, 57, 79; crossing the,
    80–85

Vagg, Jon, 3, 26, 144, 152
van Kemenade, 141, 192n. 7
Victimization: by authorities, 89–90; by
    big snakeheads, 91; by enforcers, 90;
    extent of, 89; by little snakeheads, 90;
    vulnerability to, 124
Violent Crime Control and Law Enforce-
    ment Act, 151

Waiting period, 37
Wages: in China, 14; hourly, 118, 194n. 3;
    by occupation, 117–18, 195n. 4; in the
    U.S., 14
Waldorf, Dan, 171
Wenzhou, 12–13
White Tigers (gang), 39
Wo Hop To (triad), 38
Wong, Bernard, 111
Work: benefits, 195n. 6; conditions, 116;
    employment rate, 115, 194n. 1; hours,
    116–17; occupation, 115–16

Yunnan Province, 53, 161

Zhang, Sheldon, 4, 17, 34–35, 42, 66
Zhejiang Province: 8, 26, 158
Zhou Min, 3, 111